DOUBTFUL SOUNDS

Victoria University Press
ESSAYS & INTERVIEWS

Flight of the Phoenix: Critical Notes on New Zealand Writers
James Bertram (1985)

Disputed Ground: Robin Hyde, Journalist
Gillian Boddy & Jacqueline Matthews (eds) (1991)

How to Be Nowhere: Essays and Texts 1971–1994
Ian Wedde (1995)

Doubtful Sounds: Essays and Interviews
Bill Manhire (2000)

A Dissolving Ghost: Essays and More
Margaret Mahy (2000)

In preparation:

Keri Hulme
Elizabeth Knox
Gregory O'Brien
Vincent O'Sullivan

DOUBTFUL SOUNDS

Essays and Interviews

Bill Manhire

VICTORIA UNIVERSITY PRESS

VICTORIA UNIVERSITY PRESS
Victoria University of Wellington
PO Box 600, Wellington
http://www.vup.vuw.ac.nz

© Bill Manhire 2000

ISBN 0 86473 370 4

First published 2000

This book is copyright. Apart from
any fair dealing for the purpose of private study,
research, criticism or review, as permitted under the
Copyright Act, no part may be reproduced by any
process without the permission of
the publishers

ACKNOWLEDGEMENTS
Victoria University Press would like to thank
the publishers and editors of the works in which these
essays and interviews have previously appeared

Published with the assistance of a grant from

Printed by PrintLink, Wellington

for Robin Dudding

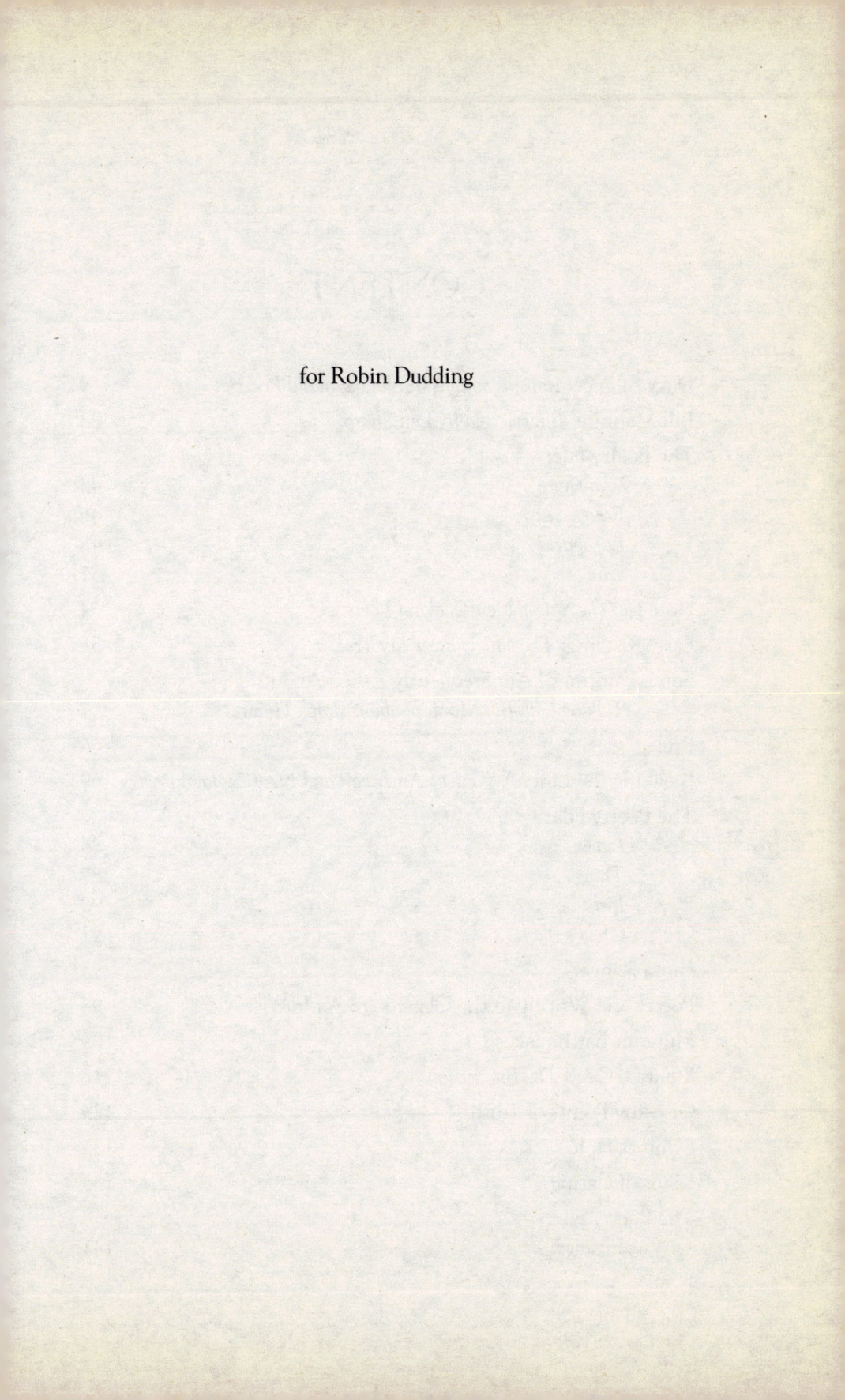

CONTENTS

Dirty Silence: *Impure Sounds in New Zealand Poetry*	9
Bill Manhire: *Interviewed by Iain Sharp*	23
The Poetry File:	
Waiwhare	43
Rough Stuff	46
Logopoeia	48
Dirt	51
Note for *The Young New Zealand Poets*	54
Early Reading: *The Magic Faraway Tree*	55
Some Paintings I Am Frequently Asked About:	
Talking with Bill Manhire about Ralph Hotere	57
Fault	66
Breaking the Line: *A View of American and New Zealand Poetry*	69
The Poetry File:	
Lines	85
Things	87
Lists	90
Child's Play	92
Laura Ranger	95
Poetry and Writing in the Classroom: *An Interview*	98
Mutes & Earthquakes	109
Maurice Gee's *The Big Season*	118
Growing Points of Truth	124
Symmes Hole	133
Kinds of Caring	135
The Poetry File:	
Endings	141

Uselessness	143
Short Cuts	145
Underground Poetry	148
Larkin at Sixty	151
Not Untrue, Not Unkind: *The Life of Philip Larkin*	155
Who is Sylvia?: *The Life of Sylvia Plath*	158
The Government of the Tongue	161
Real Hot Air	172
The Poetry File:	
Prose Poems	180
Charm	182
Finders Keepers	185
Titles	187
Events as People: *Notes on* Private Gardens	190
Smithereens	196
Stranger at the Ranchslider	199
Events and Editorials: *Baxter's* Collected Poems	209
New Jerusalem Sonnets	213
Doubtful Sounds: *The Poems of Denis Glover*	217
As If	227
The Poetry File:	
Rhyme	230
Words	232
Light Verse	234
Great Scott!	237
Snow Job	240
A Poet at the Pole	243
Wings of Gold: A Week among Poets	246
The Poetry File:	
Christmas	273
Mistakes	275
Long Poems	278
Concentration	279
Afterword: An E-mail Interview with Andrew Johnston	282
Index	290

DIRTY SILENCE

Impure Sounds in New Zealand Poetry

The only privilege literature deserves – and this privilege it requires in order to exist – is the privilege of being the arena of discourse, the place where the struggle of languages can be acted out.
  Salman Rushdie (after Carlos Fuentes, after Mikhail Bakhtin)

There is a poem by Wallace Stevens, 'The Creations of Sound', in which the following lines occur:

> Tell X that speech is not dirty silence
> Clarified. It is silence made still dirtier.

The X in these lines is sometimes thought to be T.S. Eliot, which suggests that when Stevens speaks – in poetry – of speech, he has poetry itself in mind. I don't fully understand the whole of Stevens' poem, but I think that in these lines his point is that poetry should embrace and welcome the great impure worlds of language and experience from which it makes itself, that the last and least useful of poetry's tasks is to refine or purify or clarify the silence in which it sounds.

If Stevens does have Eliot in mind, then the passage which prompted his lines may have been that moment in 'Little Gidding' when the 'familiar compound ghost' adapts a line from Mallarmé, apparently on behalf of all poets:

> . . . our concern was speech, and speech impelled us
> To purify the dialect of the tribe . . .

My intention in this talk is to make a case – less a case than an assertion with illustrations – in favour of dirty language. If the two passages from Eliot and Stevens represent an argument about purity and impurity, and about the writer's task in relation to that argument, then I want to go and stand in the corner with all the impure people.

DOUBTFUL SOUNDS

I have been invited to be fairly personal, so I plan to refer to my own work as a poet, along with the work of other New Zealand poets. I shall confine my comments to poetry, but much of what I have to say might well apply, and apply even more obviously, to New Zealand fiction and drama.

In fact, I want to begin by talking about myself, and in particular my name, since this may explain why I'm predisposed to take the side of impure language.

When I was a boy, I was both puzzled by and anxious about my surname. *Manhire* wasn't, and isn't, a common name, and New Zealanders are hardly renowned for their tolerance of those things which strike them as strange or foreign. They certainly weren't when I was growing up at the bottom of the South Island in the 1950s, a decade which seems more and more to me to have taken place entirely in black and white, in a time before colour was invented. I look at black-and-white photographic images of the period and find it hard to imagine that the original scenes were ever really in colour.

Anyway, I had this name – *Manhire* – which I knew was Cornish (and I think I knew that my father's forebears had been tin miners), but I had no idea what the name meant. Or, in a very real sense, I *did* know what it meant – it meant the fear of being thought foreign. The trouble was that if *Manhire* was translated into local terms, it became a word in English; it became the way it looks – *man* followed by *hire*. This provided rather obvious material for various weak playground jokes. Our family moved around a lot. Every year or two there was a new school and a new playground – and the same feeble jokes. I had a repeated rite of passage: I had to be a cheerful man-for-hire before I could become a simple member of the class.

The joke has pursued me into adulthood. Ten or fifteen years ago, there used to be an employment agency in Wellington which called itself Man Hire. I think it was as gender specific as it sounds. From time to time our household would get telephone calls from people who wanted a couple of big strong men to come and dig out a drain.

And there's a further variant on the joke. Several times I've had it suggested to me that with a name like mine I should set up an entirely different sort of agency and advertise it in the back pages of *Truth*.

So there was this funny name I had – *Manhire* – and it was either foreign or, if it was English, a bit silly and embarrassing.

Then it turned into another name. I noticed this first at a poetry reading in Wellington in 1974. A well-dressed Pakeha woman came up to me afterwards and said to me, full of accusation, as if the evening had cheated her of something she had some real commitment to: 'But you're not Maori at all!'

Now some people may have thought me to be Maori because I had worked with the painter Ralph Hotere. He designed *The Elaboration*, my first book of poems, and he has used the texts of my poems in a number of his paintings.

That was probably part of it. But I think the real reason for my sudden change of identity was that, in the middle 1970s, New Zealand Pakeha had begun to be aware of, but weren't especially familiar with, the world of Maori. *Manhire* still looked foreign, but its foreignness could be 'solved' if it was deemed to be a word in Maori – a language which, although it was the language of the land, was somehow felt to be alien.

For a while, people took to calling me Bill Man-hee-ray.

I didn't, and don't, speak Maori, but even I knew enough to know that a vowel was missing. All the same, I remember looking up Herbert Williams' *A Dictionary of the Maori Language* to see what Maori words my name might resemble. I scanned the various meanings.

If I followed the sound of the name, then the word *manaia* gave a range of interesting possibilities. I might be 'a grotesque beaked figure often introduced in carving; so sometimes ornamental carved work'. Or I might be a lizard, a seahorse, or a raft. As an adjective, *manaia* meant fastidious. Perhaps I was fastidious?

Then, if I looked at the look of the letters on the page, I found *manihira* (a small fish) and *manuhiri* (visitor), a word which many Pakeha now know very well. There is, too, a Maori surname – *Manihera*, which I assume is a transliteration of an English surname.[1]

Manhire manages to persist as a Maori name. If you had been listening to National Radio on Friday, 9 February 1990, you would have heard the announcer say in the course of running through the morning's programmes: 'And at ten o'clock this morning we've got 'The Venus Bird', a short story by Bill . . . Man-hee-ray.' His anxiety may have had something to do with the fact that it was just three days after Waitangi Day.

From time to time, in my etymological quest for self, I would look myself up in dictionaries of surnames, hoping to find my 'real' meaning. But the name was never there: *Manhire* wasn't even in the books! Then one day – I was now in my early thirties – I found it in a small, stapled booklet devoted

---

[1] My thanks to those present at this talk when it was given at the University of Waikato (18 July 1990), who informed me that *Manihera* is a Maori version of Mansell/Maunsell.

entirely to Cornish surnames. And there it was made clear that *Manhire* (along with *Minear*) was a variant of the Cornish-Breton word *menhir*. *Men* means stone; *hir* means long. So the name *Manhire*, in its original tongue, literally means *Longstone*.

I like to imagine that my ancestors were the sacred guardians of the mysterious standing stones of Brittany and Cornwall. Perhaps they ran the phallic cults! But, of course, if you ask people what the word *menhir* means to them, you're likely to be treated to a speech about the *Asterix* comics.

Well, that's a rather self-absorbed disquisition on my surname. But it does demonstrate, I hope, the point I want to make – that you can approach words and interrogate them for their pure essences, their original meanings; but that what you discover will probably be far less, and far less interesting, than the messy, impure range of meanings that are constantly streaming through language as a matter of course.

In a world refined to a sort of unreal, etymological purity, I'm Bill Longstone. But in fact I'm not just Bill Longstone – I'm Bill Manhire, who also includes Bill Longstone. I'm also a small fish, a grotesque beaked figure, a visitor, and, of course, a gigolo, a man-for-hire. *Manhire*, the noise that means me, doesn't have a pure meaning at all. It's a big room, a kind of sound shell, in which a range of meanings are busy having conversations with one another. You can hardly hear yourself think for all the noise.

One of the strongest drives in poetry is towards purity. Poets aspire to the 'shrill delight' of Shelley's skylark, where the bird ascends into the sky, becoming a voice you listen to rather than a material thing you see: 'Like a poet hidden,' as Shelley puts it, 'In the light of thought.' It has been a very powerful idea, I think, this notion that the world of nature has its own pure, ultimately transcendental music – and that poetry, more than the other language arts, can aspire to make such music, or be a part of it. Poets like the thought of all that sort of thing.[2]

The other thing which attracts poets to the idea of purity is the desire to keep words in full working order. There's a general feeling – not limited

---

2   Someone has probably written about birds and poetry and purity. Two texts to set against standard Romantic birdsong (and its afterlife in the work of poets like Hardy and Frost) would be Denis Glover's 'The Magpies', of which the refrain – 'Quardle oodle ardle wardle doodle' – is full of impure mockery, and Hugh MacDiarmid's 'The Caledonian Antisyzygy', which compares the writer's English-Scots inconsistencies and mixture of styles to the nightingale, 'whose thin high call / and . . . deep throb / . . . seem to come from different birds / in different places'.

to poets, of course – that language is constantly being corrupted by the worlds of advertising and politics. When a politician says, 'The fact of the matter is . . .', you expect to be told a lie. The word *fact* has somehow been alienated from its meaning.

So poets work always with the sense that the material from which they build their texts is contaminated, or in danger of contamination. Thus the American poet, Louis Simpson:

> Poets use language precisely and truthfully. Language all around us is being used hysterically. It's being used for commercial purposes. It's used to lie. The poet's own tool is always being diluted, blunted.

Simpson speaks there for any number of poets who feel that an essential part of the job description is keeping the language fresh, truthful, accurate, and therefore usable.

Here are two pieces of poetry by younger New Zealand poets. The first is from a poem by John Newton – 'Epithalamium' – which appeared in the autumn 1990 issue of the magazine *Sport*. Newton highlights the problem of language contamination by taking us on a brief visit to a West Coast rubbish dump:

> The fishing port on a still morning
> reflects the snowy guts of South Westland.
> Foreground, a pert little black & white cormorant
> cruises the edge of the local tip.
>
> He'd like to find a language clean enough to drink
> but there's always someone soaping himself upstream.
> His pronouns have been getting him in deep trouble.
> Pollution keeps sucking him into its slipstream.

The second piece is a complete short poem from Bernadette Hall's 1989 collection, *Heartwood*. She looks at the wrought-iron lacework that you see on the verandahs of some Dunedin houses, and finds in it a metaphor for the poems she wants to write:

> *Lacework*
>
> The poems must be of metal;
> Etruscan iron cut clean, sharp,
> tough as the lacework on the verandah

> at Dundas Street, bristling with mosses,
> cobbled webs, bird shit, rust enough;
> thrusting bright chunks of hills, of sky
> into my narrowed eyes; holding up my roof.

Both texts seem to speak for purity and clarity, yet neither entirely endorses what it seems to yearn for. John Newton's poem, which is much longer than the single quoted stanza, depends for its very existence on people soaping themselves upstream. It is made out of deep trouble and pollution ('snowy guts'?) and, while it talks of purity, it revels in the impurities of its own behaviour. This is even more the case with Bernadette Hall. She wants her poems to be clean and sharp so that they can bristle with impurities: 'mosses, / cobbled webs, bird shit, rust . . .'

There are problems, then, with clarity, with purity of voice. Poets like the thought but not the fact; aspirations and outcomes don't quite coincide. One problem is that purity may become a pleasant name for uniformity, homogeneity, the suppression of everything which is untidy or various or different. Denis Glover has a little poem about the BBC which, among other things, is a teasing commentary on the pure, single voice which we once heard all the time on our radios:

> *Here Is the News*
>
> When the BBC announced
> The end of the world,
> It was done without haste,
> It was neutrally, gentlemanly done,
> It was untinged with distaste,
> It was almost as if the BBC had won.

Glover speaks there against that bland, uniform tone of voice which wants to take command of all other voices – a voice of privilege which is still sometimes called the Queen's English. A pure language might be like the noise Glover describes – a composition of words which are remote, neutral, gentlemanly, devoid of feeling and experience. But then purity itself is a dangerous idea. Behind it lurk the possibilities of racism and authoritarianism, whole universes given over to the gods of correctness and correction. It does no harm to remember that the Nazis believed in purity, and that they exterminated people as part of that belief.

Dirty Silence

Poets yearn for purity, but the really interesting ones practise impurity. Often the work they produce explores both impulses. Such poets give voice to a range of voices. They revel in the messiness of language even as they try to clean it up. They cock an ear at the silence Wallace Stevens speaks of but finally choose to make it dirtier.

One way in which the lyric poem can move beyond the control of a single homogenising voice is simply to offer several voices in the course of a single utterance. Hone Tuwhare's poem 'Hotere', for example, is a monologue with a conversation, or several conversations, inside it. Appetite talks to art, poet to painter, italic text to Roman text.

Hotere

When you offer only three
vertical lines precisely drawn
and set into a dark pool of lacquer
it is a visual kind of starvation:
and even though my eye-balls
roll up and over to peer inside
myself, when I reach the beginning
of your eternity I say instead: hell
let's have another feed of mussels.

Like, I have to think about it, man.

When you stack horizontal lines
into vertical columns which appear
to advance, recede, shimmer and wave
like exploding packs of cards
I merely grunt and say: well, if it
is not a famine, it's a feast.

I have to roll another smoke, man.

But when you score a superb orange
circle on a purple thought-base
I shake my head and say: hell, what
is this thing, called love.

Like, I'm euchred man. I'm eclipsed

Part of the poem's humour comes from the enormous pleasure it takes in the insufficiency of language: words won't do as a way of replying to what it is that the paintings have to say. (Hotere himself is, of course, notorious for refusing to say anything about his paintings.) In some respects, 'Hotere' is a poem about being made speechless, a genial way of honouring the achievement of the painter, whose individual works are so powerful that words simply fail the poet. The poem's very last word, *eclipsed*, has no full stop to follow it:[3] this not only acknowledges that the paintings have 'won' the conversation, it also plays with witty elegance on the fact that Ralph Hotere is most famous for his black paintings. The poet is literally left in the dark.

Hone Tuwhare's work is full of conversations. It's not just that several voices are heard in them, or that they are often addressed to others – houses as well as people. You actually do hear a range of languages in them. A recent poem, 'Smiles Like Flowers Come and Go', is written in English but contains passages of both German and Maori, while another piece, 'Irises', includes French and Maori in a predominantly English text as it imagines a visit from Joan of Arc to the poet – while he, for his part, shows a hospitality which is lavish in its own incongruities, pouring a glass of

> dry red wine from a green bottle, and pressed from grapes off vines from Dalmatia growing on dairy flats at Kumeu.

A recent Tuwhare story, 'Don't Go Past Me with Your Nose in the Air', offers a good example of a text shifting between languages. In the course of the story an old man tells his grandson how he once gave an elderly friend a lift home from the pub on a damp, rainy day. The friend, convinced that he was about to die, invited the old man to come with him on the 'Big Journey'. 'Bloody cheek HE's got,' thought the old man, 'choosing my destination for me.'

> Sorry, I told him, I'm your slave until I get you home. Anyway, I said, I'm a 'fine weather' lover. I wouldn't like to die when the sky's black. I just like the feel of the sun warm on my body, the birds busting their heart out in the trees; close my eyes and hold on to the memory of the sun, polishing the different colour of green on the tatara-moa, the harakeke, the totara, the puriri, the karaka – kia ora begorrah! Amen.[4]

---

3   At least until recently, all printings of the poem (including the 1980 *Selected Poems* version, reproduced here) recorded no punctuation mark after 'eclipsed'. In *Mihi* (1987), however, the poem finishes with a question-mark: 'Like, I'm euchred man. I'm eclipsed?'

4   Hone Tuwhare has dedicated the story to Michael O'Leary, who first coined the greeting 'Kia ora, begorrah'.

And then the friend says: 'E hoa! You give me a good feeling saying a karakia like that for me.'

Well, there might be plenty of reasons why a karakia or charm like that would cheer you up if you were feeling preoccupied with death. But much of the life in the passage comes not from the list of forest greenery but from the exuberant mixture of languages at the very end – the Maori greeting *kia ora*, which rhymes with the Irish *begorrah* (itself a corruption of the English *begad*), and then *amen*, a word which has travelled into English (I suppose) courtesy of Latin, courtesy of Greek, courtesy of Hebrew.

That is the kind of mix that I think our liveliest poets can produce, a text which is a sort of conversation between words from different languages. That particular patch of text – 'kia ora begorrah! Amen.' – is such a conversation, and it happens to make perfect sense, although only in New Zealand. There can be no other place on earth where you could say those words and expect to be understood.

Linguists would call this kind of activity code-switching – where speakers, in the course of a sentence, shift between one language and another, one dialect and another, one register and another. Often it is simply a matter of shifting registers and tones. In another poem by Hone Tuwhare, 'In October, Mary Quite Contemporary Will Be Seven Months Gone' – the title itself is a small, code-switching narrative. The pretty noise of nursery rhyme – 'Mary, Mary, quite contrary' – shifts into the word 'contemporary' and then into the much blunter language of gestation – 'seven months gone'.

Tuwhare's poetry is full of such code-switching effects, particularly shifts between a high, formal, literary voice and a far more informal, speaking voice. He can sound within the space of a couple of lines as if he's both at church and down at the pub. And this code-switching principle extends to the way in which he organises his work when he presents it in book form. His 1987 collected poems, *Mihi*, disappointed some reviewers because the poems weren't arranged in any kind of chronological order; neither that in which they had been written nor that of first publication. If a chronological order had been adopted, readers would have been able to trace the poet's voice as it developed from its first hesitant soundings to its mature distinctive notes.

As it happens, *Mihi* is arranged around the idea of growth – it starts with a set of poems about children and childhood, for example. But it is not a book in which a single voice – the achieved, inviolable voice of the poet – displays the processes by which it found and then refined itself.

Instead, *Mihi* is a big text, crammed with voices, locations, and perspectives. Mixing the voices seems to be the central organising principle.

Many of New Zealand's best poets are code-switchers. Baxter begins as the elevated poet of a single voice, but becomes a far more interesting writer when he opens his work – in the *Pig Island Letters* and the Jerusalem poems – to a range of tones and registers. Allen Curnow is the master of code-switching in our writing. His famous early poem 'House and Land' puts several voices on the page and shows them failing to achieve anything remotely like a conversation. His later poetry moves dazzlingly, almost seamlessly, among the available registers of New Zealand English. You almost feel the need to coin a new term for the verbal performances he puts on – code-*shimmering*, perhaps.

It would be possible to talk about a whole range of contemporary New Zealand poetry in these terms, from Vincent O'Sullivan's *Butcher* poems to long collaging texts like Jenny Bornholdt's 'Land Travel' or 'From the Album'. Indeed, another contemporary poet, Elizabeth Smither, has a poem, 'Nine Postcards on a Wall', which offers a kind of collage metaphor for the code-switching effects I have been describing:

> Balancing on Mrs James Cook's bonnet
> Is Edouard Manet looking bored
> Colette with paper roses below the Magi
> Dickens' house beside the Delphi charioteer
> Turner beside a lady in a picadill
> And red buses going round the square.
>
> Details when you list them can cross borders
> Into the next postcard; often they join
> In some kind of espérance, or forlorn
> Cast their looks towards each other in the mist.
> They could have quite a party in the house of Dickens
> All but the charioteer arriving by bus.

I want to finish by reading two of my own poems, and I hope they will indicate ways in which my writing subscribes to the impure behaviour I have been describing. The first poem contains several distinct voices, including that of a racing commentary which is being broadcast on the radio. But the title, 'Magasin', is, as the text points out, the French word for shop. Like Elizabeth Smither's postcard-covered wall, 'Magasin' combines – in and between its lines – a range of unlikely things. This is a poem in which the speaker talks about learning a language, yet perhaps learns that in order to grow up and join his community he will need to acquire more than a single language. The poem, which is about an unhappy experience, ends with a disjointing, code-switching joke. A boy is visiting his father in hospital, and he has brought him some popular Australian magazines:

Magasin

I have brought my father
things to read, Pix, Post, People,
and I tell him how *magazine*

is like the word for shop
in French. I have just started high school,
I am learning a language.

My father lifts his striped
pyjama top so I can see
what looks like the map of Africa

where the doctor has traced
the shape of his liver
for the third-year students.

At the end of the ward
men are listening to the races
and from the next-door bed

the man with one leg,
the bloke my father says
might have to lose the other,

leans across to tell my father
something about
the second leg at Trentham.

I began this talk with the mixed meanings of my own name, and I've just read a poem which touches on horse-racing. I want finally to read a poem which moves among the meanings of one of New Zealand's most famous names – that of the racehorse, Phar Lap. Phar Lap's name is said to have a 'pure' meaning in Singhalese; but the poem explores the fuller, richer range of meanings which attach to the name. I should explain that there's a hidden piece of code-switching right at the end of the poem. The other language there, which is heard but not uttered, is Maori. I have in mind the time when the *Te Maori* exhibition was in the National Museum in Wellington.

Phar Lap is in the museum in Wellington, too. Or, at least, what is called his 'articulated skeleton' can be found there. Most people will know the rough outline of Phar Lap's story: a phenomenally successful racing career, first in New Zealand, then in Australia; a mysterious death in America; and then the body distributed on both sides of the Tasman, like the relics of some medieval saint. Melbourne has the hide, Canberra the heart, while we have the articulated skeleton.

I enjoyed rehearsing Phar Lap's pedigree at the start of this poem: the best words you can find in New Zealand newspapers are always on the racing page. Long before the text begins to gloss Phar Lap's name, it sets up a conversation between his various ancestors.

Phar Lap

Unlikely combinations,

Prayer Wheel and Winkie, Sentiment
and Radium: names that contract and expand
like a big heart pumping

till you get an unlikely starter,
this chestnut colt,
foaled in Timaru, October 4 1926,

by Night Raid out of Entreaty,
with Carbine somewhere
in the background.

*

The hide is in Melbourne,
the heart in Canberra.
The bones are in Wellington,

the big delicate skeleton
of a horse
who used to mean business.

Dirty Silence

*

Can the name
have been planned as a pun?

In English it is one thing.
In Singhalese, Lightning.

And they say it means
something in Egyptian.

*

But he was virtually unbeatable,
the big fellow,
winning race after race in Australia
and never fading,

even after they shot at him,
even after they missed,

*

even after he died in America
of intestinal tympany,
of theory after theory . . .

They say that for five days he ate
pasture sprayed with lead arsenate,

they say that his Australian strapper
gave him Fowler's Solution,
incorrectly mixed,

or maybe even the Mafia . . .

Well, let's say he died in California,
let's say he died of absence

*

and that when they stopped talking
they sent him home,
made him articulate
bone by bone

*

till one day up at the Museum,
it might be fifty years later,

wandering along
past the days of pioneer settlement,

I walk past Cook's cannon
and a case of muskets

and hear a woman sing
in another language

from the far side of Phar Lap's ribcage.

Well, I hope that's a poem which – to return to my title – dirties the silence. It's a text which is made impure by the languages and meanings which are busy conversing somewhere inside it. And it settles at the close not for a single resolving point of rest but for a flickering moment of double vision.

The kind of poem which most interests me, and which I have been speaking for tonight, is like 'Phar Lap': a monologue which has room for conversations. Poems don't need to be 'about' all the significant things our schoolteachers used to insist on, but they ought at least to be sociable and surprising in their behaviour, in the way they voice and acknowledge the range of languages which the community gives them to use. I'm aware that the year is 1990, the 150th anniversary of a country which calls itself New Zealand. For what it's worth, my definition of a community or nation would be consistent with what I hope to find in a good poem: a monologue made up of conversations, a voice composed of many voices.

Thank you for listening to me. And kia ora, begorrah!

Dirty Silence: Aspects of Language and Literature in New Zealand, ed. Graham McGregor and Mark Williams (Oxford, 1991). The Salman Rushdie epigraph is quoted from 'Is Nothing Sacred?', *Granta* 31, 1990. The quotation from Louis Simpson is found in *The Character of the Poet* (University of Michigan Press, 1986). Hone Tuwhare's short story is in the 1 October 1990 issue of the *Listener*. Phar Lap can now be seen at Te Papa, who have sternly challenged my poem's account of the etymology of his name.

BILL MANHIRE

Interviewed by Iain Sharp

This interview took place at Bill Manhire's home in Kelburn, Wellington, on the afternoon of 9 October 1991. A few further comments were added by correspondence later.

IAIN SHARP: *The author's note for* The Elaboration *says that you were born in Invercargill, but somehow I had the impression that Clinton was your home town.*

BILL MANHIRE: I was born in Invercargill, which I think Rudyard Kipling described as the last lamp-post in the world, but I hopped around the Southland and Otago countryside while I was growing up. My father as a returned serviceman went into the hotel trade with his wife, who was a Scottish war bride. She sailed into Wellington Harbour on St Valentine's Day 1946, on a ship packed with war brides. My father met her and they drove down the South Island. She said to me once that she remembers thinking somewhere on the West Coast that they could just drive and drive forever, and never get to Scotland. They started off in Invercargill, working for the Licensing Trust, and then moved out to Wallacetown, just outside the Trust boundary. One Tuesday morning or Monday evening when I was young, the court news in the Southland paper had three of our customers, caught travelling back into Invercargill from Wallacetown 'drunk in charge'. You could drink after hours outside the Trust district, you see. One of the customers was drunk in charge of a motor vehicle, one was drunk in charge of a bicycle, and one was drunk in charge of a horse and cart. Whenever I think of my childhood, I imagine this strange procession, heading back from the pub where I was currently living to the city where I was born. Later on, we lived in Mossburn and Clinton, where we had a pub called the Oak Tree Inn, an absurd name for a hotel. I gather that when I was a boy I had a very good singing voice, and during our time in Clinton I would occasionally be hauled out of bed late at night and made to stand in the bar, and indeed on the bar, to sing the 'Invercargill March'. Eventually we ended up in Dunedin, still in the hotel business. Nowadays, whenever I meet Lindsay Rabbitt, another poet who lives in Wellington, I have an immediate rapport with him, because we both grew up in pubs in the bottom of the South Island. There are things we know about that no one else in Wellington does.

Clinton was the place of my greatest triumphs. I learned to play the chanter with the Clinton Pipe Band. I was a senior sixer in the local Wolf Cubs. This meant that I had three stripes on my arm and when everyone squatted in a circle, I was the one who cried, 'Pack! We shall dib dib dib dib,' and everyone cried back to me, 'We shall dob dob dob dob.' I started the Clinton Junior Stamp Club and spent half my time writing off for approvals. I started a school newspaper, *The Book for Bookworms*, all written by me, including a science-fiction thriller about cosmic villains who could travel through time; it only ran to two issues. I even started a children's lending library, which worked on the happy basis that all the other kids in town gave me their books, which I then kept in a room at the Oak Tree Inn, and they could take them home to read from time to time. My world fell about me when I'd been running the Clinton Robin Hood band for a few weeks and the merry men revolted and said someone else should have a turn at being Robin Hood. I solved the problem by deciding I would be Alan-A-Dale, abandoning vast political power in favour of the arts.

In the 1960s, Ian Wedde, Alan Brunton, Murray Edmond and Russell Haley were all living in Auckland, and they seemed to constitute a tightly knit group, whereas you were a lonelier figure on the literary landscape. Did you feel isolated at all living in Dunedin?

It's true that there was a group of people I didn't know, who lived in Auckland, a big place a long way from Dunedin, and who were sort of glamorous. But the fact that I was physically distant from them doesn't mean I wasn't aware of them. I was reading their work (puzzled by a lot of it, I think), and I was in touch with Ian Wedde. At one stage we wrote what, I'm sure, were very solemn, self-conscious, self-important letters.

Fortunately lost?

I hope so. But there was a whole range of interesting writers in Dunedin as well, including people like John Dickson and Kevin Cunningham. I think there were groups of writers in all of the university cities in the '60s. The Burns Fellowship was the only writing fellowship in the country at that stage, and it brought people like Hone Tuwhare to Dunedin while I was a student. There were interesting painters around too, because of the Hodgkins Fellowship. So, no, I don't think I was a solitary figure who was somehow missing out on the action. I was never sure there was an action one ought to be part of, in any case.

You've said elsewhere that your correspondence with Wedde was partly concerned with your shared enthusiasm for Robert Creeley's poetry. With the exception of Creeley, however, I've always suspected that you were influenced by different American poets from the Auckland group. I mean, it's very noticeable that the people connected with Freed *magazine generally wrote long, sprawling, egocentric poems, whereas right from the start your work was tight and enigmatic.*

I think I was reading poets like James Wright, Louis Simpson and even the dreadful Robert Bly in those days. I read Olson too, but I never felt that I wanted to write like that or live like that. I guess I've never been very interested in that sense of self-mythologising which Baxter had, or which Alan Brunton has, where the raw material of your life becomes the material for a mythology that you offer to the world. I don't find that very useful. The American poets I read with most interest somehow used words to make the world a little more mysterious. I liked the enigmatic quality, to use your word. Living in Dunedin in the early '60s, which was really still the late '50s, you needed a bit of mystery in your life.

Dunedin wasn't sufficiently mysterious in itself?

No. Every street in Dunedin is named after a street in Edinburgh. Every street in Invercargill is named after a Scottish river, hence that short story by Owen Marshall, 'A Town of Rivers'. I lived in a fairly predictable, secure world, and I was very happy in general to be there, but somewhere inside my head I also wanted a sense of mystery.

The connection with Ralph Hotere must have been made fairly early, since your first collaborative work, Malady, *was published in 1970. How did you get to know him?*

I'm not sure now. Ralph came to Dunedin as the Hodgkins Fellow. I guess we met at parties and something clicked. He's one of those people who it's easy to sit in a room with for half an hour, or an hour, or a whole afternoon, and you don't have to make small talk, or chat about the state of the nation or culture, or whatever people feel obliged to talk about. You're just happy to be sitting with someone whose presence is agreeable. I think we've always got on in that very basic way, and presumably the poems I was writing back then appealed to him somehow, and he started using the words. But the *Malady* thing was just a bad pun, which he made interesting when he put it on canvas.

It exists as a series of paintings then, apart from the drawings in the book?

I wrote the poem as a cheap typographical display on different pages, and Ralph did some drawings to go with the text, and at the same time he did a series of canvases. I think there was an exhibition of the canvases to coincide with the publication of the book, but I was living in London by then, so I wasn't sure exactly what happened. We needed to invent a press for the book to have come from. Ted Middleton, who was a friend of Ralph's, who had been a Burns Fellow and decided to stay in Dunedin, suggested that we call it the Amphedesma Press. It's a misspelling, not Ted Middleton's, of Amphidesma, which I think has something to do with toheroa. We used the name for a number of other books we published.

Bob Orr's Blue Footpaths *was one of them, wasn't it?*

That's right. That's a good book. We also did Ian Wedde's *Homage to Matisse*. There was quite a range of titles actually. Kevin Cunningham and I were both living in London at the time, and for some reason we wanted to publish little books of poetry. We had a very helpful arrangement with John Griffin, who was then the managing director of the University Book Shop in Dunedin. If we produced 200 copies of a book and sent them to him, he would simply buy them outright for a sum of money and then distribute them. That was a very cosy and fantasy-world way of being a publisher, where we didn't have to face up to how we sold the books or how we raised the money for the next project. But I think we put out some good titles at a time when not a great deal was happening.

Your second book, The Elaboration, *was published by* Square and Circle. *Who was behind that?*

Charles Brasch wrote to me in London from Dunedin, asking for a poetry manuscript. He and Janet Paul, who had been heavily involved in publishing with her husband, formed a small company called Square and Circle. The joke was always to wonder who was the square and who was the circle. I don't think it's known to this day. They wanted to publish small books of prose and poetry which also involved artists' contributions. Brasch wrote with the proposal that I should supply a text and Ralph Hotere would supply some drawings. As well as my book, Square and Circle did *The Loners*, Ted Middleton's collection of short stories, again with drawings by Ralph. Then Brasch died.

Had you known Brasch quite well in Dunedin?

I don't think I was ever very close to him, but in some way he was quite an important figure for me. I remember sending him some dreadful poems when I was in my first year at university, or perhaps my last year at high school. I'd heard there was this person who lived in Dunedin who was a poet and an editor, so I decided to send him a few of my things. I may have written them specially for the occasion. I can't remember the exact contents, but I think they had lines like 'I stalk the streets of the midnight city' and were full of soiled sheets and neon and terrible things like that. He wrote back a very nice note, which said very politely and very grammatically, 'This stuff is rubbish, but I admire you for trying. Do keep at it.' For some reason I was enormously encouraged by this straightforward response, which nevertheless approved of my desire to write. I think what I learned from Brasch was that it was proper to take yourself seriously as a writer.

He belonged to quite an interesting, floating group of writers in Dunedin, which met once a month and which I went to. Iain Lonie was there; Trevor Reeves, who had started Caveman Press. Baxter would occasionally turn up when he was in town. At one meeting Brasch proposed a game to me. I can't think why. He would supply three lines of poetry from a little working notebook, and the idea was for each of us to go away and write a poem in the manner of the other. I still have my poem somewhere, and I still think it's rather good – you know, not a bad imitation of Brasch's manner, insofar as I understood it. But I remember eventually getting his version of me, which I've lost, unfortunately. I was just horrified by it. Again, I can't recall how it went exactly, but I think it was full of lines like, 'I stalk the streets of the midnight city.'

You were still pretty young when you first appeared in Landfall, *weren't you, March 1968?*

It was a huge symbolic moment to have a poem in *Landfall*. It meant somehow you really were a writer. I owe this great rite of passage to Robin Dudding, who replaced Brasch as *Landfall*'s editor.

Dudding seems remarkably astute in how early he picked up on not just you but Wedde as well.

I think he's just a brilliant editor. It's a pity he's not still doing it. I think it was partly that he had time to shape an issue. He wouldn't lumber it with a great thematic idea; he just let it slip into place as an arrangement of parts with somehow its own shape and logic, which wasn't an obvious logic. I think every issue he did of *Landfall* and *Islands* had a centre to it. You felt like you were reading a book rather than just a gathering of things that had come to hand over the last three months. But you do need a lot of time for that to happen. I guess that's why *Islands* slowly subsided twice. But, yes, I think Robin Dudding is a very important figure in New Zealand writing, and at some stage someone will have to sit down and try to work out just what his presence consists of, apart from the considerable beard.

There seems to be a similar shaping principle behind each of your books of poetry. The order of poems in your books is often at variance with the chronology of their first appearances in magazines.

I think I started off with the idea that a published book had to be a selection from published work, so that if you had published fifty poems in magazines you would put only thirty-five in your book. It's probably not a bad idea. It might improve quite a few books of New Zealand poetry if that principle were applied retrospectively. But I also had a sense that books needed a shape and a particular kind of poem needed to be in a particular place, and if it wasn't there in the work I was producing at the moment, I would grab it from somewhere else. I think I've even grabbed poems from earlier books once or twice and moved them. There's some kind of editorial, anthologising instinct in me, I think, which isn't necessarily distinct from whatever it is that makes me want to write imaginative pieces of literature.

Your career as an editor seems to date back almost as far as your career as a published poet, what with the Amphedesma Press.

Yeah, and John Dickson and I edited the University Arts Festival yearbook in 1969, and I co-edited the capping book at Otago University too. I enjoy anthologising. I even get some pleasure out of helping to plan the programme for the Writers and Readers Week in the Wellington Arts Festival.

I've always had the impression that certain kinds of literary criticism don't interest you at all. Is that so? My guess is that you would much rather be engaged in some kind of editing work than face yet another critical essay which interprets whoever's great poem or novel.

I think I've always felt uneasy about literary criticism. I never wanted to do the literary criticism paper at the University of Otago, for example. In my day it was just Aristotle through to T.S. Eliot, of course. Theory doesn't interest me greatly; I think partly because too much of it seems to me totalitarian in its behaviour.

Were you a reader of And?

Oh, I quite liked *And*, because it misbehaved. *And* was a kind of vehicle for literary theory, but it became part of the variety of things that were going on. I liked it because it made life more various. I liked the essays *And* ran by Roger Horrocks. I think *And* took its own life at just the right moment as well. But a lot of people who get involved in theory seem to be at odds with variety.

Because they can't bear to be contradicted?

Well, there's lots in the way of totalising discourse, as they say. I suppose if you've got enough theories, all competing with one another, it doesn't matter. I think there's some point, though, at which theory represents the academy's revenge against the imagination. I know it's terribly old-fashioned, but I actually do believe in this thing called the imagination. If you work in a university and teach in a department of philosophy, presumably at some point you can see yourself as primary material. You're just as important as Aristotle or Wittgenstein or whoever. You can interpret them, of course, but ultimately you're all sitting on the same shelf. But English literature is rather different. Why should you have to teach John Keats? You might be more intelligent than he was. I notice that a number of students who get into literary theory actually believe themselves to be wiser than the books they study. I can't cope with that kind of arrogance. It just seems appalling.

I can quite enjoy it when it reaches the level of magnificence that Leigh Davis sometimes achieved.

Oh yeah, that was terrific – very bouncy. And there are some great minds working in literary theory, there's no doubt about it. But the minds that aren't great seem to me less interesting than the minds that aren't great in other areas of human activity. Do you believe there's such a thing as the imagination?

I guess so. It's hard to see how anything at all could be invented otherwise.

Yeah. I've never really understood what people like Coleridge are going on about when they start constructing elaborate theories of the imagination, but I do think it's important to be capable of imagining what it's like to be other than you are. That's why poetry matters to me, I think. It constantly says that imagination is important. I think there's a problem in general with the imagination in New Zealand society. It's thought of as a bad thing. Or not even thought of. You notice this attitude in our driving habits, in our failure to learn languages other than English and in the way the government tries to introduce superannuation reform without being able to imagine what the likely reaction will be. There's a general inability in this country to imagine other ways of being. One of the functions of poetry is to ask us to imagine, and imagine actively – read these words and create a world from them.

You would be strongly out of sympathy then with the Wystan Curnow kind of postmodernism which declares the imagination redundant?

I just find most of the Language poets very boring. I get no pleasure of any kind from reading them. I guess that's a very sad thing for me to say. But it's like any other kind of activity. Some people do it well, and some don't. I've really enjoyed some of Lyn Hejinian's writing.

She gets taught in the American poetry course at Auckland University, along with Ron Silliman. Do you like Silliman?

Yeah, I do quite like him. It's hard to get hold of stuff, though. You have to live solemnly within the various information networks if you want to keep up. But who's the one who came round New Zealand not so long ago? Charles Bernstein? I think he's awful. He's just boring.

He did a pretty weird reading at the Gluepot in Ponsonby.

Language poetry overlaps a lot with theory, I guess, and he's in there overlapping as madly as he can. I think that theory and Language poetry are two areas where people are thought to be interesting simply by dint of declaring themselves part of the activity. I find that rather annoying. I'm very happy to make distinctions between those who are interesting and those who aren't.

Distinguishing between lesser and greater talents isn't very fashionable at the moment, of course. We're all supposed to be democrats.

What's the phrase that's used? False valorisation? Who knows? Some of the words are great fun. I was very pleased when people started to pick up on the phrase I used in one of my stories, 'Ventriloquial' – 'discourse substitute'. It's sort of a racing term.

There's a lot of racing terminology in your work. Where does it come from exactly? Do you go out to the racetrack every weekend and bet furiously?

No but I used to go to the races when I was a kid. It was a really exciting family event. Or in Clinton there was the Railways picnic. We would get onto the steam train and chuff out to Lake Waihola, where there would be a lolly scramble and overheated people playing bagpipes. But pubs are centres for gambling as well as drinking in New Zealand. Every pub has its in-house bookie, the radio's relaying the track commentaries. A lot of the conversation in pubs has to do with the races. So you could say I grew up in a racing atmosphere. Actually, my father was the part-owner of various horses at various times, none of which ever did him any good. One of them was called Detain, which was a perfect name, because it always came last. All that stuff from my childhood has somehow lingered on in my poems. I agree that racing is everywhere in my work – 'Wingatui', for instance.

The old Wingatui railway station was up for sale about four years ago. I wanted to send you a window or something, but I couldn't afford to be lumbered with the expense of removing the whole station. But how did you feel when 'Wingatui' appeared in Private Eye's Pseuds' Corner?

Oh, I was deeply flattered.

Was there a New Zealander on the staff of Private Eye *at the time, do you think?*

No, although I have an idea that one of the current editorial people is a New Zealander. I think 'Wingatui' appeared in Pseuds' Corner as a bit of surrealist waffle. There was a poem by Paul Muldoon in the same column. Probably both entries came from the same outraged *Times Literary Supplement* reader.

A quotation from Allen Curnow turned up in Pseuds' Corner not long afterwards – the one about having to be in the Mediterranean to understand the Pacific.

Oh bugger.

You thought you were the only New Zealand poet to be featured? I'm sorry to disillusion you.

But, as Ian Wedde and others have pointed out, there was a language problem with 'Wingatui'. Poems sometimes need more translation than we initially realise when they move from one English speaking country to another. I think this is especially true with the Poms, who have become parochial and provincial without noticing it. I think the area where horses parade before a race, which we call the bird cage, is known as the paddock in England. Of course, that means something else again here. Someone said to me the other day that if Rupert Brooke had been a New Zealander, instead of 'some corner of a foreign field', he would have written 'some corner of an overseas paddock'.

The Brits often make the complacent assumption that they know best. The English guy who replaced Anne French for a while at Oxford University Press and worked on *Dirty Silence*, for example, made all sorts of happy, blithe changes and sometimes got things wrong. When I said I was born in the South Island, for instance, he changed it to 'in South Island', because he assumed it was just like 'in Northern Ireland'. One of my other favourite stories about this kind of thing concerns Maurice Gee's second novel, *A Special Flower*, which in the published version has a chapter that begins, 'At Christmas the Frasers rented a beach on Waiheke Island.'

They must have been remarkably rich.

Eventually you realise it's a misprint for 'bach'. When Maurice sent his manuscript to Hutchinson's in London, the English editors obviously thought, 'Bach? This word is not spoken by anyone we know. Therefore it doesn't exist. In the colonies, where Maurice Gee lives, you probably can rent a whole beach quite easily.' Maurice corrected the mistake on the galley proofs, but eventually when the page proofs came back for him to check he found that the editors had changed it to 'beach' again. He made the correction a second time, but it still appeared as 'beach' in the final published form. I guess that's what I mean about the Brits being parochial without realising it.

On the whole, though, your work seems to have had quite a good response in Britain?

Yeah, people read the stuff there and publish it.

You've published much more in Britain than in the States, haven't you?

Yeah. It's probably just that I knew which British magazines to send stuff to, because I lived in London for three years in the '70s, and I was there again for another year in 1981. I've published a couple of stories in America, and I did a reading tour there.

Who was that with?

Keri Hulme, Witi Ihimaera and Lauris Edmond. We must have made a very strange troupe. We were mostly reading at university campuses, and it was all brilliantly timed to coincide with their vacations, so I don't think it was a big promotional success.

Has any of your work been translated into foreign languages?

I don't think much of it has. I've seen some funny translations of things into Russian and Chinese. There was a time when the Russians and Chinese were translating everything they could find. But I can't imagine my poems would translate very well. There's too much tonal shifting. Loose versions of some poems might work, I suppose, but it would have to be a language which let irony exist.

You've done some versions of Old English poems – 'Wen' and 'Wulf' and 'The Anglo-Saxon Onion'. Do you plan to do any more translating?

Occasionally I think I might want to. I have a rough version of a long, early Danish poem somewhere. What I'd really like to translate is some skaldic verse, but it's so complicated I can't even understand it properly let alone translate it. A surface translation might work, just following the wild image patterns without worrying too much about the sounds or what the images refer to. But I'm very bad at languages. I've half-started learning a great many and given them up at the point where some real work was involved.

What made you want to translate Camille Flammarion?

Oh, 'Contemplation of the Heavens' isn't an actual translation. Rather, it's theft from a translation. I didn't translate from the French either, but from the English. The subtitle says 'After Camille Flammarion', so that's probably where the confusion comes from. I just wanted to acknowledge the source of the misty phrases I was using. Flammarion wrote the most wonderful, romantic astronomy texts the world has ever seen.

I'm not quite sure of the chronology. When was it that you began to teach at Victoria University?

In 1973 – a long time ago now. I came straight to Wellington from London, where I'd been doing postgraduate work on Old Icelandic.

Your teaching career seems to favour the practical over the theoretical. You teach people Icelandic, and you run the creative writing workshop. Has this been a deliberate policy on your part?

I think it's all been fairly accidental. I mean, the original composition course was set up by Don McKenzie, one-time professor of English at Victoria, who wanted something like the arrangement at Cambridge, where students could submit a manuscript of creative writing as part of their degree, so that Sylvia Plath, for example, submitted a book of poems. There was a stage where the English Department at Victoria had a creative writing course, which I think was a third-year course, but there was no real exam and there were no classes. As a prerequisite, students needed to have passed a course in eighteenth-century poetry.

As proof of their sincerity?

Yes, as proof that they really were English students. If they submitted a folio of writing, they were given six credits out of the 108 credits they needed for their arts degree. But after a year or so the students began to feel lonely. They wanted to talk to one another and have someone teaching them. I was the person who ended up co-ordinating a number of meetings between the students. Eventually the meetings got more structured, and I started having power fantasies and started suggesting things they might like to try and write about. Over a period of a few years, we changed the prerequisites, so that now anyone can apply for the course. You don't have to be an English major. A lot of people do apply. Twelve people are accepted each year, and in the last couple of years seventy-five people have applied. It's been very hard work choosing the right people, and obviously the right people have sometimes been left out.

The course seems to me to have developed real power, so that now Wellington appears to be the place where most of the action is, as far as young New Zealand writers are concerned. It's almost as if there were a Wellington school of writers.

Whatever the effect Charles Brasch had on me when I was young, that's the effect I would like to have on the people that come through that workshop. Again, I think it's very much a matter of getting them to take themselves seriously as writers. That doesn't mean pompously, solemnly or self-importantly. I'm not talking about a po-faced seriousness, but just that I'd like to make them aware that writing is something their lives can consist of. But I'd hate it if there were a Wellington school, *your* phrase, where everyone sounded the same, because the one thing I do believe very strongly, and again it's not a fashionable thing, is that each writer has their own voice, and in an important way everyone's task is to find out what that voice is. I try very hard to make sure that the students in the course chase off in a direction that is theirs, and to that extent I keep myself separate from the assessment procedure. There are ways of teaching courses like this where the person in charge simply says to the students, 'You write as you wish during the year, and we'll have exercises and meetings and so forth, and I'll just give you a grade, but pretend it's not happening.' Well, at that point, of course, they all try to work out how to please the person awarding the grades. So I've devised a useful system where I'm not involved in the assessment programme, and students can go in whatever direction they feel they want to. Though, again, I keep trying to change the direction they came into the course with, because I think there's often a problem with younger writers that they have a very limited sense of their capacity. They think they can do only one thing, and probably they're capable of many others.

We do a lot of exercise work. I try to set exercises which make the students jump the tracks imaginatively and do things they probably wouldn't try otherwise. I think this has been very successful. It's surprising how, when people are faced with a set of constraints, they become astonishingly inventive and powerful in the way they use language, much more so than if they're simply given a sheet of white paper and told to get creative and imaginative and deeply meaningful. It's always interesting to see pieces I remember being set as exercises turning up in magazines or winning short-story contests. I immediately ring up and ask for a ten per cent cut! No, I'm only kidding. But rather than acting as an imaginative straitjacket, the exercises usually work as a release mechanism.

I'm very happy to take some of the credit for persuading people to take themselves seriously as writers, or to take language or the fact of an audience seriously, or to take a few imaginative risks. But I'm not at all happy to be seen as some kind of mentor figure. Finally the students have to find a voice that is theirs, and that's their business and no one else's.

Do you regularly participate in the exercises yourself?

No, no, I'm just the crazed authority figure who sets them. I wouldn't have the time. I make them work far too hard. I couldn't work as hard as that. Although they're given six credits at the end of the course, they do about eighteen credits' worth of work. You can really take advantage of people's desire to write.

The students must have a lot of literary ambition to get into the course in the first place?

Yeah, but equally they can be very tentative about showing their work for the first time. There's a lot of real coming-out-of-the-closet, stuff with people who have previously shown their writing only to their mums or their best friends, who of course just say, 'Well done! I always knew you were a genius.' Reading their work aloud to the class and having other people make comments on it is often a huge step for the students. I think it would be strange if it wasn't.

Did you have people you could show your work to when you were young?

Just friends. We all knew we were total geniuses and so on. Actually, there's a part of me which totally disapproves of this creative writing workshop culture which is now growing up.

Under your supervision?

Yeah, there's part of me which doesn't like it at all. And yet some extraordinary work comes out of it. I think it's important that people don't become totally wedded to the group, where there's an instant audience, and everyone tends to be too nice to one another. For that reason, the workshops at Victoria stop at the middle of the year, and after that the students work by themselves, putting together quite substantial folios of their writing without the support of the group. Of course, strong friendships often develop between people in the course who find one another's writing interesting, but I think it's healthier if these friendships take place outside of the organised occasion.

Speaking of jumping the tracks imaginatively, was it a conscious decision on your part to switch from poetry to prose, at least for a while, in the mid-'80s?

There was a stage where I felt, rightly or wrongly, that my poetry was becoming stale. I could do very good copies of my own poems – you know, I could do a good impersonation of Bill Manhire – but it began to feel as if I were becoming a cheap imitation of myself, although it might have been the case that I was the only one who could tell the difference. I wanted to go on writing, and ultimately I wanted to go on writing poetry. Switching to prose was just a noble idea, really, to set me off in what I hoped would be new directions. The mania for short-story competitions also started around that time, so there were these wonderful deadlines for me to meet and there were carrots of money dangled in front of me. My book, *The New Land*, began to shape itself while I was on sabbatical leave in 1987. Stepping outside of New Zealand somehow helped me to see the patterns and to realise that New Zealand would be at the centre of the book. I think that being overseas partly accounts for the sort of disenchanted-cum-whimsical-cum-satirical tone of those stories. At some point I must have decided that I would try to come at New Zealand in a variety of different ways. I'd have my science-fiction story, my total realism story, a crazed surreal piece, a phoney literary interview, and so on. *The Brain of Katherine Mansfield* was originally going to be part of the book too, but then I decided it would be nice to publish it separately. I'm very pleased with *The Brain of Katherine Mansfield* actually.

The timing ended up perfect, with The Brain of Katherine Mansfield *coinciding with the Mansfield centennial and* The New Land *coinciding with New Zealand's 1990 celebrations*

Maybe I'm just opportunistic. I must have arrived in London just before Christmas in 1986. My brother works for a publishing firm in London, and he gave me a big cardboard box full of science-fiction, including some choose-your-own-adventure books. For some reason, I went to New Zealand House – I suppose all New Zealanders go there when they're in London – and it was in the middle of some kind of promotional exercise where there were lots of brochures about New Zealand, which were all very sunny and colourful and presented a stupid fantasy-land in stupid tourist language. I think I was feeling rather homesick at the time but the only evidence of home I could find was this nonsense. I was also feeling middle-aged. I remember going to the British Museum on 27 December, which was my fortieth birthday, to look at the latest bog person that had just been discovered – the one they were calling Pete Marsh. I thought he was better preserved than I was. So I was feeling rather aged and homesick when I started to write *The Brain of Katherine Mansfield*, which is a half-nostalgic, half-satirical story about people romping about in the bottom half of the South Island, which I've always regarded as my home territory, since it's where I had my childhood adventures.

When you returned to poetry in Milky Way Bar, *the general mood of your work seemed to have changed. At least, your previous book,* Good Looks, *struck me as generally pessimistic in tone, whereas* Milky Way Bar, *although not necessarily optimistic, is much more playful.*

Yeah, I think writing prose must have shifted me around somehow. Some of the poems in *Milky Way Bar* developed an oblique narrative behaviour.

Very misbehaved narrative, though?

Yeah, but there's still a sense in which 'Hirohito' tells the story of Hirohito's life, for example. I don't think I'd written anything with that kind of clear shape to it before. I didn't set out to write narrative poetry, but somehow the idea of narrative crept into my poems.

Perhaps you should attempt a Norse saga?

That would be all right, but it would be very pessimistic – total fatalism, in fact. I think prose writing generally attends to the physical and social surfaces of the world more readily than poetry, which tends to drift into a private universe. I think the short stories I wrote helped to bring the world back into my poems. I started writing about things outside myself.

Including things which don't usually appear in poems, such as reference to B-grade westerns and 'lowbrow' magazines like Pix, Post *and* People.

Yeah, I wonder why there's so much of that stuff.

Perhaps it's the result of a fierce dislike of preciousness?

It must have something to do with the fact that simply as a reader I have felt very, very strongly that poetry's important, and therefore I object violently to the kind of precious, poseur element that gets into the poetry business. I don't like that high cultural view of poetry at all, where it becomes a vehicle whereby people offer their superior wisdom to the world, saying, in effect, 'I am a poet, therefore I am wiser than you are.' I don't think poets are necessarily any wiser than people who read poetry. I think that some poems can be pretty resourceful, of course.

I've never had the impression that any older New Zealand writer has had a powerful effect on your writing, not at least in the way that Baxter and Curnow were obviously powerful presences which helped shape C.K. Stead's approach to poetry, or that Kendrick Smithyman has been an important presence for Murray Edmond.

I don't like the idea of being part of a literary salon, and I don't think it matters much whether it's a salon consisting of contemporaries who live in the same city or a chronological salon located in your culture. I've always enjoyed reading a range of poets who probably wouldn't speak to one another if they were in the same room. I think Philip Larkin's terrific, for example, but equally I like John Ashbery. And I like both Ashbery and James Fenton, who certainly wouldn't get along together. It's never seemed to be a problem to me. I guess it's amazing that I have any sort of voice of my own, given the diversity of my reading interests. And it may be that I don't. Perhaps I just make a range of mimic noises. In fact, I was quite a good mimic when I was a boy.

As well as being a fabulous singer? You could perform the 'Invercargill March' in different voices?

Yes, and I'm also a brilliant ballroom dancer. You should ask my wife. But I think a certain mimic skill is part of writing anyway. Some writers are afraid to let any element of mimicry into their work, because they're desperately trying to be original. They confuse originality with authenticity and integrity. I think you acquire your voice as a writer by listening to and imitating other voices, just as in the most literal sense you acquire your voice as a child by mimicking the various noises you hear around you, as well as the size of your diaphragm, or however that mechanism works.

You were commenting before on a sense of staleness you had with your poetry in the mid-'80s. Actually, I felt that the steam had gone out of English language poetry just about everywhere at that time. Did you share that feeling?

I guess so, but I don't feel it so much now as I did a few years ago. To suggest it happened everywhere seems a bit sweeping, though. What happened in New Zealand, I think, was that the idea vanished of one generation having to front up and take on the generation before it, in order to speak at all. I'm one of the so-called 'young New Zealand poets', who with a bit of luck have all finished their mid-life crises by now, but in the '80s there didn't seem to be a generation coming after us telling us we were middle-aged. There wasn't a new group who were thinking collectively in a different way and displacing the one before it. Instead, there was a kind of broadening out. People were saying, 'You haven't looked here, and you haven't looked over here.' Women and Maori poets came along, for instance.

I did think American poetry had lost its edge in the mid-'80s. Instead of the range of voices that had amazed me in the '60s, the American poets all seemed to be speaking with a similar, synthetic sort of voice. Actually, I suspect creative writing courses had something to do with that – places like Iowa.

Do you have much contact these days with the other so-called young New Zealand poets?

When someone invents a title like that and sticks you in an anthology, people tend to assume that you spend a great deal of time drinking in pubs with the other poets in the collection and attending one another's parties. People assume that I see a great deal of Ian Wedde, for example, and in fact he is a friend, but I see Ian only about four or five times a year. We feel comfortable with one another when we do meet, as people do who have a certain amount of shared experience, which might just mean being born in the same year. I try to steer clear of affiliations and tribal groupings, but I suppose people only understand the world by inventing tribes, affiliations and categories, assigning X to this one and Y to that one.

In the last few years something odd seems to have happened to the notion of the line in New Zealand poetry. Younger writers like Jenny Bornholdt and Virginia Were produce texts which are a curious typographical mixture of verse and prose. I don't think it's just a matter of carelessness about lineation either. Particularly in Jenny's case, the various pauses and breaks seem carefully worked out.

I'm not sure where that comes from. Dinah Hawken does it too. Perhaps it's not so important now for New Zealand writers to opt for one thing or another. I make a point in the original composition workshops of mixing things up. The poets have to have a go at prose, and I make the prose writers produce some poetry. Sometimes some lovely hybrid work results.

But you continue to make clear distinctions between poetry and prose in your own writing?

Oh yes, I even like to have very tidy stanzas. I suppose what I really like is to set up a system which looks wonderfully secure when you first encounter it on the page, but within the framework there are crazy things which tip the reader off balance. I like to have steady three-line stanzas marching down the page, but within that apparent regularity everything's all over the place, and readers continually have to regain their balance. Or I like to say crazed and illogical things in a very logical, pedantic, grammatical kind of way. I do care very much where lines break and how the stanzas look on the page, but I also like that tension between security and insecurity, or between incoherence and a patient tone of voice.

One of the things I like about Milky Way Bar *is the way the lines often sound off-hand, even chatty, but each word is craftily chosen.*

Maybe that's just a rhetorical device. When I give lectures, I have everything written out beforehand, but I like to deliver them as if I'm improvising.

Do you revise much?

Ah, I was hoping you would ask that question, since it's one of the ones I included in 'Some Questions I Am Frequently Asked'.[1] I think I used to work very fast to get a text that I would then fiddle with, but now I inch along slowly. Perhaps I take much longer to write a poem than I used to because the process has become one of accretion these days. But I actually

---

1   The 'phoney literary interview' referred to earlier.

enjoy revision, especially when I feel I'm working on something which is quite good anyway. It's a much less anxious business than getting the first draft. Facing that sheet of white paper can feel like a bad movie of Scott going to the South Pole.

You seem not to revise your poems after they have been published; the magazine version is the same as the book version.

I think I probably go along with whoever's notion it is that poems are never finished, only abandoned, but there comes a point when you have to let a poem get by on its own. There's a funny kind of conflict where you're looking for the continuities in your life, but you don't want to create continuities at the expense of the differences. I don't want to go back and smother the person I once was, any more than I want to take a photograph of myself in 1975 and rub out half my hair to make myself look mildly bald.

Did you see the interview Robert Mannion did with Michele Leggott recently in the Dominion Sunday Times, *where he expressed his outrage at that piece of yours, 'The Asterisk Machine', which appeared in* Landfall 177. *Robert wasn't at all impressed by two pages of Xs followed by a page with just an asterisk on it.*

Oh, I got great pleasure out of that. You've probably noticed that I like to put asterisks in my poems from time to time. I like asterisks. I think they're a much under-rated device. I was offered a fabulous sum of money to do something for the *Now See Hear!* exhibition in the Wellington City Art Gallery. So I thought I'd set up a text machine which simply sat in the corner and produced a screenful of Xs and then one tiny solitary asterisk. It continued to work away steadily while people were taking their cappuccino, eventually producing something like 120,000 asterisks. The other pieces in the exhibition were much more manic and outrageous. My machine was just hard-working – a steady little trundler, to borrow one of Maurice Gee's phrases. *Now See Hear!* was designed partly to subvert various conventional ways of thinking about language, but I think the asterisk machine may have had the effect of mildly subverting the exhibition itself, since it couldn't produce words at all, only this hopeless little star. The *Landfall* version simply represents – rather lamely – what happened.

You seem to enjoy technology generally, using a computer, for example, to generate that poem 'Allen Curnow Meets Judge Dredd'.

Yeah, but I don't think I'm very good with technology. I couldn't tell you how a car works, for example. It's just a magical thing that happens. I've sometimes wondered what Curnow made of that poem. Really, it was just intended as an affectionate tease.

He probably pretends he's never heard of it.

But, yeah, I like the things that technology enables you to do with a text. They can be good fun. I was going to produce a whole string of those poems at one stage: 'Lauris Edmond Meets the Dancing Wu-Li Masters', 'Leigh Davis Meets Matthew, Mark, Luke and John' . . .

Are the mechanical devices a means of getting started with your poems?

There might be some truth in that. I've never been able just to think of a topic I want to write about and then find the words to do it. And the writing I don't like in other poets is often manifestly that sort of writing. But if you constantly want to surprise yourself with what you write, maybe that does mean it's very hard to get going and some kind of artificial trigger is needed. Perhaps I should start going to my own creative writing workshops to pick up a few trigger ideas.

You do seem to use more trigger ideas than other poets – everything from found language to the battery-operated crystal ball you mention in 'Life with Madame Rosa'.

It's probably also a way of stopping me from becoming a hopelessly soggy romantic. Give me half a chance . . .

And you'll be back stalking the streets of the midnight city?

Yeah, I guess it's a matter of striking a balance between being a soggy romantic and being a technological smartarse. I don't want to be either.

In the Same Room, ed. Elizabeth Alley and Mark Williams (Auckland University Press, 1992)

THE POETRY FILE

'The Poetry File' was a monthly column on poetry, commissioned by Stephen Stratford for his magazine *Quote Unquote*. The columns were published – sometimes in a more occasional than monthly manner – between 1993–1997.

Waiwhare

The Koppio sorrows for lost Wolloway,
    And sigheth in secret for Murrurundi,
The Whangaroa wombat lamenteth the day
    That made him an exile from Jerrilderie;

The Teawamute Tumut from Wirrega's glade,
    The Nangkita swallow, the Wallaroo swan,
They long for the peace of the Timaru shade
    And thy soft balmy airs, O sweet Mittagong!

Sweet Nangwarry's desolate, Coonamble wails,
    And Tungkillo Kuitpo in sables is drest,
For the Whangarei winds fall asleep in the sails
    And the Booleroo life-breeze is dead in the west.

Cootamundra, and Takee, and Wakatipu,
    Toowoomba, Kaikoura are lost!
From Oukaparinga to far Oamaru
    All burn in this hell's holocaust!

Narrandera mourns, Cameroo answers not
    When the roll of the scatheless we cry:
Tongariro, Goodiwindi, Woolundunga, the spot
    Is mute and forlorn where ye lie.

These stanzas are from Mark Twain's 'A Sweltering Day in Australia' – '(To be read soft and low, with the lights turned down)'. Twain travelled and lectured in Australia and New Zealand in the late 1890s: 'A Sweltering Day' was one of the results. He started out with a list of eighty-one Maori and Aboriginal words, and managed to get sixty-six of them into the finished poem.

In one sense Twain's poem is a version of the well-known 'I've Been Everywhere' song. But it depends for its effect on using words which don't belong in poems. The word 'bicycle' was once deemed dangerously unpoetic. How much more unpoetic, then, are words like Tongariro and Oamaru! Even so, Twain's greatest problem is technical. He can only include Maori and Aboriginal languages in his poem by rejigging them rhythmically, thus domesticating them within the English line. In the first stanza, 'Whangaroa' has to be pronounced as a three-syllable word (Whang-a-row) if the line is to work metrically; while Te Awamutu has been turned, deliberately or not, into Tee-wah-mewt.

Not many contemporary writers would use Maori words in English texts with Twain's happy abandon. Nineteenth-century Pakeha were less bothered. Writers like Alfred Domett and Thomas Bracken barely hesitated when it came to incorporating Maori stories, characters and words into their work. Bravest of all was Arthur Desmond, who offered a repeated refrain which ran: 'Exult for Te Kooti, yo-hoo!' No doubt 'yo-hoo!' represents a piece of Polynesian exultation; but it looks and sounds for all the world like a friendly greeting from Coronation Street.

Maori has had even stranger moments in twentieth-century poetry. Not only did the Dada artists who flourished in Zurich during the first world war invent 'sound poems', like this one by Hugo Ball, where the noises are not inhabited by conventional meanings

> gadji beri bimba
> glandridi lauli loni cadori
> gadjama bim beri glassala
> glandridi glassala tuffm i simbrabim
> blassa galassasa tuffm i simbrabim

but they also gave chanted cabaret performances of Maori waiata, partly because the sounds made no sense to them, and partly because the words came from the South Seas and thus had 'primal' qualities which might challenge the stranglehold of European culture.

The Dadaists also composed poems in several languages – 'simultaneous' poems in which nonsense texts in English, German and French were recited by three voices at once. In fact, the practice of writing poems in more than one language has a long and respectable history – and even the great poems of the twentieth century move between languages quite deliberately. T.S. Eliot's *The Waste Land* ends, famously, with Latin, Italian and Sanskrit embedded in a wild mixture of Englishes, and this simply summarises the essentially polyglot behaviour of a poem which has already included French and German.

One of the strangest ways in which poetry touches more than one language is through what is sometimes called 'surface translation'. The American poets, Louis and Celia Zukofsky, translated the Latin poet Catullus into English. But rather than translate the content, they translated the *sound* of the Latin. Thus the form of the Latin produced a strange, disrupted set of English meanings:

> Newly say dickered my love air my own would marry me all
>   whom but me, none see say Jupiter if she petted . . .

Another version of this practice comes in a clever book called *Mots d'heures, gousses, rames*, which translates the surfaces of English nursery rhymes into French: 'Un petit d'un petit / S'étonne aux Halles . . . '

Back home, the name sometimes given to sea- or lakeside baches, Waiwhare, is not only a case of surface translation ('why worry'), it's also a cross-language pun, insofar as 'wai' means water and 'whare' means house. But for poets, the problem of inviting English and Maori to inhabit the same space, the same musical structure, remains considerable. Those who are best at it, like Keri Hulme and Hone Tuwhare, live and move between the languages as a matter of course. Even Mark Twain, challenged in 1895 by a New Zealand journalist 'to try his hand at some Maori rhymes', was defeated (like Rudyard Kipling before him) by Paekakariki. Still, there have been some advances in the last 100 years. The first playground rhyme my children ever brought home went like this:

> *Paekakariki*,
>   the boys are cheeky;
> *Wainuiomata*,
>   the girls are smarter.

Rough Stuff

The Voice

Woman much missed, how you call to me, call to me,
Saying that now you are not as you were
When you had changed from the one who was all to me,
But as at first, when our day was fair.

Can it be you that I hear? Let me view you, then,
Standing as when I drew near to the town
Where you would wait for me: yes, as I knew you then,
Even to the original air-blue gown!

Or is it only the breeze, in its listlessness
Travelling across the wet mead to me here,
You being ever dissolved to wan wistlessness,
Heard no more again far or near?

    Thus I; faltering forward,
    Leaves around me falling,
Wind oozing thin through the thorn from norward,
    And the woman calling.

'The Voice' comes from the remarkable group of poems which Thomas Hardy wrote after the death of his wife, Emma. Many of them are memory pieces; and though they are poems of loss, they often recall the wonder of what has been lost, the way things were 'at first, when our day was fair'.

    The poem is typical of Hardy in that it is marked (but never marred) by deliberate moments of awkwardness. It starts, rhythmically at least, in a fairly bland, agreeable manner: the stresses fall as we expect, nothing seems out of place. But in the fourth line things begin to go wrong – the line itself feels short, and in fact there are only nine syllables to set against the ten syllables of the second line. The rhythm loses its regularity because something – to borrow the poem's opening words – is 'missing'. The fact that 'fair' makes only a half, half-hearted rhyme with 'were' is also part of the poem's quiet, sudden stumble.

    And so it goes on – a harmony is always being indicated in the stress patterns, which the poem refuses to live up to. Perhaps this is strongest in the decidedly 'unpoetic' last line of stanza three, 'Heard no more again far or near?', with its rhythmic and questioning awkwardness and banal diction. And then the final stanza switches metre altogether; and at the same time, by referring to the speaker 'faltering forward', accurately describes the poem's own behaviour. This is a poem which tries to sing a sad song, but, in order to be true to its feelings, ends up speaking them. Or it mixes singing and speaking in ways which actually create the feelings referred to.

Hardy often looks gauche and clumsy on the page, always falling short of the mellifluous sounds that poets are supposed to make. (He makes noises more often than sounds.) But this gives his work a sort of dogged integrity – you see the effect, and at the same time you see the *work* that produces the effect. It's rather like seeing the brush marks in an oil painting; or it's as if you've been allowed to see the front and back of a tapestry at the same time.

Perhaps an even better analogy is the one that Lawrence Jones reports James K. Baxter offering in response to a University of Otago student who had complained about Hardy's rhythmic roughness. 'Hardy,' said Baxter, 'is like a skilled cabinet-maker, who makes beautiful objects; every detail is perfect, but he refuses to fill the nail holes – he's not going to hide the kind of work that's gone into it.' This is a lesson that Baxter must have taught himself. His own early poems are full of high-flown, unworldly, musical grandeurs. He had to learn to leave things a little unpolished – as he did in the poems he wrote from *Pig Island Letters* onwards. His interest in ballad and polemical verse and folk forms would no doubt have led him in such a direction.

There are plenty of poets who mix polish and roughness in their work. William Blake is one; in very different ways, so are poets like Wordsworth, Robert Browning, Walt Whitman ('one of the roughs,' he called himself), Bertolt Brecht, Stevie Smith, Les Murray and Philip Larkin. Closer to home, we have writers like Elizabeth Smither – or Denis Glover who, for all the lyric grace of his 'Sings Harry' poems, is probably going to be best remembered for putting the words, 'Quardle oodle ardle wardle doodle,' inside a poem.

Here is a poem by Stevie Smith that makes dazzling use of awkwardness:

I Remember

It was my bridal night I remember,
An old man of seventy-three
I lay with my young bride in my arms,

> A girl with t.b.
> It was wartime, and overhead
> The Germans were making a particularly heavy raid on
>   Hampstead.
> What rendered the confusion worse, perversely
> Our bombers had chosen that moment to set out for Germany.
> Harry, do they ever collide?
> I do not think it has ever happened,
> Oh my bride, my bride.

This poem's force probably depends on our assumption that the girl is dead at the point when the speaker, presumably now very much older than seventy-three, begins talking. But that force also depends on the poem's willingness to be gauche and banal. The first and last lines sound like conventional poetic music; but almost everything in between sounds prosaic – words stumble through a rhyme scheme, but never reach the status of 'poetry', and the rhyme scheme itself (perversely/Germany) fails to achieve even the most ordinary harmonies. When Stevie Smith performed this poem at poetry readings, her audiences would start roaring with laughter, only to be caught flat-footed by the extraordinary, un-awkward power of the final line.

The American poet, Carl Sandburg, once wrote that poetry was 'the achievement of the synthesis of hyacinths and biscuits'. I think I disagree with him about the need for a synthesis; but I do agree that poems need plenty of biscuits alongside the hyacinths.

Logopoeia

'Janet Waking', written by John Crowe Ransom in the 1920s, is one of a large number of poems which deal with a child's first apprehension of death. But unlike most others – Wordsworth's 'We Are Seven' or Hopkins' 'Spring and Fall' or Peter Bland's 'Death of a Dog' – its tone jumps and shifts and lurches, so that the poem seems to mock and tease the very grief it records.

> *Janet Waking*
>
> Beautifully Janet slept
> Till it was deeply morning. She woke then
> And thought about her dainty-feathered hen,
> To see how it had kept.

Logopoeia

One kiss she gave her mother.
Only a small one gave she to her daddy
Who would have kissed each curl of his shining baby;
No kiss at all for her brother.

'Old Chucky, old Chucky!' she cried,
Running across the world upon the grass
To Chucky's house, and listening. But alas,
Her Chucky had died.

It was a transmogrifying bee
Came droning down on Chucky's old bald head
And sat and put the poison. It scarcely bled,
But how exceedingly

And purply did the knot
Swell with the venom and communicate
Its rigor! Now the poor comb stood up straight
But Chucky did not.

So there was Janet
Kneeling on the wet grass, crying her brown hen
(Translated far beyond the daughters of men)
To rise and walk upon it.

And weeping fast as she had breath
Janet implored us, 'Wake her from her sleep!'
And would not be instructed in how deep
Was the forgetful kingdom of death.

As the title suggests, this is a highly sophisticated poem, alert to all the resonances words can manage. Janet is not simply waking in the morning. She is also waking into an awareness of the fact of death, the final sleep from which there'll be no waking. But why is the death at the centre of the poem described in such ludicrous language? Why does Janet's 'daintyfeathered hen' get translated into a clapped-out old chook called Chucky? Are we really expected to take this grief seriously?

In fact, the poem is wiser than either the quizzical adult narrator (Janet's father?) or the distressed child whose cries we witness. Its point, I suppose, is that both perceptions of the tragi-comic Chucky are true, and that any fully capable view of the world will have to accommodate them both. Janet herself, the poem suggests, will one day have a far more complex sense of the world than she has at present; and she may well have to cope with the loss of far more crucial companions – for example, the mother, father and brother to whom she apportions kisses with such deliberate exactness in the second stanza.

'Logopoeia' is a fancy pseudo-Greek term coined by Ezra Pound, and it seems to me not a bad way of describing what is happening at the level of language in Ransom's poem. Pound once suggested that there were three main kinds of poetry. Poems where musical elements are preponderant, he placed under the heading 'melopoeia'. Poems in which visual images are central were examples of what he called 'phanopoeia'. But 'logopoeia' he glossed as 'the dance of the intellect among the words' – meaning poems which are not only interested in the direct meanings of words but also take account 'in a special way of habits of usage, of the context we *expect* to find with the word, its usual concomitants, of its known acceptances, and of ironical play'.

Logopoeia is a kind of poetry where language draws attention to itself, where different tones of voice, different registers, different sets of associations inhabit the same moment of utterance. Pound's own controversial *Homage to Sextus Propertius* is an extended example of such writing, deliberately mixing low and elevated styles, modern and classical allusions, in a manner which once infuriated classical scholars:

> We have kept our erasers in order.
> A new-fangled chariot follows the flower-hung horses;
> A young Muse with young loves clustered about her
> ascends with me into the aether . . .

Pound thought of logopoeia as an extremely up-to-the-minute thing, and I expect he would have judged John Crowe Ransom to be rather old-fashioned. Yet Ransom's poems often seem like textbook models of logopoeia, especially in the way they set up etymological clashes, mixing together words of Latin and Anglo-Saxon origin. In 'Janet Waking', the mock-heroic syntax and diction which record Chucky's death undermine and tease; yet the emotion of the bereaved child, especially as it is worded in the second-to-last stanza, has all the genuine dignity of classical tragedy. And of course, despite the narrator's wry deflations, the poem's most pompous and silly words (like 'transmogrifying' – which, any friendly dictionary will tell you, means 'changing, often surprisingly or grotesquely') are never attached to Janet. It's as if the poem fills itself with impurities of diction, in order to let the grief itself stand pure.

So here is a poem which very deliberately mixes its positions and perspectives. Truth, it says, is a mixed business: tenderness and scepticism, passion and irony, tragedy and comedy, aren't at odds with one another; they walk about the planet hand in hand. But the poem doesn't simply tell us these things; it *shows* them to be so. The extremes and contradictions of human experience are written into the text in the detail of the diction, in the switching tones and textures of the words.

Dirt

We are often taught to think of poems as somehow purer than other forms of utterance – music lifting above the earth, unchained and rising on its wings. Frank O'Hara is thus mildly unusual. Or the following poem is – for in it he has penned what amounts to a dirty song: an everyday, downmarket ode to dirt.

Song

Is it dirty
does it look dirty
that's what you think of in the city

does it just seem dirty
that's what you think of in the city
you don't refuse to breathe do you

someone comes along with a very bad character
he seems attractive. is he really. yes. very
he's attractive as his character is bad. is it. yes

that's what you think of in the city
run your finger along your no-moss mind
that's not a thought that's soot

and you take a lot of dirt off someone
is the character less bad. no. it improves constantly
you don't refuse to breathe do you

Of course, people still think of poetry as ethereal stuff. Poets (or some of them) are supposed to be absent-minded, dreaming creatures. Thus their work will have to do with clouds and flowers and a range of more or less transcendental experiences, but will hardly concern itself with the mundane business of, say, eating breakfast or catching the bus to work. Leave that sort of stuff to the novelists. That's to say, some topics are appropriate for poetry, and others aren't.

Tennyson once wrote a poem called 'Saint Simeon Stylites', about a deranged fifth-century Syrian saint who spent thirty-six years of his life on top of a fifty-foot pillar in the hope that his extreme display of piety would guarantee a fast-track journey straight to Heaven. It certainly turned him into a tourist destination. Tennyson was fascinated by Simeon's hypocrisy, the richly human mixture of self-denial and self-regard. Yet one Victorian reviewer attacked the poem precisely because a figure like Simeon was unsuitable for poetry:

> We find exhibited Simeon's loathsome yet ridiculous attempts at saintship, all founded on an idea of the divinity fit only for an African worshipping a scarecrow fetish made of dog's bones, goose-feathers and dunghill rags. This is not a topic for Poetry; she has better tasks than to wrap her mantle round a sordid greedy lunatic.

Another view of poetry, of course, is that it gets a great deal of its life from the world of dog's bones, goose-feathers and dunghill rags. One of James K. Baxter's prototypes for the poet was 'not the magician or dreamer – rather the emu, who digests stones and old boots . . .'; and Frank O'Hara (born like Baxter in 1926, though he died younger, aged forty) was very much a poet with an emu-like digestion system. His poems are full of clutter and trivia; they are made up of all the contradictory human stuff that meets his gaze as he saunters along the pavement.

In fact O'Hara is best known for his 'I do this, I do that' poems, in which he simply records his lunchtime walks along the streets of central Manhattan: 'It's my lunch hour, so I go / for a walk among the hum-coloured / cabs . . .' O'Hara's poems hum with everything they encounter. They approve of dirt – 'You don't refuse to breathe, do you?' – and of the squandering, impure randomness of life. 'What is happening to me,' he once wrote, 'allowing for lies and exaggerations which I try to avoid, goes into my poems. I don't think my experiences are clarified or made beautiful for myself or anyone else, they are just there in whatever form I can find them.'

Dirt

The argument is as much about language as subject matter. Pure subjects need pure diction, words without sweat glands. It's a tall order – a desire for innocence that can only exist if the body doesn't – but of course the fact that something is unattainable doesn't stop people yearning and making their gestures. The Austrian poet Karl Kraus once said, 'My language is the universal whore whom I have to make into a virgin.' Now there's a challenge for poetry! In reply it's tempting to quote Sylvia Plath's line, 'Perfection is terrible, it cannot have children.'

Perfection, purity, innocence – they seem to have very little to do with inhaling the actual human atmosphere. The playwright Dennis Potter is dying at the moment, vehemently writing his way through terminal cancer. His great works for television – among them, *Pennies from Heaven* and *The Singing Detective* – are stunning accounts of the contending forces of purity and impurity. Potter's imperfect human beings yearn, impossibly, to be otherwise – and their yearnings are often articulated in song. But it is finally the impurity of things which sustains all of Potter's work. 'The wonderful thing about words,' he once said, 'is that they've been in so many other people's mouths.'

NOTE FOR *THE YOUNG NEW ZEALAND POETS*

A good friend describes a climbing trip in the Southern Alps, and an electrical storm late at night – the mountains clear and naked in sudden bursts of light (and so forth) – and recalls shooting off a roll of film, nervously excited, attempting to capture the light as it came, and the landscapes it set forth. Not one coincidence, however, was exact, though this was only apparent when the film was developed and discovered blank. (Moral: darkness is easy to capture.) He offers this as an image for the creative process: a snap, as it were, at the right moment, in the awareness that the disposition of such moments is not in any sense within the control of the artist. Guilty of theft, and inadequate description, I pass it on.

Lately, I have found it necessary – at any rate in writing – to approach a condition which borders on narcolepsy, where it seems possible to relax into some generous relationship with words. In this state, the head grows independent and vigorous, for a few moments anyway. This may explain why so many of the poems are short, though it is not my intention to apologise for their brevity. The chief joy of the shorter lyric I take to be its ability to carry the reader out of the sequential, linear world into its own moment: as it were, snap.

It is no new thing to remark that; nor to suggest that one writes out of a number of such instances, in time and place, which prove tenacious. But one lives there, also: so that I sometimes wonder what a New Zealander is to make of a line such as Pound's 'Dawn enters with little feet like a gilded Pavlova'. An appropriate response to that simile is no doubt a Cultural Admission, but suggests that we should not strive too earnestly for a cosmopolitan poetics. If the vision granted is of meringues, equipped with legs and ankles (and somewhere, surely, wrists), we must wave our cake forks, and approve it.

The Young New Zealand Poets, ed. Arthur Baysting (Heinemann, 1973)

EARLY READING

The Magic Faraway Tree

As a kid, I read comics with most delight: they offered a nice mix of security and excitement – the characters stayed the same but got around. I read books, too, lumbering – often with not much more than a sense of duty – across the solid platform of children's 'literature'. The author who gave me the greatest pleasure was Enid Blyton. Her books weren't – presumably still aren't – available in public libraries. But this was all to the good. It meant that to read them I had to *own* them: they could be possessed, physically (and therefore imaginatively), in ways that library books couldn't.

The books I owned were the 'grown-up' ones – *The Secret Seven, The Famous Five*, the 'Mystery' series – and I suppose the fact that they looked and felt like adult books was important. Certainly, the Noddy stories always seemed to me silly and childish, and infinitely so when the author took to reading them in a squeaky, impossibly English voice over the 4ZB Breakfast Session. It hadn't crossed my mind that her stories weren't set in some corner of New Zealand.

There was one book, *The Magic Faraway Tree*, which was always very special. The Faraway Tree itself grew in an enchanted wood, and on the edge of the wood lived a fairly ordinary family – mother, father, three children. Mother and father were irrelevant, but the children, along with a visiting cousin, had endless adventures in the company of a host of creatures who lived in the tree: Silky, Moon-Face, Mr Watzisname, the Saucepan Man. Halfway up the tree there lived an old lady who made a habit of pouring her washing-water down the tree – which made climbing a risky and comical prospect. Like this lady, most of the tree's inhabitants resembled real people. They had endless rounds of tea parties, scoffing a range of sweet things: Pop Biscuits, Google Buns and the like. Top of the confectionery list came Toffee Shocks, a kind of toffee in reverse. As you sucked one, it

55

grew larger and larger until it filled your whole mouth: then, when things seemed well beyond hope, it would explode – leaving your mouth empty.

The Faraway Tree had a kind of fairground interest. But the remarkable thing about the tree was that a ladder at the top gave access to other worlds. You climbed through cloud to find yourself in whatever land, good or bad, happened to be there. The lands rotated constantly, so that when you started up the ladder you didn't know quite what would be waiting. It might be the Land of Spells or the Land of Topsy-Turvy, the Land of the Snowman, or the Land of Do-As-You-Please. The lands seemed to be infinite, but they all meant adventure, sometimes adventure of a very sophisticated sort.

In the Land of Dreams, for instance, the children find themselves in a field of red poppies, across which the mysterious figure of the Sandman is moving. He scatters sand in their eyes; they fall asleep, and awake to find an ice cream man approaching. Their pockets are full of marbles but, happily, this is just the kind of payment the ice cream man requires. He hands over packages which, once unwrapped, prove to be large whistles. The children blow the whistles and six large policemen come puffing up, asking if help is needed. When their offers are declined, they take the children to the local swimming pool and tell them to get in and swim. 'Don't be silly,' says one of the children, 'there's no water!' The policemen are mightily distressed and begin to weep; their tears fill the pool and the children push them in. As they hit the water, the policemen are transformed into tiny blue fish which swim off into the distance, flicking their tails.

The imaginative power in such episodes makes the usual criticisms of Enid Blyton – as stylist and moralist – irrelevant. The things that happen in her books are right and remarkable. Her real strength – the thing which pleased me as a child, and continues to please me – is the way she overrides – as much as Dickens ever did – our habitual distinctions between what is real and what is fantastic. If children can climb a ladder into other lands, the people of those lands can as easily descend to ours. In Enid Blyton's work there's an easy two-way traffic between the world of the everyday and the world of the imagination – something found also in the greatest works of literature. Faraway is quite close by. Or, as one of the children in *The Magic Faraway Tree* puts it, 'It's so queer being awake and having dreams.'

'Early Reading', *Education* 26, no 10, 1977

SOME PAINTINGS I AM FREQUENTLY ASKED ABOUT

Talking with Bill Manhire about Ralph Hotere

GREGORY O'BRIEN: *How did you come to meet Hotere in Dunedin?*

BILL MANHIRE: I don't remember any particular moment. But the late 1960s was an interesting time in Dunedin. Ralph and Michael Smither were both using an old house in Castle Street for their studios. Jeffrey Harris was there too so it was an interesting territory to wander into. I've always liked hanging around artists' studios – not that I do it much. It feels like you're standing inside your own head at the moment when you're writing a poem or something.

I must have felt a temperamental affinity with Ralph, I guess. The first thing we did together was called *Malady* – though that's the wrong way of putting it, because we've never exactly collaborated. I don't think Ralph works as a collaborator. He has friendships and people he works with; he brings things to life in the gaps and spaces and accidents that other people – and circumstances – make available. Anyway, I had written this concrete/pattern poem which was just three words – four words, actually, but three articulations:

> *malady . . . melody . . . my lady*

And I'd made them into a typewritten booklet – pages of word patterns. I must have given a copy of the *Malady* book to Ralph at some stage. He presumably flicked through it and started making the paintings which became the *Malady* series.

Did he ask your permission or just bowl on into it?

He might have mentioned it to me after he started. At some stage we seem to have come to an agreement that he can help himself to my words when the mood takes him and I can pinch his images to use on book covers or whatever. I used a drawing of his on the cover of The Old Man's Example [a limited edition collection of Manhire's early poems, published by the author in 1990] and told him I was doing it, but I didn't feel I had to ask.

It's not as if Ralph bumped into my poem, 'Malady', and then started putting words on paintings. There's a history of that sort of thing in New Zealand painting, and in Ralph's earlier work too . . . the word *Polaris*, for instance, appeared in paintings from the early 1960s and then there was the astonishing *Sangro* series, where you have not only the name of a place but also inscribed numbers, which are the ages of the New Zealand dead buried in the Sangro cemetery in Italy during the Second World War – Ralph's brother is one of them. *Sangro* is both the name of the place and of a river, I think. The word looks alien at first, but it also fills with meaning once you're aware of its context and can see it repeating and repeating – this dark word with a catch of lamentation at the end.

In your work, both you and Hotere seem intent upon setting up something that, at a glance, might appear very simple but is in fact very complicated.

The word play on *malady* is a simple statement that gets more complex the more the words play against one another. Though maybe the effect there is different – as if the familiar word becomes stranger and more interesting. And I guess there's a point where it empties of meaning altogether and simply becomes patterned marks on paper or canvas. Though it's a very sloppy old love poem, really.

I'd gone overseas before the first *Malady* exhibition some time in 1970. So the first series of *Malady* paintings must pre-date the images that were used in the book. Ralph did some drawings to go with my text; there's actually a nice continuity between those drawings with their vertical lines and his later work with corrugated iron – all of his work seems continuous with itself in that sort of way. The book was published in a limited edition to coincide with the exhibition opening.

The *Malady* paintings went on for a while – Ralph was in Dunedin and I was living in London. And a few other things happened. There's a poem without a title I must have given to him at some stage:

> February, May and the birds of ice
> The moon drowns in its voices of water

and there are quite a few Hotere drawings and paintings around that use that text. Several of my early poems keep on surfacing in Ralph's work – for instance, 'The Wind II', which I don't think I've ever published in book form:

The Wind (II)

A wind goes out over the fields.
A shadow grows where I touch you.
What is this distance?
Whose hand is quietly waving?

It reappears later in his *Baby Iron* paintings . . . barely visible marks floating across these narrow corrugations. One of the things that's both interesting and frustrating with this deal we have is that I have no idea what has been used, where it is, and all that sort of stuff. But Ralph probably doesn't know either.

It seems a very loose arrangement – perhaps that openness is an essential part of the collaboration?

At one stage, while I was living in London in the early '70s, I sent Ralph a piece of poetry each week. Every so often I would put in the mail a postcard with the word *pine* on it – plus a line: 'empty of shadows and making a shadow', 'in the labyrinth, at the destruction'. Some of the lines were awful. Ralph did a series of works – mostly stuff on paper – using bits of that text. I've always found pine forests really scary and interesting in the way that Janet Frame did. There was always a plantation near where we were living when I was a child. In the forest the sound quality changed – it was scary and safe all at once – cathedral, underwater stuff. That was what was in my mind when I wrote the words, but I don't imagine they would have meant that to Ralph – it must have been strange for him to receive a weekly line about a European tree.

Maybe there's a statement about colonialism in your sending the word pine *regularly from England?*

Could have been. I'm not sure if it was an issue or not. I liked all the resonances of the word pine – sadness, torture. Maybe it was me pining for home. Actually the distance at which Ralph and I have worked from each other seems important.

Distance allows the meanings to change more, I guess – it's not like you're stuck with each other in the same creative space.

Yes, there's a sort of healthy freedom. Some years later I remember playing on the typewriter with the word *sunrise* – columns of the word below and above a sort of horizontal line. I must have sent this to Ralph – eventually it worked its way into some of his work (along with lots else) in relation to French testing in the Pacific.

Certainly the one occasion we tried to do a direct collaboration didn't come off at all. Alan Loney suggested we make a book for his Hawk Press in the late 1970s. I went down and stayed with Ralph at Careys Bay and I was going to write a sequence and Ralph would produce drawings. It didn't work at all. The kind of poems I'd wanted to write had shifted a lot and I don't think they suited Ralph. They were busier, more aggressive poems . . . making a great noise about themselves. But it was all somehow far too deliberate.

The series was going to be called 'Loss of the Forest' – and indeed there is a poem in *Good Looks* called that. Some of the titles of those poems would turn up later in Ralph's paintings, although I don't think any of the poems themselves made it. I think Ralph needs room to move that those poems simply don't allow. He needs time and space to contemplate the view and just to let things happen.

I was thinking the other day, after you talked to me about doing this interview, that there's some connection between Ralph's work and the fact that he's a trained pilot – there's a great photo I have a very fuzzy photocopy of, which shows him sitting in the cockpit of an aeroplane. I'm not sure when he got his pilot's licence, whether he was a trainee after the war . . . but you can look at his paintings sometimes and think they've lifted way up above the territory they're dealing with. They're not remote from it, they're certainly not ignoring it, but they've managed to bring a whole territory into view which hadn't been entirely visible before. And there's a kind of contemplative wisdom about what's going on. It might be spiritual or emotional or political, but there's usually that kind of lift off and looking back. He's hovering above the forest, not clomping around at ground level.

Your writing is often quite playful and ironic. When Ralph uses your words he seems, perhaps, to take them into a much darker, angst-ridden zone.

I think that darkness is already there in my early poems. What you say is true of most of the poetry after *The Elaboration* – it's much more textured tonally, probably more playful even when it's being dark. Those early poems were written when I was an emotional teenager. Even if you think about *Malady* . . . logically, the title ought to be *My Lady* and then malady and melody would be the emotional states that the title (or the beloved in the title) was generating and resolving. But I never had any doubt that the key word was *Malady*. I suppose I can look back at it now and think that it might be a poem about worship with a bit of mischief lurking in the margins. But I don't really know.

How did your first collection, The Elaboration, *which Ralph 'illustrated', come into being?*

It was published by Charles Brasch and Janet Paul under their Square and Circle imprint. Quite a few of the Hotere drawings incorporate the square and circle. He had to provide a portrait of me for the book and, as I was in England, he had to work from memory.

He did two portraits – a standard dreamy young poet line drawing [later used on the cover of *The Old Man's Example*], then he did this much wilder, murkier, messier image . . . I'm not sure if he or the publishers decided to go with the murkier number but it was a prescient decision because that was the territory my poetry was about to move into in *How to Take Off Your Clothes at the Picnic*.

It's interesting Hotere picking up on the square and circle and using it in the portrait of you. He seems to often operate on suggestions, taking very plain or commonplace ideas or forms and making a motif out of them.

You only need to think about his use of stencilled words. There may be some sort of high-cultural pedigree for that, but I suspect that it has a lot to do with stencilling place names on export produce: destinations on wool bales and things like that. Lots of New Zealanders have seen those stencilled letters – often pointing elsewhere – in freezing works, in wool stores, in orchard packing sheds, down at the wharf. I'm sure there's a connection there.

His deployment of words seems to be the antithesis of the fully brushed expressionistic handwriting of someone like McCahon. Hotere's use of stencils and wooden printing blocks and his avoidance of the 'heroic' brushstroke make the works quieter and more self regarding, postmodern in their detachment, you could probably say.

He's using something that is there already, I suppose. It's a kind of scavenging impulse . . . looking around and picking up what's at hand and using that as part of the process of making a thing, rather than having it all flow from the mind and soul of the 'genius' who's producing the 'master artwork'.

Some of his best scavenging, if that's the word, is with actual buildings.

His various studios, especially the one that was destroyed at Port Chalmers, have been astonishing constructions – always older buildings that have been adapted and reworked, often by having bits of other buildings, windows for example, incorporated into them. And often the buildings have some other, earlier function still implicit in them – ecclesiastical, say, or even mercantile, like the old stone bank he now has in Port Chalmers.

Perhaps Ralph's major scavenging act is *Black Phoenix* . . . you know, the burned boat that he resurrected (without fully *redeeming*), and which I guess will be a key thing in whatever happens inside the Te Papa building.

How did you feel about your words entering the fine arts arena?

I was very pleased to see my words have a life beyond the page – I thought that was great. And occasionally Ralph would give me a painting or drawing by way of royalty, which was pretty satisfactory.

I suppose you have to relinquish your control over the specific meanings of these words once someone like Hotere runs off with them? I recall reading a review that implied the Malady *paintings were an anti-nuclear statement.*

I don't mind what meanings he attaches to them. Or other people. I think the idea that the *Malady* paintings are an anti-nuclear statement is just silly. But you can see how someone might get to it. It's clear that Ralph did the *Polaris* series with that issue in mind and that he's a very political painter at some times and a very political person. But being a political person doesn't mean that you're not also a personal person.

If New Zealand artists put words on paintings they're expected to make pronouncements. Statements. But Hotere's work incorporating your words has never played to that notion – it's far too ambiguous.

The early poems – 'Malady', 'The Elaboration', and the various crossovers into 'Song Cycle' – they are very lyrical poems that sit waiting for someone else to contextualise them or texture them somehow, or articulate them. I don't mean they're inadequate in their own terms but they're available for other people to voice. And it's interesting that those are the poems that Ralph keeps going back to. They're the ones that composers keep on setting in various ways, too.

Would it be fair to say you're both after a spareness . . . some of Hotere's work could be described as minimalist.

There's a certain spareness that produces resonance, I guess. I feel uncomfortable with the word minimalism, which seems to imply a closing

Some Paintings I Am Frequently Asked About

down of options. A spareness of utterance that produces endless potential and possibilities – I feel Ralph's paintings work like that . . .

Some of his paintings are actually called windows, and lots of them behave like that – you feel you have to look through them, which also implies that something has the capacity to look back. Sometimes the windows behave like mirrors – buffed, shiny surfaces of one kind or another, so that you see your shadowy self reflected in them, plus these coils of light moving beneath the surface.

Following the Malady *paintings,* Song Cycle *was the next major instance of your words and his paintings getting together . . .*

The long canvases incorporating my poems came out of the *Song Cycle* project, which involved the dancer John Casserley, composer Jack Body, a guy called Barry Margan . . . Ralph was to do the stage design, which he never quite got around to doing . . . At the last minute he produced some rather abstract slides that he had painted, then dripped acid on (or something that reacted to it in some not quite controlled way), and these were projected across the bodies of the dancers. He produced a programme with a couple of dancer drawings and handwritten versions of the poems. He did a lot of dancer drawings and some of them are pretty good – again continuous with those drawings of women he's been doing over the years. One day someone will get together an exhibition of Hotere's 'Woman' drawings – and it'll be one of the great shows.

Ralph produced the *Song Cycle* canvas banners later, well after the show had finished. They were to have been hanging on the stage at various depths with the dancers moving among them.

It's typical of Ralph that the paintings appear later, after he has, well, lifted off. He gives people something to be going on with but doesn't pretend he's got somewhere when he's in fact still working his way towards it.

The *Song Cycle* paintings have words on them but also lots of accidental stuff. There are metal eyelets in the edges, and this is because they were nailed flat and lived for long periods of time out in the weather on the hill at Port Chalmers. So the paintings are sort of made up of wind and sun and rain and grit, as well as paint. They've got the days and the nights and the weather in them. That strikes me as very characteristic of his work – that what they are is partly what has *happened* to them – they're not totally deliberate effects of a controlling mind. There's a lot of accident and chance. I guess that's a kind of scavenging, too.

That's quite an organic approach . . .

Yes. It's not some sort of intellectual bricolage, it's an organic attentiveness and picking up and gathering in. I'm sure Ralph likes the fact that his corrugated iron paintings are going to go on rusting. I imagine conservators are busy trying to stop them rusting! There's a lot of process in them – they're not static.

That organic thing is part of his politics anyway – how he felt about the proposed smelter at Aramoana and so on. It's political but it could also be seen in traditional Romantic terms.

Hotere's paintings have an oracular quality. There's a sense that they are meaningful without yielding their meaning very easily. They're also very beautiful, but it has to be a difficult beauty.

Yes, and oracles offer enigmatic statements that require interpretation – they don't gloss their own meanings. Like the cover for *Landfall* 100, which looked to some people at the time like a stained-glass window and to others like the headstone on a grave.

People want reductive solutions to his paintings. They want to say that everything is political. So the *Malady* paintings are seen as something to do with the anti-nuclear stance of some of his other work. Or because he does black paintings, some people think it must have something to do with his being Maori. Or we're to see a set of influences: Ad Reinhardt and Mark Rothko. Or the darkness is seen as tragic darkness, or threatening darkness. But it might just be the night sky. But there is this difficult beauty, as you called it. Except it's not difficult. It's only difficult if you want a straightforward answer. It's only being itself. It's certainly not more itself if it stands absolutely still and says one very simple, very clear thing.

You recently wrote a text after a piece of work by Ralph Hotere.

Yeah. That was my revenge – a reversal. I was commissioned to write something for a catalogue to mark an installation called *Fault* by Ralph and Bill Culbert, which slipped very silently into its place [on the facade of the Wellington City Gallery].

You need to see it at different times of day and night, in the different weathers. Like lots of Ralph's work, it shifts depending on what situation you're in. The text I made takes up this sort of thing – teasing out meanings, all of which have their moments but none of which will finally do. The bit I was most pleased about was the discovery that the one window on the facade that isn't incorporated into *Fault* is the staff tea-room. There are still some sacrifices that can't be made for art. I imagine Ralph will eventually strike late one night and paint it black.

Given that you've appeared in person in Hotere's art, is Hotere likely to ever make an appearance in your writing?

Well, he turns up as a surreptitious joke in a story I wrote, 'Some Questions I Am Frequently Asked', where one of his paintings masks a secret doorway. The index to *The New Land* points it out: 'Hotere, Ralph, allusion to'.

At one stage I wrote a short story for the Hawk Press pamphlet series. It wasn't very good and I'm glad the Hawkeye series ended before it got around to my story. The piece was called 'Ralph Hotere at the Intensity Centre' and it was a kind of attack on what we would now think of as New Age art. It was a satirical piece about self-therapy and self-advancement. The one thing that was going to end the story and contradict the shallow world the characters had moved through was an image based on a dream I had. Ralph was standing in front of a dartboard in a hotel bar – as well as playing golf, he used to be a member of the Careys Bay pub darts team. So there he was perfectly poised in this dark smoky bar – hat on his head, cigarette in his mouth, and a beer in one hand and a dart in the other – intent on the board and balanced and throwing the dart and watching it fly towards the board. But in this image the board doesn't have a back to it, somehow there is just infinite depth behind it, like a horizontal well. So that Ralph is throwing darts at this wired, geometrical, numbered, circular board, but the darts just carry on. The feathers retreat further and further into the distance, lots of them, all at different distances.

And that was where the story was going to end. But I couldn't get it properly on the page; this man launching his missiles which kept on going past the obvious and immediate destination.

The other thing is that, of course, this isn't high, remote genius-on-a-cloud stuff. Wherever they're going, the darts are being thrown from a smoky public bar with other people present.

Gregory O'Brien conducted this interview late in 1995, and it appeared – with illustrations – in *Landfall* 191 in the following year. O'Brien's groundbreaking book, *Ralph Hotere: Out the Black Window. Ralph Hotere's Work with New Zealand Poets*, was published by Godwit in 1997 as the catalogue for the major exhibition (of the same name) which O'Brien curated.

FAULT

PHILOSOPHY

Whose fault is it? There are two of them (two artists/two lines) and probably they are both at fault. That is, though they would not choose to be called collaborators, they have certainly drawn the line between them. Those dark rectangles of glass might have their history in canvas or hardboard or corrugated iron. Like any Hotere painting, the blacker they become, the more they seem to entertain reflection. And that lifting line of light, the neon, has made its way along other corridors, in other countries, in and out of the Culbert family suitcase. Sky and cloud step out at either end.

RELIGION

They were correcting a fault – abandoned sheets of glass, a house made up of openings that wouldn't work. But how did they set about it? Did they stand in silence, for example? Did they walk about a lot? Did they hum and ha? Did they sit late at night and stare out the window? Was there wine? Perhaps a star? Did one say dark and the other light?

SOCIOLOGY

They left ghosts in the facade: a world of borrowings and books still haunts the words above the windows. The letters themselves are carved in stone. Thus the line of light lifts from Philosophy to History. I used to come here with my kids every Saturday morning. If we were lucky we would park the car out here, just where I am standing to admire the fault (jet trail, song, pure note rising on a string). There was grass (still is). You could see people inside the building. They walked around with books and newspapers, keeping quiet. We filled the car with books. I never noticed the names above the windows; I just looked through. It always looked to me as if they threw the whole place in through the windows.

SCIENCE

The fault is full of power. It's working. It uses about as much electricity as a modest two-bar heater.

[LITERATURE]

USEFUL ARTS

But is it one work or many? I want to know and they won't tell me. There's the promise of narrative and rhythm: chapter headings, the line ascending left to right. Page after page, and each window with its title, each like the last but different, like a row of pictures hanging on a gallery wall. So what's the story? Maybe they've turned the inside out? I go up close and look. Matt black. Osram. Hellweiss/Cool White. Some of the neon tubes are 'Made in Italy' and some 'Australian Made'. Then I come and stand back here. They're working late at the gallery: dark windows and all the light is on.

COMMERCE

Or maybe Civic Square is the meeting house, the wharenui? Maybe the windows are tukutuku panels – ribs and tears, teeth and stars – and the dark panes of glass are lattice webs that shine with everything they capture. It looks like an exhibition. This and this and this. But no one's selling anything. No one's taking money at the door.

DOUBTFUL SOUNDS

FINE ARTS

Shriek in the dark, lightning frozen in the glass. The sleepy light at dawn. The way things shift and change. The banister shines above the staircase, the wave beside the shore. The earth goes quaking on its faultline, which is also the line on which the child will learn to write. His first word is underlined before he gets it out. Crevasse. How small he is, with his chalk, his crayon, that quiet gleam already in his eye. At dusk the fault softens, shivers at the edges. Light spills across stone. Surreptitious warmth. The kids have all gone home. The way things shift and change. You notice the windows high in the opposite building. Bright electric light inside a frame. Curtains. Look, there's a man inspecting a sheet of paper: my latest parking fine.

HISTORY

One small window has escaped both the darkness and the line of light. Is it faultless, or a mild mistake? Look high, the second row, the upper row, top right-hand corner, there, the one without black, without neon, where the building is tied to a horizontal sail, tugging against sky and water. It's the tea-room. The gallery staff are up there, clutching their mugs, chuckling to one another, glancing down into the square. They are pleased and anxious and transparent, safe for the moment, which is of course only the moment: there may be dangerous men on the streets with cans of paint, women with bricks, librarians, artistic children. The gallery staff watch the square, the citizens coming and going. They stare out at the contemporary weather. They note how the light changes, and they see their own building reflected in the windows opposite. How history wavers! Look, there's a woman inspecting a sheet of paper. Undertow. Oh soon the night will come: the dark with its moon, the dark with its streetlights and headlights, the dark with its stars. When that happens, they can go.

First published in 1994 as a small book by the City Gallery, Wellington, at the launch of *Fault* by Bill Culbert and Ralph Hotere, on the facade of the Gallery.

BREAKING THE LINE

A View of American and New Zealand Poetry

I want to begin with two poems. Each places its writer in a certain relation to a wider community of writers. The first is by Walt Whitman; it dates from about 1860:

Poets to Come

Poets to come! orators, singers, musicians to come!
Not to-day is to justify me and answer what I am for,
But you, a new brood, native, athletic, continental, greater than before
    known,
Arouse! for you must justify me.

I myself but write one or two indicative words for the future,
I but advance a moment only to wheel and hurry back in the darkness.

I am a man who, sauntering along without fully stopping, turns a casual
    look upon you and then averts his face,
Leaving it to you to prove and define it,
Expecting the main things from you.

The second is by R.A.K. Mason. It was first published in 1925, when Mason was twenty years old:

Song of Allegiance

Shakespeare Milton Keats are dead
Donne lies in a lowly bed

Shelley at last calm doth lie
Knowing 'whence we are and why'

Byron Wordsworth both are gone
Coleridge Beddoes Tennyson

Housman neither knows nor cares
how 'this heavy world' now fares

Little clinging grains enfold
all the mighty minds of old . . .

They are gone and I am here
stoutly bringing up the rear

Where they went with timber ease
toil I on with bloody knees

Though my voice is cracked and harsh
stoutly in the rear I march,

Though my song have none to hear
boldly bring I up the rear.

    R.A.K. Mason is the poet we think of as being the first genuinely New Zealand poet. Allen Curnow, introducing Mason's *Collected Poems*, calls him 'his country's first wholly original, unmistakably gifted poet'. He is certainly the first New Zealand poet I read with enthusiasm (at a time when it was a matter of revelation to me that New Zealand poets existed at all), and at some deep level he remains my favourite New Zealand poet. I have a copy of the first edition of his *Collected Poems*, which I bought at Whitcombe and Tombs' annual sale in Dunedin in 1963. I was in my last year at high school. Mason's best poems, it seems to me now, are wonderfully adolescent, and I read them at a time when I was pretty wonderfully adolescent myself. So it was a very satisfactory coincidence.

    It will be easy enough to see, I suppose, how unencouraging a piece like 'Song of Allegiance' might be for a young New Zealander who hoped to write poetry. I am sure there is something attractive to the New Zealand temperament in the dogged stoical tone of Mason's voice, and in its awkward modesty. But that roll-call of great English poets leaves the New Zealand poet no place to be but at the end of the line – bringing up the rear, as the poem puts it, at the end of its own last line. The metaphor is really rather dispiriting. And the further up the line you go, the more dead you seem to get.

One local alternative to Mason's metaphor exists in Allen Curnow's often-quoted couplet, 'Not I, some child, born in a marvellous year, / Will learn the trick of standing upright here.' But the child projected in that poem is something absolutely special – a figure of redemption and miracle, forever to be deferred, and forever to be deferred to. Unless you are in the habit of confusing yourself with Jesus Christ – and the confusion is sometimes apparent in the world of poetry – you may find Curnow's lines almost as discouraging as Mason's.

I was reading Walt Whitman avidly at the time I was reading Mason. I had my own 1900 edition of *Leaves of Grass*, complete with portrait of the author and a fold-out facsimile autobiography in Whitman's own hand. I had rescued it from a large heap of books which had been dumped behind the school woodwork room. An old boy had made a gift of his private library to the school, and the school had responded in the only way it knew how – by deciding to make a bonfire of the books.

'Poets to Come' was in my bonfire edition of Whitman and it occurs to me now that it must be an extraordinary experience for young American poets to meet that poem for the first time, to find themselves being encouraged and challenged, imagined, by this poet who addresses them directly, who declares that it is from them that 'the main things' will come.

I suppose my argument, insofar as I have one, is that New Zealand poetry, in order to begin producing its own 'main things', needed to escape from the sense of tradition which is declared in Mason's poem. It needed to abandon its place at the rear; it needed to step out of line. It had to stop paying homage to the whole metaphor. I think that all of this has happened, and that one of the reasons is that New Zealand writers began to read the work of those American poets whom Whitman addresses in his poem. Those American poets had already abandoned the line that Mason declares in 'Song of Allegiance'. Theirs was, and is, a world of pluralism and possibility.

I do not think there are signs of Whitman in the poetry I myself write. But he is a wonderfully encouraging poet to read – if you are another poet, or would-be poet. He insists, for example, that a poem can be extremely personal, yet thereby be a public rather than a private statement. 'Song of Myself' begins:

> I celebrate myself and sing myself,
> And what I assume you shall assume,
> For every atom belonging to me as good belongs to you . . .

Later in the poem he calls himself, 'Walt Whitman, a kosmos'. Whitman also insists on the importance of inclusiveness and variety:

> Do I contradict myself
> Very well then I contradict myself,
> (I am large, I contain multitudes.)

An emphasis on the importance of contradiction and diversity has been very strong in American poetry. There is a little poem by Louis Simpson, for example, called 'American Poetry', which begins prescriptively:

> Whatever it is, it must have
> A stomach that can digest
> Rubber, coal, uranium, moons, poems.

Or there is the idea of 'impure' poetry expressed by the Chilean writer Pablo Neruda, who in my mind keeps company with a large number of North American poets:

> It is well, at certain hours of the day and night, to look closely at the world of objects at rest. Wheels that have crossed long, dusty distances with their mineral and vegetable burdens, sacks from the coalbins, barrels and baskets, handles and hafts for the carpenter's tool chest. From them flow the contacts of man with the earth, like a text for all harassed lyricists. The used surfaces of things, the wear that the hands give to things, the air, tragic at times, pathetic at others, of such things – all lend a curious attractiveness to the reality of the world that should not be underprized.
>
> In them one sees the confused impurity of the human condition, the massing of things, the use and disuse of substances, footprints and fingerprints, the abiding presence of the human engulfing all artifacts, inside and out.
>
> Let that be the poetry we search for: worn with the hand's obligations, as by acids, steeped in sweat and in smoke, smelling of lilies and urine, spattered diversely by the trades that we live by, inside the law or beyond it.
>
> A poetry impure as the clothing we wear, or our bodies, soupstained, soiled with our shameful behaviour, our wrinkles and vigils and dreams, observations and prophecies, declarations of loathing and love, idylls and beasts, the shocks of encounter, political loyalties, denials and doubts, affirmations and taxes . . .
>
> Those who shun the 'bad taste' of things will fall on their face in the snow.

So poetry can be a bad-taste operation. It can be impure and various, breaching decorum at every point. I think that this is something I first found out about from Whitman.

I want to mention one other aspect of Whitman's poetry which I find important – and this is the way in which he offers what he writes as a conversation with the reader. 'Song of Myself', which is a long poem in fifty-two sections, begins with the word 'I' ('I celebrate myself and sing myself') and ends with the word 'you' ('I stop somewhere waiting for you'). The whole poem represents a transfer of energy from writer to reader; and as reader you are constantly being reminded of your responsibility to be active, to contribute to the whole process by which the poem's meaning is constructed.

This idea of the poem as conversation, as intimate address from writer to reader, has been very important in American poetry. I think you can see signs of it in the work of several New Zealand writers since the 1960s. James K. Baxter's *Jerusalem Sonnets* are a clear example. Much more obliquely, in my own writing, I am struck by the frequency with which I use the word 'you'. It is an odd, shifty pronoun: it can refer directly to the reader; it can signify a specific figure within the poem, even the writer of the poem; or it can do the generalising job that the English 'one' does. I am never quite sure just how the word 'you' operates in my poems – sometimes it seems to shift between the various possibilities, rather than opting for any single one of them – but it is certainly there.

So in Whitman, whom I read at the age of sixteen, I can recognise many of the assumptions I was going to find in later American poetry. Poetry could quite properly be an instrument for subjective exploration, yet this subjectivity was not necessarily the same thing as narcissism or solipsism; it might even be a means to a truly public voice. And poetry could be messy, contradictory, various, inclusive. It could also be conversational in its voice, not measured and managed like a newspaper editorial. I do not think that any of these senses of possibility were present in the poetry being written in England during the 1940s and 1950s; and since New Zealand poets were still waiting politely in place at the end of Mason's English line, the possibilities were not especially evident in New Zealand poetry either.

I find myself asserting New Zealand ignorance of the example of American poetry. But I think I can give an interesting instance of that ignorance.

The most influential figure in New Zealand writing after World War II was Charles Brasch, through his editing of *Landfall*. Now I do not want to suggest that Brasch was a man of narrow sympathies. He was generous and encouraging to a whole range of younger New Zealand writers (even publishing my own first book of poetry). He translated poetry from Russian, German, Italian and Punjabi. But I think he had a blind spot when it came to the work that had been and was being produced in the United States. Brasch, of course, had a considerable private income and was a considerable benefactor. When I was a student at the University of Otago, no one seemed to have any doubt that he, almost alone, constituted the 'anonymous group of local businessmen' who had endowed the Burns Fellowship. One of Brasch's benefactions at this time was a grant to the university library, which was designed to enable it to buy every book of verse published in Britain and the Commonwealth over a ten-year period. What struck me about this was the absence of American verse.

Others must also have been struck by the very European nature of Brasch's sensibility. In the December 1966 issue of *Landfall*, the second-to-last which Brasch edited, there appeared two poems by a certain C.G. Gibson. They had pride of place at the front of the magazine. The first was called 'Low Paddocks and Light'. Here are the first three of its seven stanzas:

> I think it is in Otago, that place
> That lies upon the eye of my mind
> Now, like a grey blade set to the
> Sea's shifting oneness,
> Like a glass plain touching,
> Crowning all that is.
>
> Crowning, but capped by its own
> Cloth of morrows: how still it lies.
> The long paddocks run out
> To the sea there. The bush is not dense.
> The flat paddocks, dark between fences, run
> Out to the pale snug of the mapped water.
>
> And the fences go on up, rising slowly,
> With a sheep-bird halfway, on a stunted
> Post, watching. (Birds take some knowing.)
> – Watching how the light slides through them
> Easy as weeds, and the tall wires sighing.
> How sharp the salt seems, how
> The grasses cluster.

The only problem is that anyone at the time who had read much contemporary American poetry would probably have come across a poem by W.S. Merwin, called 'Low Fields and Light'. The difference between 'field' and 'paddock' in the two titles fairly sums up the difference between the two texts. Here are Merwin's opening stanzas:

> I think it is in Virginia, that place
> That lies across the eye of my mind now
> Like a grey blade set to the moon's roundness,
> Like a plain of glass touching all there is.
>
> The flat fields run out to the sea there.
> There is no sand, no line. It is autumn.
> The bare fields, dark between fences, run
> Out to the idle gleam of the flat water.
>
> And the fences go on out, sinking slowly,
> With a cow-bird halfway, on a stunted post, watching
> How the light slides through them easy as weeds
> Or wind, slides over them away out near the sky.

Needless to say, Merwin's poem pre-dates the work of C.G. Gibson.

My assumption at the time was that someone had set out to make a point. Perhaps C.G. Gibson was really one of the poets anthologised in Charles Doyle's 1965 anthology, *Recent Poetry in New Zealand*. Perhaps C.G. Gibson was 'C.G. Gibson'. More recently, however, I have realised that the dust-jackets of an expatriate novelist, Colin Gibson, offer a biography (born in Invercargill, advertising copywriter in London and New York, etc.) which accords with the *Landfall* note on the poet C.G. Gibson. Presumably novelist and poet are closely connected.

Whatever the origins of C.G. Gibson, *Landfall* itself never acknowledged that it had printed a pair of American poems in error. I believe Charles Brasch thought there was nothing to apologise for. He had accepted the poems in good faith: that they turned out to be, more or less, by well-known contemporary American poets merely confirmed the acuteness of his taste.

The Brasch view – which was Eurocentric, and which essentially affirmed, I think, Mason's roll-call – was what I met at the University of Otago. The very first written exercise I faced as a first-year student of English was clause analysis of several stanzas from Spenser's *Faerie Queene*. In a note on the magazine *Freed*, Murray Edmond has pointed out the importance of Auckland University's American poetry course to writers associated with the magazine. Alan Brunton, Ian Wedde, Jan Kemp, Russell Haley and Edmond himself took the course. I do not recall that sense of focus and revelation at university at all. In fact, I think it was somehow important to me that American poetry, or the part of it that I was reading, was not taught in the Department of English, and would not in any case submit meekly to the analytical techniques I was being trained in as a student.

I had grown up reading comics, many of them American. Once I sent to America for a Phantom skull ring. This glowed in the dark. If you were ever placed in a situation where it was necessary to despatch some evil-doer with a clean, well-timed blow to the jaw, you were well equipped. Your opponent woke up with a head full of clouds and asterisks; on his chin was the imprint of a skull – sign of the Ghost Who Walks. I read American comics, watched American movies, listened to American music. American poetry therefore connected quite comfortably with the rest of my imaginative life – though not with my formal education in English literature. To read it was normal – but also a mild defiance, a private excitement. American poetry was hard to come by, too. You might have to send away for it, just like a Phantom ring.

My life then, as now, was made up of all kinds of incongruities and disjunctions – not grand or dramatic but the stuff of everyday experience. There was a continuing gap, for example, between the university, where I studied the *Faerie Queene*, and my home life. 'Home', in my case, meant a central-city hotel, which was run by my parents. The gap between pub and university was obvious enough. But it had none of the romance that James K. Baxter attributes to it. For me it was normal; I made the journey every day as a matter of course. Because the hotel sometimes displayed in the bar posters for travelling music shows, there were plenty of free concert tickets. So I went to show after show in the Dunedin Town Hall. That seems pretty incongruous in retrospect, too. On the one hand, I would go happily to Del Shannon or the Everly Brothers. On the other hand, I would go just as happily to Jimmy Shand and his band or the Howard Morrison Quartet. Or there might be a Mozart opera at His Majesty's Theatre.

In fact, that musical world was mixed in ways that the literature we were taught and could buy in bookshops was not. The reason American books were unobtainable in local bookshops was tied up with the convenient way in which British and American publishers had carved up the English-speaking world. The London publishers owned the Commonwealth, and in many respects still do. This meant that British poetry was well distributed here, while American was not. Even more insidiously, it tended to mean that American poets first had to face the test of English taste. Those of them who became known in New Zealand had to be anthologised in London, or be taken on by a firm like Faber and Faber.

The anthology of American poetry which is sometimes said to have transformed poetry in English is Donald M. Allen's *The New American Poetry*, published by Grove Press in 1960. In New Zealand and Australia poets seem to compete as to who was first to read it. I am sure I was not one of the first although I remember encountering there the Beat poets, the Black Mountain poets, the New York poets, and a whole range of statements and manifestos. I remember poring over Charles Olson's essay on projective verse – it was busy and somehow badly behaved, like much else in the book.

The anthology which meant more to me, however, and which made a context for Allen's anthology, was a 1962 Penguin, *Contemporary American Poetry*, edited by Donald Hall. Inside my copy I have written (unusually) the date of purchase: 1963, my last year at high school. It was a rather more catholic choice of contemporary American verse than the Allen anthology. As well as sampling New York, San Francisco and Black Mountain, it documented a range of other initiatives: Robert Lowell, for example, and writers like Galway Kinnell, James Wright, Robert Bly and W.S. Merwin. (In fact, 'Low Fields and Light', the poem pirated by C.G. Gibson, is printed there.) Donald Hall's was a less polemical, less single-minded anthology than *The New American Poetry*. In some ways it was more decorous. But it also let more performers into the concert hall – quite deliberately. In his introduction, Hall speaks of an orthodoxy which has ruled in American poetry, and then suggests that the control of this orthodoxy has recently been broken (he is writing in 1961):

> We do not want merely to substitute one orthodoxy for another . . . but we want all possibilities, even contradictory ones, to exist together. The trouble with orthodoxy is that it prescribes the thinkable limits of variation . . .

I took all this very much to heart. 'Do I contradict myself? / Very well then I contradict myself, / (I am large, I contain multitudes).' I think I probably had a go at writing like every American poet I came across: I could show you my John Crowe Ransom poem, my John Berryman poem, my John Ashbery poem, my Robert Bly poem, my Gary Snyder poem, my Denise Levertov poem, my W.S. Merwin poem, my Allen Ginsberg poem . . .

DOUBTFUL SOUNDS

In fact, here is one of my Robert Creeley poems. Creeley is probably the American poet who meant most to me when I was learning to write. He seemed American and Elizabethan all at once. What I particularly liked, though, was the way he could get syncopated, musical effects by playing the pauses of his line endings against the more conventional cadences declared by the poems' syntax. I found the hesitant, delicate rhythmic system of his poems very attractive. My poem is called 'The Proposition', and I will place against it a typical piece of early Creeley.

The Proposition

the week it
snowed, the day the
footpaths didn't matter.
I wanted to get

a number of things
straight, but didn't:
and the next day, when
people were out

again, driving, you said
let's take ourselves
off, into the country,
to a cave, or that

kind of expedition: I bent,
tentative, over the
table, and cracked my
knuckles: would you

care to be more
precise about whatever
it is you are
saying, I said

The Rain

All night the sound had
come back again,
and again falls
this quiet, persistent rain.

What am I to myself
that must be remembered,
insisted upon
so often? Is it

that never the ease,
even the hardness,
of rain falling
will have for me

something other than this,
something not so insistent—
am I to be locked in this
final uneasiness.

Love, if you love me,
lie next to me.
Be for me, like rain,
the getting out

of the tiredness, the fatuousness, the semi-
lust of intentional indifference.
Be wet
with a decent happiness.

Let me show you one more theft, from the Jamaican-born American poet, Louis Simpson. He is one of many American poets who have engaged in a kind of verse conversation with Walt Whitman: 'Where are you Walt? / The Open Road goes to the used-car lot.' He is what is sometimes called a deep image poet, but with a Chekhovian edge. 'I have the poor man's nerve-tic, irony,' he says in one poem. The first poem is Simpson's; the second is mine.

DOUBTFUL SOUNDS

Tonight the Famous Psychiatrist

Tonight the famous psychiatrist
Is giving a party.
There are figures from the sporting world
And flesh-colored girls
Arriving straight from the theater.

And many other celebrities . . .
The Jew looks serious,
Questioning, always questioning, his liberal error;
The Negro laughs
Three times, like a trumpet.

The wife of the host enters slowly.
Poor woman!
She thinks she is still in Hungary,
And clings to her knitting needles.
For her the time passes slowly.

The Cinema

The Americans make many spectacular movies:
the surroundings of the town are beautiful,
the lake is enclosed by trees.

The other night we went
to a realistic, pitiless film. The spectators
cried, 'Encore!' Afterwards,
we felt we had risked everything.

Early in the morning, we weighed anchor.
We were on board a Russian steamer,
trying to find our sea-legs.

On shore there were many hardened criminals.
Many fields were under water,
many faces lit by summer lightning.

Breaking the Line

American poetry was read by a whole range of New Zealand writers in the late 1960s and early 1970s, but for those of my generation it had an absolutely transforming effect – partly because it made sense in the context of all those other American influences to which we were being exposed as a matter of course. It would have been abnormal *not* to read American poetry. Arthur Baysting wrote in his introduction to *The Young New Zealand Poets* (1973) that '. . . the Americans are producing work which is more interesting and exciting than that of any others writing in English.' Most of the twenty or so poets in the anthology would have been happy to agree with him.

There are dissenting voices, of course. One argument runs that New Zealand poets were simply being derivative in a thoroughly shallow way, that they were learning only to be fashionable. The poet Brian Turner, for example, says in a recent interview that, when he began writing, other New Zealand poets were impatient 'to be seen to be writing in a style that was up to the minute. Anything that gave off even the faintest whiff of the Georgian was abhorred. Most English poetry was insufferable: stodgy, pedestrian, dull, and so on. Beat and Black Mountain was what we should be responding to. I found it all rather shameless, silly and a bit weird. Adolescently arrogant.'

Yet, a little later in the same interview, he himself acknowledges considerable influences. 'Personally I have been attracted by a good many overseas poets, especially Americans. In particular I might mention W.S. Merwin, Galway Kinnell, James Wright, Philip Levine, Donald Justice, Charles Wright, some of William Stafford and Wendell Berry.'

The inference I draw from this is that Brian Turner has read American poetry as avidly as any other New Zealand writer of his generation. Some parts of it speak to him, other parts do not. The real value of American poetry is the number of parts it has. And if you look at 'the young New Zealand poets' you are struck as much as anything by their diversity. If I put my own poetry next to the work of three other poets also born in 1946 – Alan Brunton, Sam Hunt, Ian Wedde – I find the differences between us far more striking than the similarities.

I do not believe that American poetry made the poets of my generation into American clones – despite the sample thefts I have indicated. What it did do was make diversity and possibility available, and, in so doing, it freed New Zealand poetry from the single line represented by the English tradition. None of the poets listed by R.A.K. Mason in his 'Song of Allegiance' was discarded. But the long line in which they stood was broken. Somehow all the poets were present in a single room, and you could walk across and interrogate the ones you found most interesting. A literary tradition was something you might construct for yourself; there was no need to place yourself at the rear of a chronological metaphor.

In the 1960s and 1970s, one of the ideas that writers worked with (I expect it was an American idea) was that each writer had to find her or his own voice. I do not know very clearly what my voice is, but I do know that it is composed very much of other voices. The idea of the artist which most attracts me is that of the *bricoleur* – the figure who lurks around the edges of the human settlement, scavenging all the bits of tribal junk and discards, constructing something new from them. The work of art is composed out of used and second-hand items; yet the finished piece is 'new' and 'original', however old and derivative its parts.

My own poem, 'The Cinema', is actually composed to a large extent from a list of 'common English idioms' which I once came across in a book for foreign language students. I put some of them together, along with a few of my own devising, and found that it was possible to imply a narrative. And I found that phrases which originally bordered on cliché, in combination took on a quite new life.

When the film *Utu* was reviewed in *The Times* last year, the reviewer made the observation that 'an ability to move freely between dark drama and banal comedy' characterises New Zealand and Australian films, and perhaps the New Zealand and Australian temperament. I do not want to speak for other temperaments, but I am happy to speak for my own and say that the remark strikes me as true. The poetry I write is strongly marked by tonal drifts and lurches, and I think that these come mainly from the diversities, disjunctions, juxtapositions and incongruities which constitute my experience. Much of my experience is derivative, a matter of influence and imitation. I think that is a fairly normal thing, not a matter for apology. An important part of my experience has been an avid reading of American poetry, which itself is full of diversities and incongruities.

Perhaps I can put my own case best, however, by placing one of my own poems alongside Whitman's 'Poets to Come' and Mason's 'Song of Allegiance'. It deals with one of the ways in which a writer might go about acquiring an 'authentic' voice:

On Originality

Poets, I want to follow them all,
out of the forest into the city
or out of the city into the forest.

Breaking the Line

The first one I throttle.
I remove his dagger
and tape it to my ankle in a shop doorway.
Then I step into the street
picking my nails.

I have a drink with a man
who loves young women.
Each line is a fresh corpse.

There is a girl with whom we make friends.
As he bends over her body
to remove the clothing
I slip the blade between his ribs.

Humming a melody, I take his gun.
I knot his scarf carelessly at my neck, and

I trail the next one into the country.
On the bank of a river I drill
a clean hole in his forehead.

Moved by poetry
I put his wallet in a plain envelope
and mail it to the widow.

I pocket his gun.
This is progress.
For instance, it is nearly dawn.

Now I slide a gun into the gun
and go out looking.

It is a difficult world.
Each word is another bruise.

This is my nest of weapons.
This is my lyrical foliage.

Perhaps as an afterword I can say that the influences from America are still making themselves felt in New Zealand poetry – but not in the overwhelming, transforming way that used to be the case. This is partly because American poetry itself is at a low ebb at the moment, and partly because of the current confidence of New Zealand literature. Two very specific influences are the Language poets, who are closely associated with recent developments in theory, and the poets associated with the women's movement. For me, however, a 'young New Zealand poet' just turned forty, it is over. The *excitement* of reading American poetry finished about fifteen years ago. The most interesting American text I have come across recently was in the men's room of a Chicago restaurant a couple of months ago. I looked at my face in the mirror and saw, inscribed on the glass above the face that was staring back, a thoroughly conspicuous message: NO WONDER YOU'RE GOING HOME ALONE.

The passage from Pablo Neruda is quoted from *Selected Poems of Pablo Neruda*, edited and translated by Ben Belitt (Grove Press, 1962); the Louis Simpson passages are from his *Selected Poems* (Oxford, 1966); Robert Creeley's poem is quoted from *Poems 1950–65* (Calder and Boyars, 1966).

Murray Edmond's essay on *Freed* is in SPAN 16/17, 1983. A good example of Baxter's view of the pub and the university can be found in his 1948 poem, 'Envoi' – 'Lost, one original heart and mind / Between the pub and lecture-room'. On Australian poets and American poetry, see *The American Model: Influence & Independence in Australian Poetry*, edited by Joan Kirkby (Sydney, 1982). The interview with Brian Turner is published in *Talking About Ourselves: Twelve New Zealand Poets in Conversation with Harry Ricketts*, (Mallinson Rendel, 1986). The review of *Utu* is in The Times of 26 April 1985.

THE POETRY FILE

Lines

Poems come in lines. A line ending, like a comma or full stop, is a sort of rhythmic interruption, a device to make the reader pause. You wait a moment, then read on. This is true for poems written in conventional metre, like William Blake's 'The Tyger'

> Tyger! Tyger! burning bright
> In the forests of the night,
> What immortal hand or eye
> Could frame thy fearful symmetry?

though here of course the lines simply confirm what is already clear in the movement of the words. Even if Blake's words were written out as prose, we would still pause after 'bright'. We see on the page what our ear already knows.

Things are different with free verse. The line remains the unit of attention, but line breaks are more flexible and have more particular point than they do in formal verse. In Robert Creeley's 'I Know a Man' there is no necessary relationship between the line endings and the pauses which are there in the poem's single sentence. Creeley visited New Zealand in the mid-'70s. I remember him talking about line breaks to a hall of three hundred first-year students and holding their attention. Imagine, he said, that after each line I go out and walk around the block. 'As I sd to my (round the block) friend, because I am (round the block) always talking . . .'

> *I Know a Man*
>
> As I sd to my
> friend, because I am
> always talking, – John, I

sd, which was not his
name, the darkness sur-
rounds us, what

can we do against
it, or else, shall we &
why not, buy a goddam big car,

drive, he sd, for
christ's sake, look
out where yr going

Lines and line breaks are tied up with the time a poem takes, with a poem's pacings and pausings. They enhance that sense of performance happening on the page. In Creeley the result is a range of musical effects – like counterpoint or jazz syncopation – where the line endings play against the given rhythms of the grammatical sentence. The effect can be wonderfully subtle and satisfying – especially in a poem like 'I Know a Man' which seems to set sudden leaps of nervous possibility against an underlying sense of powerlessness.

The way Creeley shapes his lines also gives you the impression that his poem is thinking itself into existence as it goes along. It's not so much a considered statement as an utterance working its way off the tongue. There's a feeling of effort, of the stuttering difficulty involved in articulating our sense of how we find ourselves in the universe. Creeley himself has said that the lineation of his early poems connects with his feelings. 'The short, seemingly broken line I was using in my first poems comes from the somewhat broken emotions that were involved in them.'

Other American poets of Creeley's generation – Charles Olson, Robert Duncan, Denise Levertov – talk about the line, often connecting it to the writer's physical as well as emotional make-up. Sometimes this can sound both arcane and silly. Yet there is evidence to suggest that there is a neurobiological basis for such assumptions. Professor Fred Turner, who flew in to New Zealand from Dallas recently to give a keynote address at the Federated Farmers' annual conference, has been involved in research on the relationship between poetry and the human nervous system.

Professor Turner and his team have produced some clear results. Every culture in the world has poetry. Every culture produces its poetry in lines. And the length of a line of poetry is constant: usually three seconds in duration. Poetry's three-second line is explained by the fact that the human brain physically processes information and constructs verbal phrases in three-second units. Three seconds is also the standard length of individual communications between a mother and her new-born child. Maybe advertisers who have been busy reducing our attention spans are on to something.

Line endings can sometimes be treacherous. Meanings depend on them. Years ago, when I was a student in London, a friend from Oamaru fell in love with a handsome Italian. We couldn't afford to travel to her wedding, but some of us decided to send a telegram. We were told that whatever message we sent would be mangled by the Italian postal services. We thought deeply, then decided on the exclamatory noise for which Barry Humphries' character, Barry Mackenzie, was famous: *Whack-oh-the-diddle-oh!* The message caused great consternation at our local post office, but eventually off it went. *Whack oh the diddle oh love Bill Marion Brent and Charlotte.* Then we settled back and waited.

Some weeks later we learned that the telegram had got through not only word-perfect but also letter-perfect. However, telegrams are lined out just like poems, and this telegram's lineation had changed both the rhythm and the meaning of our message. Our cry of South Pacific triumph and acclaim had become a tiny poem, a sigh of sad commiseration:

> Whack oh the diddle
> oh love Bill Marion
> Brent and Charlotte

Things

The following fourteen words (or sixteen – it depends how you count your wheelbarrows) were published by William Carlos Williams in 1923. They constitute one of the most famous short poems of the century – one which has probably been reviled and admired in equal measure.

> *The Red Wheelbarrow*
>
> so much depends
> upon
>
> a red wheel
> barrow

87

>   glazed with rain
>   water
>
>   beside the white
>   chickens.

James Fenton, recently elected Professor of Poetry at Oxford, is squarely in the opposition camp. He reckons that the wheel (new line) barrow gets up his nose. (His words, his nose.) The critic Elizabeth Drew, in her influential 1959 guide, *Poetry*, wrote that Williams' poem proved 'only that words can't take the place of paint', then promptly printed the poem without the gaps between its stanzas – a pretty effective piece of death-by-layout.

One of Williams' sins is that he has done so well with such a small, apparently casual piece of poetry. The British poet and critic Donald Davie recently declared it a 'trivial and self-preening squib', partly because it has had 'so much grave and reverent attention from so many critics'. I'm sure, though, that Williams' greatest sin is to write a poem which teases the pretensions of critics and poets alike. 'So much' is promised – big answers and colossal truths – but the poem delivers something far more modest. A red wheel/*what?* Oh close the book; this can't be poetry.

'The Red Wheelbarrow' reads like a version of Williams' famous slogan, 'No ideas but in things.' Very little, it seems to say – especially in the world of poetry – depends on conceptual statements; but an enormous amount depends on our noticing what is local and concrete and specific. This isn't just any old wheelbarrow but a red one. Nor is it a red wheelbarrow alone on the page; it's a red wheelbarrow glazed with rainwater beside white chickens. And not just any old chickens: these are specific farmyard creatures – *the* white chickens.

And so on. There are plenty of other observations we could make about the poem. For example, it's extraordinarily symmetrical: each stanza consists of two lines only – three words followed by one of two syllables. And then the line breaks seem to carve compound units into their constituent parts, as if to foreground the individual items which make up the larger thing: a wheel/barrow; rain/water.

In fact, the way the poem sorts things into their parts suggests that it wants to show how every 'thing' is composed of smaller particulars. We are offered a single moment, in which a wheelbarrow of a particular colour, textured by the passing weather, is glimpsed beside a few white chickens. Presumably the rain has just fallen – that glazing effect won't last. Likewise, the wheelbarrow has been left there by Farmer Brown, who is sheltering in the barn and may come along and move it shortly. The chickens are just passing by. The brief juxtaposition of shining red and feathery white won't last. Look a moment later, it's gone.

Pay attention to the world, the poem seems to be saying. Notice things. Select what counts. (And leave other things out: the green trees in the background, the orange tractor parked in the distance.) Observe the relationships between your chosen things. Show the links between wheelbarrow and chickens, between wheel and barrow. Williams' poem is a piece of quiet advice to poets and readers alike. Be alert to the world. Look hard at what you see. No ideas but in things.

And so on. Certainly, when you see what politicians and advertisers can do with vagueness, you begin to understand why poets are sometimes so opposed to abstract language. A friend of mine was recently sent on a writing course run by one of those new consultancies for high-flying public servants. After the class had been trained to use bullet points in place of sentences and punctuation, they were instructed in the skills of writing vaguely, how to sound impressive yet actually say nothing. Bullet points mixed with evasive waffle: it's a lethal combination.

Another friend of mine once worked at an assessment centre attached to the Great Ormond Street Children's Hospital. There was a child there who had an odd language problem. There's no doubt a clinical term for it, but it came down to the child's need to individuate and name everything. He couldn't abstract and generalise; he didn't understand that language deals with categories. If he was shown a blue sphere, made of rubber, ten inches in diameter, and told that it was a 'ball', he was perfectly happy. But if he was then given a *yellow* sphere made of rubber, ten inches in diameter, he had no word for it. He had the same problem if the ball remained blue but was made of plastic; or if the ball was suddenly smaller. There were too many things in the world. Words failed him.

No ideas but in things. It's not a deep or complex proposition, yet it seems to work for artists. That child would never have turned into a philosopher or a policy analyst or a politician; but he might have become a poet.

Lists

> The pure contralto sings in the organ loft,
> The carpenter dresses his plank, the tongue of his foreplane whistles its wild ascending lisp,
> The married and unmarried children ride home to their Thanksgiving dinner,
> The pilot seizes the king-pin, he heaves down with a strong arm,
> The mate stands braced in the whale-boat, lance and harpoon are ready.
> The duck-shooter talks by silent and cautious stretches,
> The deacons are ordain'd with cross'd hands at the altar,
> The spinning-girl retreats and advances to the hum of the big wheel,
> The farmer stops by the bars as he walks on a First-day loafe and looks at the oats and rye,
> The lunatic is carried at last to the asylum a confirm'd case,
> (He will never sleep any more as he did in the cot in his mother's bedroom;)
> The jour printer with gray head and gaunt jaws works at his case,
> He turns his quid of tobacco while his eyes blur with the manuscript;
> The malform'd limbs are tied to the surgeon's table,
> What is removed drops horribly in a pail;

This is the opening of section 15 of Walt Whitman's great poem, *Song of Myself*. In the first line someone is singing, and in a sense the fifty or so lines which follow go on to sample the singers who make up America's music. But the most remarkable thing about Whitman's song is that it comes as a list. There's plenty of delicate variation – the lines grow longer or shorter and sometimes, as above, a pair of lines will come together to focus on a single thing. But most of the time it's just one thing after the other: a catalogue of people and the things they do.

Most of Whitman's poetry uses the list as its organising principle. This sets up a wonderful sense of capacity and richness: things repeat and accumulate and come in crescendoes. There's a sense of order, but without the plod of uniformity. Whitman himself compared his lines to waves. If at first they look lawless, 'on closer examination a certain regularity appears, like the recurrence of lesser and larger waves on the seashore, rolling in without intermission, fitfully rising and falling'. Whitman's lists (especially if you say them aloud) also produce a sort of rhapsodic factuality. Incantation is mixed with the inevitable line after line of accumulating detail – this and this and this . . . As orators know, the list is a powerful rhetorical device: it makes people agree with you.

Because a list is a set of accumulations, it can build to a climax. But equally often it will work in an anti-hierarchical way. Things are never subordinated in a Whitman list: each item is equal; the word 'and' – whether visible or invisible – holds together both text and vision. This dovetails nicely with Whitman's declared position as the poet of democracy. He doesn't admit differences of class into the America he celebrates; and his use of the catalogue keeps such differences out of the poetic architecture. Later in this passage we get an opium eater, a prostitute and the President – one after the other, each equally there, each with equal rights in the poem.

The list can be a wonderfully encouraging device for new poets. Kenneth Koch has used it with schoolchildren to astonishing effect. Because it offers a way of organising words and ideas which is different from sentences and paragraphs, a list teaches the novice poet that the line is the unit of attention. And it never inhibits. In fact, it encourages forward movement: a poem can grow quickly, then be revised. Write a poem, says Koch, in which every line begins with the words, 'I wish'. Write one where each line is based on the structure, 'I used to . . . but now I . . .' And so on.

It's not only children, of course, who write in lists. Some of the greatest poems – from the Old Testament *Song of Solomon* to Bob Dylan's 'A Hard Rain's A-Gonna Fall' – are composed as lists. A list can be carefully ordered – like a recipe or a spell or a set of instructions for assembling a model aeroplane – or it can be loosely ordered, disordered even – like a shopping list. And it's not just wishes that a list accommodates. The list can be a wonderful weapon for insults. Witness this vituperative catalogue from the spleen-ridden thirteenth-century Italian poet Cecco Angioleri:

> If I were fire, I would set the world aflame;
> If I were wind, I would storm it;
> If I were water, I would drown it;
> If I were God, I would send it to the abyss.
> If I were Pope, then I would be happy,
> For I would swindle all the Christians;
> If I were Emperor, do you know what I would do?
> I would chop off heads all around.

> If I were death, I would go to my father;
> If I were life, I would flee from him;
> The same I would do with my mother.
> If I were Cecco, as I am and I was,
> I would take all the women who are young and lovely,
> And leave the old and ugly for others.

In its original language Angioleri's poem is a rhyming sonnet, which only goes to show that a list isn't so much a poetic form in its own right as a way of organising words that can live inside a range of forms. And, needless to say, a list doesn't guarantee quality simply as a matter of course. Sometimes lists quickly wear out their welcome. At any rate that's the idea that lies behind one of my own list poems, 'Declining the Naked Horse':

> The naked horse came into the room.
> The naked horse comes into the room.
> The naked horse has come into the room.
> The naked horse will be coming into the room.
> The naked horse is coming into the room.
> The naked horse does come into the room.
> The naked horse had come into the room.
> The naked horse would of come into the room
> again if we hadn't of stopped it.

Child's Play

Telephone Wires

> In the far away distance
> I can hear the telephone wires
> Singing in churches
> like pakehas.

This quiet little poem is written in English. But in the last line it's suddenly clear that the perspective isn't 'English' at all. In fact these four lines give a much more persuasive account of cultural difference than most of the sociological texts which set out on the same mission. For a moment we glimpse the familiar from an unfamiliar point of view.

Child's Play

A literary critic could probably say a lot about this text. Its linkage of technology and worship is immensely interesting; likewise its quiet acknowledgement of the strange beauty that can attach to what is alien or remote. Formally there's real sureness of touch – in the way that the very last line is also the shortest; or in the way in which the poem actually evokes the eerie noises it refers to, especially through the sibilants which mark the line endings: distance, wires, churches, pahekas.

But it's a safe bet that the author would be extremely puzzled to hear such talk. The poem was written by a twelve-year-old, Mary, and I first came across it in Elwyn Richardson's wonderful book, *In the Early World*. Richardson taught at the small Northland school of Oruaiti in the 1950s, and his book records the astonishing work his pupils produced.

Children's poetry sometimes appeals to us as naive art does: it is cute; we enjoy something which the author really never had in mind. What is remarkable about the poetry produced by the children at Oruaiti is that they knew what they were doing. They worked hard. They knew that craft was involved. They discussed their work with one another. They understood their material – language – in exactly the ways that potters understand clay.

Richardson must have been a marvellous classroom teacher, finding out what worked as he went along, rather than operating by a set of rules. He decided to encourage his students to write out of their own experience. He showed them poems (Chinese and Japanese verse, work by other children), but never poems written by adults for children. He encouraged 'thought writing' – fast, free associative writing. He encouraged the children to use their own, natural speech rhythms. Above all he discouraged the use of rhyme, because it usually produced 'erroneous and senseless statements'. (An even better reason to discourage rhyme in children's poetry is its tendency to make writers boringly conventional. As Oscar Wilde said, there's a curious connection between piety and poor rhymes.)

Another great teacher of poetry writing is the American Kenneth Koch. His work was done with schoolchildren in Manhattan, and is recorded in several books – most famously in the 1970 collection, *Wishes, Lies, and Dreams*. Koch, too, banned rhyme, though he introduced his students to ideas of formal structure – especially the use of repetition and lists. He talked about technique, but not by way of intimidation. For example, his children wrote poems built on comparisons (but never spoke of metaphor); they explored all sorts of sound patterns (but never agonised over alliteration and assonance). Koch often suggested particular topics – a poem made up of wishes, a poem made up of lies – but he kept his children alive to imaginative play:

> I used to be a fish
> But now I am a nurse
> I used to read *My City*
> But now I am up to *Round the Corner*
> I used to be as silly as David
> But now I am sillier than David

Plenty of well-known adult poets began writing early. Elizabeth Barrett wrote her first poem at the age of six. Sylvia Plath was well under way by the time she was eight. James K. Baxter wrote his own first verse at the age of seven. But the evidence isn't always wildly encouraging. Here is my own seven-year-old attempt to describe an aeroplane:

> Like a giant metal bird
> it flies along, unseen, unheard;
> far below, a patchwork quilt,
> which seems to rise and fall and wilt.

Wilt? I still sometimes wonder if I could do some sort of rescue job on the poem. The syntax of the second couplet, and its relationship with the first ... Perhaps if I ... ? But of course the poem's beyond redemption, cursed by all the staleness that a dutiful, conventional sense of what's poetic can supply. Where were Kenneth Koch and Elwyn Richardson when I needed them?

Poems on the page often seem effortless – so that you begin to think that writing poetry itself ought to be child's play. It's not, even when it's being done by children. Poets ought to be willing to be playful – and sometimes they do have moments when they feel inspired. But most of the time, it's plain hard work. However you go about it, you have to go to school.

LAURA RANGER

I first heard about Laura Ranger's work from Brent Southgate. He was editing the *School Journal*, had come across her poems somehow, and was going to publish some of them. I didn't quite believe the claims Brent was making for Laura's poems: a six-year-old? But then he showed me some.

In fact, there's no doubt about the quality of Laura's work. She's a real poet, and plenty of people think so. The first poem she wrote, 'Sands', was published in the American magazine, *Stone Soup*; her second poem, 'Autumn Leaves', shared first prize in the Whitireia Poetry Competition with a poem by Lauris Edmond. And when I included her 'Two Word Poem' in *100 New Zealand Poems*, it quickly became for many readers the hit poem of the whole anthology.

> The toad sat on a red stool
> it was a toadstool.
>
> The rain tied a bow
> in the cloud's hair
> it was a rainbow.
>
> Which witch put sand
> in my sandwich?
>
> I stood under the bridge,
> then I understood.
>
> I sat on the ledge and
> thought about what I know.
> It was knowledge.

The accomplishment there is quite extraordinary. We are given images, things to look at. Not only that, the way the poem moves along is well-nigh perfect. There isn't a word out of place; there are deft and delicate, hidden sound patterns (bridge/ledge/knowledge); and – above all – the stanzas are in exactly the right order, perfectly paced. Try rearranging things – swapping the first and last stanzas, for instance – and you begin to see how absolutely right the poem is, just as it stands.

'Two Word Poem' also takes its life from the pleasures of language itself. It manifestly enjoys words and plays with their possibilities – not to be smart or clever, but to arrive at a quiet point of wisdom which it even decides to name: knowledge. You feel, rightly or wrongly, that the poet has had a good time with a dictionary in the course of making the poem. Punning is sometimes said to be the lowest form of wit, but in some places, like poems, it can be the highest. This poem even ends with a pun it probably never had in mind: no ledge/knowledge.

Laura Ranger plays with words elsewhere, even coining her own, like unileaf, or nevergreen. She says of her poems, 'They are just ideas that came into my head' – which is a practical way of talking about inspiration. But you have to catch inspiration as it comes, and Laura has always kept a notebook, especially when travelling, so as to write down ideas and images when they do come into her head.

The difference between these poems and the work of some other poets is that, wherever the ideas and images initially come from, they are then worked on. Laura's first poems were written by hand – a pretty time-consuming and exhausting labour when you are only six. But by the time she was seven, she was using a word processor – typing on to the screen her initial phrases and thoughts, and then working on them. What seems effortless in Laura's poems has been worked at – and this must be partly responsible for the absence in her writing of those twin curses of children's poetry: clumsy rhymes and adjectival overload. Thus the crucial processes of revision, which reasonably enough bore and infuriate small children, along with quite a few large adults, were made possible, and even interesting, by computer technology. Changes could be made quickly on the screen, a text printed out, considered, then quickly changed again.

Poets have always liked bribes and needed patrons. The British Poet Laureate used to do his job for an annual supply of sherry. The parental bribe that kept Laura Ranger encouraged was permission to stay up for an extra hour or so if she was working on a poem. It's possible to imagine the determined, sleepy poet at the word processor, images drifting into her mind and on to the shining screen. Maybe this is where the last verse of 'What I Would Take Out of the World' comes from:

Laura Ranger

> I would take sleep
> out of the world.
> I would put rings around my eyes
> so they never close.

Like most poets, Laura likes her recent work best; at the moment 'Blue' is her favourite. But this book, as much as one by Jenny Bornholdt or Seamus Heaney, is filled with poems which talk to one another, even as they chart the changes in a life. The poem 'Disappear', for instance, is a progression from 'Pete and Me'. And subjects recur: there are poems about zoos and pets, parents and little brothers, the beach, Christmas, and – in particular – the seasons. And these are the poems, not of a pale, bookish child, but of someone who is leading a normal, busy New Zealand life – climbing trees, going to the beach, riding bicycles.

I think that these are wonderful poems, full of life and liveliness and intelligent, alert good humour. They set a standard for poetry by young writers – but also for anyone of any age who has begun writing poems, and is even now sitting up late, dreaming at the screen.

Introduction to *Laura's Poems* (Godwit, 1995)

POETRY AND WRITING IN THE CLASSROOM

An Interview

ROD MCGREGOR: *Perhaps we can begin by talking specifically about poetry. Of all the literary genres in secondary school, and primary school as well, poetry is the least taught.*

BILL MANHIRE: Is that because the teachers are scared of it, do you think?

Well, I was going to ask you whether you had any ideas on why that might be?

Well, I do think there are a lot of teachers who are scared of poetry and I think that's probably because they were taught by teachers who were scared of it or by teachers who were vicars in disguise who were busy drawing morals out!

So what can we do with poetry to stop learners being scared of it?

I think, and this is very personal, I think that teachers ought to try teaching poems that they haven't read before. I mean, it's perfectly understandable – people get out their lecture notes on *The Waste Land* or whatever and . . .

In other words we should get away from that situation 'I know but you don't' sort of thing.

That's right. That's the professional situation a teacher is put in. The teacher is meant to be the wise person, but I don't think it works for poetry because there's the poem in the middle. A teacher can say, 'Here is a poem. I haven't read it before. I don't know what it's about. Let's read it, let's talk about it, let's work out what the different reactions to it are, and arrive at perhaps a point of agreed understanding.' That's one thing. But if the students come to class and the teacher says, 'Here's a poem. I teach it every year. It's a very difficult poem. I know what it's about and you don't. Now you're going to read it and then we're going to have a class and I'm going to take you to the point of understanding which I already have.' Well, it seems to me that most quick-minded students are going to try and go around the edge of the poem, and just find their way to the understanding that the teacher already has.

So the only way to avoid the students taking that path 'around' rather than 'through' the poem is for the teacher to say, 'Here's a poem. I've never been through this wood either. Let's do it together and if we get lost in the forest, we'll all get lost together. I certainly won't be on the other side waving at you, saying you're stupid.'

Wouldn't that be even scarier for teachers?

I think it would, but they might have more fun, you know. Of course, I know it's very easy for me to say that.

So that suggests that what's making the poem off-putting or boring for the students is not the text itself but the way the teacher presents it?

I think we have all been trained to think of poetry as a higher form of wisdom and therefore we stick these things called 'themes' on them and students, well, have got to find what the theme is, and perhaps they have to learn to spell onomatopoeia and alliteration on the way, but they never make any connection between the craft and the content really. So there's this sort of rote learning about craft or formal matters and then there's this pseudo-churchy stuff about themes and moral wisdom and lessons and so forth. I don't think that any fifth-formers who have problems with poems have any problem with a piece of new music. They just listen to it and say, that was a good experience. So I suppose what I'm saying very simply is, let them have the experience of the poem first and then talk about it. How can a teacher persuade them that they are entitled to have the experience first? Well, maybe you have to say, 'I haven't had this experience yet either. I haven't worked out my position. I haven't worked out the theme. I don't actually know what I think.'

What are some sorts of questions that we might ask when we read it together – if it's not going to be, what is the theme or can you find examples of alliteration? How can we begin the dialogue?

It might be interesting to work out how the poem sets you up as a reader. If the poem is written in the first person – I mean, I don't think one would want to choose Wordsworth's 'Daffodils' but if it says, 'I wandered lonely as a cloud', what does that mean in terms of the reader entering the text? Do you have to become the 'I' of the poem in order to get the meaning? Do you undergo the experience with the first person in a lyric poem or can you stand off and watch it? Stuff like that might be interesting. Or at the start of Eliot's 'Prufrock' – Who are the 'I' and the 'You'? I think that sort of question, which I'm afraid I'm not talking very well about, that question of how the reader is tempted and led through the poem, how the reader in the current jargon is constructed by the poem – that is very interesting and it might be that seventh-formers anyway would find that a very fascinating thing to think about and it would be quite distinct initially from whether there is alliteration or what the theme of the poem is; it would be to do with how the poem manipulates your experience of it. I don't think anyone would have any trouble looking at a piece of oratory and talking about it in those terms or a piece of advertising. You would be asking how a poem works its design on the reader. And eventually you would start talking about sound patterns and musical elements and inevitably the thing the poem seems to want to say and persuade you about.

That still leaves us with the problem of selection. It's interesting that, year after year in Bursary and School Certificate, you get the same very narrow range of poets being used – Baxter, Tuwhare, Eliot, Plath, Donne and war poets, especially war poets.

Is that because teachers feel secure with those poets? Those are the ones they studied a bit at university and they've got their lecture notes?

I suppose it is.

I mean, that's probably to insult a lot of teachers but that suggests to me that the teachers aren't doing any reading of their own, that they themselves don't like poetry, that they themselves feel a bit scared of it. I mean, why aren't they teaching Jenny Bornholdt?

So, contemporary, local poetry is a good place to start, would you say?

I think so, yes. And if you can get a good poet into the classroom and actually speak to the poet who you are studying at the moment, that would be a terrific thing as well. But it is very hard to keep up with contemporary local poetry and often the edges of the contemporary are busy being so avant-garde, no-one can keep up at all, so there's always a problem.

In the curriculum we have this phrase 'established critical reputation'. We can feel reasonably confident that Seamus Heaney will still be being read in 2097. Will Jenny Bornholdt still be . . . ?

I think she will be, too. I tell you what she has. She has a kind of playfulness which doesn't damage a kind of deep seriousness either and I think that is a note that has got into New Zealand poetry in the last fifteen years.

Deep seriousness.

No, no, the playfulness mixed with the deep seriousness. And you find it in someone like Tuwhare actually. I don't think you find it in someone like Baxter, and I think it's very interesting. We were talking about this the other day, that with people like Baxter, Curnow, Glover, Fairburn, there is a big serious thing called Poetry, very solemn, sometimes pedantic, sometimes a bit difficult to cope with. And then there's another thing called verse, sometimes called light verse, where the poets are very high spirited, very funny, very occasional, commenting on public events and terrifically entertaining in likeable ways. None of those writers put those two things together much. They don't let the serious and the comical inform one another. They don't let them into the same room. I think people like Jenny Bornholdt do.

You do that in your writing too, don't you?

Well, I try to. Because you see, poetry, whatever else it is, and of course it is all the high and wonderful things people say it is, is also part of the entertainment business and that's why Sam Hunt is such a good person to have around – (a) he's a terrifically good poet, but (b) he's a true entertainer and he doesn't apologise for it.

Just to make it more personal, have your own children, who have recently been teenagers, though are slightly past that stage now, did they inherit your love of poetry like when they were twelve, thirteen, fourteen, fifteen – did they pick this up? Are they keen readers of poetry?

I think my daughter – who might kill me for saying this – when she was twelve, thirteen, fourteen, she read *Sweet Valley High* all the time actually.

Did that worry you?

No, not at all. I'm all in favour of people reading all sorts of things.

She's grown out of that, has she?

Yes. She is now in graduate school at Rutgers in the States but it must all still be lodged within her somewhere. I hope so. I read Enid Blyton, Biggles and Tarzan. I'm all in favour of that. Maybe that's another problem in the classroom. Maybe we don't get a range of things in. I don't know.

We're trying to. The new curriculum is trying to but it still has this phrase 'established critical reputation', that we have to have a certain amount of.

Well, I'm all in favour of that, too. I think the idea that you should throw Shakespeare out and just bring in Chris Knox or something, that's equally silly.

They inherited that?

I don't know. I mean, they don't think of poetry as a funny thing to be interested in whereas my father was totally puzzled about the fact that I had such an interest. He was slightly worried about it. Did this mean I was going to be someone who couldn't lock the scrum or something? But it's no problem for them at all. Poetry just goes along with every other element in the world as far as they are concerned.

You would be more worried if they were locking the scrum?

Oh, I wouldn't mind. I think Greg McGee is probably right though that the writer's position is at full back, watching the game and occasionally sort of roaring into the line and dashing the length of the field. You know, Christian Cullen mightn't be a bad model for a poet!

So do they read your books?

Yes, they do, but we don't talk about it much.

They don't complain they can't understand them?

No, no, they don't.

I just wondered if you had any impressions either in your own education or your children's education about how they were taught in those critical teenage years, literature in general or poetry in particular?

Well, I think I was taught English mostly by teachers who did not like reading books, which I think was a huge problem for my generation, and may still persist as a problem. I think my children did meet teachers who love books. I think a problem they had – maybe this is where the problem of a text-based curriculum falling away surfaces a little – I think they both had the experience of each year a new teacher saying, 'I have got a treat for you. This year we're going to study the work of Author X.' But they had studied the work of Author X the year before and the year before and so on. Author X was wonderfully teachable, wonderfully relevant, wonderfully contemporary, but maybe teachers should follow their own hunches again rather than just repeat the teachable author, and the teachable text. I guess that's how the war poets go on surviving – they are great poets of course but if you're getting Wilfred Owen every year of your life in high school, that's perhaps a bit much . . . or a bit little!

Perhaps we could look at the teaching of writing now, Bill, and especially your course at Victoria. I am interested in the name of the course, Original Composition. Did you have any problems with that – coming up with a name? Naming of writing has been a real problem within the curriculum.

I think in fact we've lost any argument over that. These days everybody refers to it as 'creative writing'. The Victoria course was set up by Don McKenzie back in the mid-'70s as an untaught paper – a paper without course work – and I think he modelled it on the music idea. If you go up to the School of Music they talk about the Composition students when they're discussing the students who are training as composers. I myself am extremely uncomfortable with the word 'original' – partly because I think that people who are just starting to write need to be encouraged to read hard, find the work and authors that matter to them, and learn from them. If that involves writing under the influence, as it were, that's all to the good.

So that the word original bothers you because the writing may not be original?

Well, I think originality is a dangerous goal to have in mind, really. I just don't believe it. I mean, God might be original, if God exists, but I don't think the rest of us are. I think we're distinctive, we're ourselves. I think we are individual, characterised by particular things, but the idea that we are all original doesn't connect with the day-to-day world that I move around in.

That's interesting because I remember when the curriculum was being tossed about, original writing or creative writing was dropped because somebody argued that all writing is creative and that it doesn't distinguish enough between what we mean by creative writing, which has tended to be . . . what is now called 'poetic' writing. So we've got this distinction between poetic, transactional and expressive. Do you have any feelings about that?

That just sounds awfully fussy to me. And it sounds like false professionalisation, I guess. I mean, I'm speaking totally as an outsider, as somebody who doesn't know about these discussions, but if someone puts language like that on a sheet of paper and gives it to me, I just think there is professional anxiety in the background somewhere, producing stuff that looks like jargon. And though I don't like the phrase myself, 'creative writing' seems to be the one that has currency everywhere and which people understand.

Would you concede that journalistic writing is creative? Report writing is creative?

Yes. I wouldn't have any problems about conceding that, but I would then still say that when people talk about a creative writing workshop, they know that most of the time you are not going to be learning feature writing, though there are lots of creative writing programmes in the States where you study poetry in one workshop, feature writing in another workshop, screen writing in another one. Also what they call creative non-fiction is very big in the States – memoir writing, very good travel writing, that sort of thing.

That's the way writing is tending to go in the schools now, under the influence of the concept of genre – teaching learners various types of writing rather than writing as a global activity, how to write a report, how to write an argument, how to write a story. Does that seem to you a helpful approach?

Well, it makes sense to me to the extent that it foregrounds the idea of an audience – a market, I suppose. If there are different kinds of writing, then clearly they are going to be governed by the audiences they are for. I feel slightly uneasy, I guess, in the sense that in a schoolroom that audience is always absolutely hypothetical, whereas in a creative writing workshop which is focused on poetry or short-story writing each writer is developing what they can do, but they are faced with an actual audience of specialist poetry readers or specialist short-story readers. We are back to the old problem of the teacher being the immediate audience all the time, and how does one overcome that?

   I find that when I am teaching students at Victoria in ordinary literature tutorials, and they are having great trouble with their essays, it's usually because they are writing the essay for me and they have got a false conception of what I am; so they either spell things out very pedantically because they think that's what I want, everything explained, or they leave all the stages of the argument out because they don't want to insult me by assuming that I don't know them. My response often is to say the imagined reader for their essay has to be someone intelligent and interesting – that is, *you*, before you began thinking about this topic. But I think that's true, isn't it, that with a piece of discursive prose you are saving an intelligent person from doing the 'think' work that you, the writer, have done.

Poetry and Writing in the Classroom

I think that English teachers today try very hard to set up often imaginative contexts in which audiences are different from that of a teacher. And in publication we try to dream up different ways in which the writing can be published.

That's very helpful, I think.

We have this phrase in the curriculum called 'authentic contexts', which is trying to take the writing out of that classroom situation and give the writer a sense of context in the audience, even if it is imagined.

Well, I'm all in favour of that. One of the things that I've done with the Victoria workshop is to get what I think of as marketplace experts in to run a session. So over the years, for example, I've had Brent Southgate, who was editor of the *School Journal* for many years, come up from Learning Media and spend the whole two- or three-hour workshop talking about the kind of work they're looking for, discussing the different genres as they apply to children of a particular age group. He then sets an exercise, usually relating to something he is particularly short of for the *Journal*, and everyone does it and the results are discussed by the group, of course, but they also go off down to Learning Media and Brent reads them as submissions for the *Journal*, and each year he has found one or two or three pieces that he's wanted to publish. And something like that really brings the idea of a specific audience absolutely alive for the writers in the group. I've done the same thing with television or radio.

Right. That must be very useful for the students because outlets for writing in New Zealand aren't all that common, are they?

No. Well, we have the odd position where there is a marketplace. You know, it really is a marketplace with particular requirements and all the rest of it, but it's not a marketplace in which anyone makes any money.

Can I ask you – keeping on the topic of this course, original composition, what sorts of things do you seem to do that are most helpful in terms of facilitating or motivating original writing? What can the leader of the group do that helps?

Well, I use a whole lot of specific exercises – I don't say let's all sit around and be sensitive and write about the thing that matters to us most at the moment. I use exercise work as a sort of ice-breaking activity in the first weeks of the course so that people learn the workshopping process through work that doesn't matter to them personally or intensely.

What happens to it?

People write between workshops, not during workshops usually. So I will set an exercise like the five-item exercise that is described in the *Mutes & Earthquakes* book. And people grizzle and groan and say, 'This is no good. This makes us all come out the same as one another. You've taken control of our imaginations.' They grumble a wee bit. So they go away and do this, come back with it and they bring twelve or thirteen copies to the group, so that everybody gets a copy. They read it aloud and then they have to listen to people respond to it, critique it.

The whole group does this for each piece?

Yes.

So if there are only twelve of you, it's reasonable.

That's right, it's manageable. And I put a space limit of two or three pages. And it has to be typewritten and printed. No handwriting is allowed in the room!

Are they allowed to respond in any way they feel is genuine, or are they obliged to be supportive or positive?

I think we set up a pretty positive atmosphere and that probably happens because I behave in certain ways. Yes, I think it's important for them to be supportive. Each person needs to find out what it is that they want to do as a writer, but equally as readers, as members of the audience in a workshop, they have to find out what it is that the other writers are aiming to do or are aiming to become.

So you are essentially training them as readers as well, aren't you?

Oh yes, I mean that's the real activity in a way. They are reading texts just like ordinary literature students, and once they work out what that writer over there is aspiring to do, then it seems to me they are in a position to say, 'I don't think this bit works,' because they are saying it on behalf of the piece of work or on behalf of what the piece of work wishes to become. But they are not really in a position until half-way through the workshop to critique each other's work in helpful ways, so it's very good again to have exercises where they can be learning to do it but on pieces of work that don't matter deeply to them.

They also learn from these early exercises that if they work with strange constraints and don't just emote on to a piece of blank paper, they can do the most astonishing things that surprise them as much as their readers and, despite the apparent controls, are totally distinctive to them. They find out more about their writing voice by doing some strange, common exercise than if they are just told to go off and be deeply individual.

You said 'whatever the writer is trying to achieve'. Do writers always know what they are trying to achieve or is it possible for a reader to say to a writer something like, 'It seems to me that what you are writing about here is this,' and for the writer to be a bit surprised?

Well, this comes back to another thing that I believe, that the writer who has thought deeply and fully and in complex ways about something may not write well about those things at all. You know, novelists talk about characters taking over. Poets say they don't know where a particular image came from. If people aren't using the act of writing as a way of exploring something they don't fully understand, they might write very badly too – which again is a good reason for funny exercises, making people jump the tracks imaginatively a bit.

So what have we got? We've got things that you do, you set up an exercise situation which has constraints of one kind or another.

Yes.

Then you set up a readership feedback; so everybody gets a response. What happens after that?

At the end of the workshop the students have to present a folio. They have to, as it were, submit a manuscript of writing; and again I model that particular moment, which I suppose is also the assessment and examining moment on the course, on the marketplace. I take the part of a publisher and workshop members submit a manuscript which I then send out for reading. So each year I've asked two members of the staff of the Victoria English Department to read each folio and I've asked Fergus Barrowman, as a real publisher, to read each folio and eventually the students get their folios back with three readers' reports and I, as the publisher, can then say, well you pass or you fail. Of course everyone passes. They would have to choose to fail really. But I try to model the course's assessment on the publishing process.

But I've missed out another whole stage in the workshops, which is that when we've stopped doing the exercises, we move on to people's 'serious work', that's to say the work that's going to be in their folios, and by that stage, with luck, we've learned how to talk to one another. People have got a livelier sense of their own capacity. So people put up their work for discussion. Again they bring twelve or thirteen copies to the class, distribute their work, read it aloud and sit back and hear what people have to say about it. I think that would be a disastrous thing to do in the first workshop, but it's quite productive once people have begun to respect one another and have a sense of who's doing what.

English in Aotearoa, No 33, 1997

MUTES & EARTHQUAKES

A couple of pieces of advice:

1. Write what you know, and
2. Write what you don't know.

Write what you know is easy. If you want to write a novel set in an Icelandic fish factory, you had better know something about Iceland and fish factories. Write what you don't know is a bit harder, but much more rewarding. I started teaching writing at Victoria University twenty years ago. I had no idea what I was doing.

The course began in 1975 as a sort of undergraduate thesis paper, giving recognition to students' own writing. There were no formal classes, but the students – who had to be third-year English majors to enrol in the first place – were able to submit a folio of original writing and receive credit towards their degree.

The next year, the students who were enrolled in the course, half-a-dozen of them, began to feel lonely and I was asked by the department chairperson, Stuart Johnston, to arrange some informal meetings where they could share problems and discuss their work. It proved a good place to be, the shabby prefab room where we all gathered. To start with, everyone actually wanted to be there, which was never something you could safely say of tutorials on *Richard III* or the nineteenth-century novel. And the students were interesting, too. They talked about literary texts, their own, without having to worry about what the approved, time-honoured judgements might be.

Somehow or other the idea of exercise work began to develop. It was interesting to see what each writer did with the same set of challenges, and as we went along I began to get adventurous. I introduced cranky constraints, strange systems of chance. For instance: 'Write a haiku using only the words you can find on the racing page of the *Evening Post*.' And so, in 1977, Helen Gabites wrote this:

> A tamed life moored in
> shifting dark horizons, this
> quiet lady.

My memory is that we were all surprised by the quality of the work this exercise produced. But of course we shouldn't have been. New Zealand's best words are there on the racing page: much of the nation's most strenuous creative endeavour has gone into the task of naming horses.

We were beginning to enter the gaming halls of the imagination. Soon I was asking people to make large cardboard dice, write words on them and throw short poems:

> Stones in distance, or
> just blue stones. As you touch them
> they attach their wings.

Then I was asking students to 'find' poems and bring them to class. I was asking for riddles, for spells.

By the early '80s I began to have some sense of what was going on. I didn't know what I was doing; but somehow I did know, sort of. The course had changed in certain ways. It had moved to 200-level, and was available not just to English majors but to anyone. The prerequisite was now 'any twelve credits', along with something even vaguer: 'a required standard of writing'. This was simply a way of coping with admissions. There was space in the workshop for twelve students only, and many, many more were applying. Students submitted poems and stories, as samples of their wares. By 1996 there were over 150 applications for the course each year, and we were turning away large numbers of talented writers.

Still, the exercises had become more formal, a key part of the early stages of the course, and I had begun to understand more clearly what I was doing with them, and just how they might be useful to new writers meeting in a group. Creative writing workshops depend on their members behaving in certain ways. They have to read their work aloud; they have to be willing to listen to a dozen other people making comments on it. In turn, they have to be willing to make comments on the work of everyone else in the workshop; they have to be honest (or honest enough) without being damaging, and they have to be encouraging without being false or fatuous. Students also have to let their work be published. By this I mean that they bring a dozen copies of their work to class, then two or three hours later watch the other members of the workshop leave the room, taking copies of all the poems or stories with them. This can be a hard moment. Not only have you had to listen to comments a little less gratifying than those your mother might offer, you also have to watch your work departing into the universe. Now anyone might read it.

For a range of reasons like this, it helps if the first pieces of course work produced are exercises – and, in some respects, the sillier the better. If you are forced to write a story that somehow incorporates a child standing in water and the *Oxford Dictionary of Saints*, and several people express disappointment with the second-to-last paragraph, you needn't feel personally hurt or deflated. After all, it's not the heartfelt poem you wrote about your last disastrous love affair, or the meditation on your pet budgie's death, that evocative piece which mattered so much to you but you never quite got right. So the exercises give us conversational practice. People learn to talk about one another's work in – I hope – civilised ways. Eventually we move on to discuss the 'real' work that people have been getting on with, and which will be in their end-of-course folios.

Of course, the exercises are real work, too, and often the results find their way into course folios and, in many cases, into books and literary magazines. For me, one of the great satisfactions of the Victoria workshops has been to see, year after year, the amount of surprise and pleasure people get from producing work that copes with – and often transcends – the arbitrary demands of an exercise idea. Our culture has inherited the dangerous assumption that the only work which matters – and, by extension, can be any good – is the stuff which is sincere, which springs from something deep within the writer, which is, indeed, somehow *inspired*. But how can you be inspired or sincere when you are made to write an exercise?

Well, Stravinsky is supposed to have said that inspiration is what happens when you are working really hard. I'm sure this is true for writers. The hopeful writer who waits for inspiration may end up waiting forever. This is one of the big reasons why writers should write what they don't know. If you know too much before you begin, you won't find your way to characters or stories which you yourself find interesting, or – especially if you are a poet – you will write in the stale phrases we've all heard somewhere else, rather than letting the words be instruments of exploration, part of the actual process of discovery. The need for creative ignorance is something which all kinds of writers seem to agree on. Poems are like dreams, says the American poet, Adrienne Rich; in them you put what you didn't know you knew. Or, as the Australian novelist David Malouf says, 'You have to fall out of that part of your mind where you know too much, into an area where you don't know anything before the best writing can happen.' And here is the great New York short-story writer, Grace Paley, making the same case:

> Lucky for art, life is difficult, hard to understand, useless and mysterious. Lucky for artists, they don't require art to do a good day's work. But critics and teachers do. A book, a story, should be smarter than its author. It is the critic or teacher in you or me who cleverly outwits the characters with the power of prior knowledge of meetings and ends.
>
> Stay open and ignorant.

Exercises are a way of encouraging new writers to stay open and ignorant, to write what they don't know. Constraints seem to prompt inventiveness; we use our imaginations because we need to solve problems; we don't simply put on paper the things we knew we knew already. And, in the Original Composition exercises, quite a bit of genre-jumping goes on. Poets are made to try prose fiction, fiction writers, poetry. (It's the fiction writers who get most anxious about this.) There is another advantage here. Writers who are made to jump the tracks imaginatively can develop a broader sense of what they might be able to do. Occasionally a poet walks into the course, and a novelist walks out – or even a playwright.

I get a perverse pleasure from the range of things some of the Victoria graduates are able to do. Vivienne Plumb has published highly successful fiction and poetry, as well as drama. Anthony McCarten isn't just the co-author of *Ladies' Night*; you can also find his poetry quoted admiringly in the *Oxford History of New Zealand Literature*, while a collection of his short fiction has been published in both the United Kingdom and New Zealand. Barbara Anderson was writing poems and stories when she did Original Composition; then she became a successful writer of radio plays; now she's a novelist.

My greatest pleasure comes, however, from watching new writers find and begin to explore their own voices. This is a slightly different thing from finding the genre that they write best in, though that can be part of it. Voice is simply the unmistakeable, distinctive sound that a writer makes on the page: an almost unanalysable combination of effects – tone, cadence, texture – of language and of subject matter. We each have our own voice as a writer, just as we have our own voice on the telephone or tape recorder. The problem is to find that voice, and to speak in it, in a world filled with noise.

Creative writing is big business in the United States. There are over 400 degree courses, and they say that some American publishers can pick 'the Iowa voice' or 'the Stanford voice' when a new manuscript thuds onto their desk. The implication is that teachers of writing busy themselves producing clones. I can see that this is a danger, but an even greater danger would be for a workshop teacher simply to keep quiet, and avoid expressing opinions. I'm pleased by the variety of voices and writing styles which can be heard on the far side of Victoria's Original Composition course. Elizabeth Knox does not sound like Chris Orsman who does not sound like Forbes Williams who does not sound like David Geary who does not sound like Gabrielle Muir who does not sound like Jenny Bornholdt who does not sound like John Macdonald – and so on.

One explanation for this is my decision to keep my own workshop role separate from the assessment process. There are three examiners for each end-of-course folio (a little like publishers' readers); they write reports, which often differ from one another and which may or may not make individual writers happy. Equally, students simply pass or fail: there are no grades like B- or C+ or straight A. All this means that I am free to say what I think in workshop sessions. No one need feel pressured – at least in terms of grades – to take particular account of what I say. If they have found what they can do, they can go on doing it.

Voice shouldn't be confused with originality, another of those big ideas like inspiration and sincerity. We all learn to speak by mimicking the adult figures around us. We hear a noise and copy it. We are shown approval, or not. When we grow up we can hear our parents inside the sounds we make, and yet we are still ourselves – distinctive, and distinctively different from the voices which shaped us. The writing voice is like this, too.

This is why imitation can be very useful for a writer. You find your way to your voice by being influenced, by copying. The twelve-year-old Frank Sargeson started copying out Sir Walter Scott's *Ivanhoe* into an exercise book, which is going a bit far; but the idea has a strange sort of merit. Poets, especially, can be silly about this. I have met plenty who declare that they never read other poets: their own pure, original voice might somehow be contaminated. People who talk like that aren't writers. They simply like the idea of calling themselves writers. If you read a hundred poems by Seamus Heaney and write in his influence for a month or even a year or two, that's fine. It may be part of the process of finding out what to do. I don't imagine there are many aspiring screen writers who decide not to go to films on the grounds that the experience may destroy their art. The only person who will never become a writer is the one who doesn't read. Concert pianists listen to music. Great chefs like to eat.

So I encourage people to read widely. We talk – sometimes formally, more often informally – about the people we are reading. We recommend writers to one another the way some people recommend restaurants. Have you tried Lorrie Moore, Raymond Carver, Beth Nannestad? Carol Ann Duffy can make a good night out; or Donald Barthelme, if you're in the mood.

I hand out sheets – thoughts by writers about writing. I pass around an essay by Ursula Le Guin, called 'Why Are Americans Afraid of Dragons?', which emphasises the importance of fantasy and the imagination. Or I distribute a sheet of advice from Grace Paley, which includes various pieces of genuine wisdom. There is the piece about ignorance quoted above. Or this:

> Literature has something to do with language. There's probably a natural grammar at the tip of your tongue. You may not believe it, but if you say what's on your mind in the language that comes from your parents and your street and your friends you'll probably say something beautiful.

Or this:

> It's possible to write about anything in the world, but the slightest story ought to contain the facts of money and blood in order to be interesting to adults. That is – everybody continues on this earth by courtesy of certain economic arrangements, people are rich or poor, make a living or don't have to, are useful to systems, or superfluous. And blood – the way people live as families or outside families or in the creation of family, sisters, sons, fathers, the bloody ties. Trivial work ignores these two FACTS and is never comic or tragic.
>
> May you do trivial work?

I also have a sheet I occasionally distribute called 'Two Works of Art'. This contains Homer's astonishing description of the shield of Achilles from Book 18 of *The Iliad*:

> Next [the artist] depicted a large field of soft, rich fallow, which was being ploughed for the third time. A number of ploughmen were driving their teams across it to and fro. When they reached the ridge at the end of the field and had to wheel, a man would come up and hand them a cup of mellow wine. Then they turned back down the furrows and toiled along through the deep fallow soil to reach the other end. The field, though it was made of gold, grew black behind them, as a field does when it is being ploughed. The artist had achieved a miracle.

and Wallace Stevens' deliberately flatfooted poem, 'Anecdote of the Jar', whose opening suggests the way in which a work of art can bring the messy natural world to order:

I placed a jar in Tennessee
And round it was, upon a hill.
It made the slovenly wilderness
Surround that hill.

Then there is a sheet containing poems by children from Elwyn Richardson's wonderful book, *In the Early World*:

Grass

Green grass
Like the grass in my painting:
Green in the top of the trees;
Blue through the spaces.

Baby Birds

Baby birds open their beaks
Like open buckets;
The buckets waiting for water
And the baby birds for worms.

Night

The stars hide in the cattledrains
The moon prowls
By a blue spiked leaf.

Thistles

I saw thistles noses sniff with cold.

Stars

I said to myself
I could jump and get
One of them stars.

Untitled

The frightening of a flower:
Bees' muscles singing.

The idea with poems like this is to indicate a standard that we might all aspire to. If we can do half as well, we'll be doing extremely well. But in fact I don't discuss this sheet or others like it in class. They simply get carried home in the writers' bags. But my hope is that they will supply contexts and points of focus which will help students as they set about their work.

Most writers I know have had the experience of recklessly answering the question, 'What do you do?' with the words, 'I'm a writer', only to be faced with the follow-up question, 'Yes, but what do you *really* do?' Aspiring writers enrol in workshops for a range of reasons, but one reason must be that a workshop legitimises the desire to write; at last that novel can be given priority, and not simply be the thing you are going to do 'one day', when everything more pressing is finally out of the way. Workshops *make* you write, too. There are regular deadlines. If you don't produce work week by week, you are failing in a social obligation, one you may also be paying for. Writing is a solitary business – you work in what Eudora Welty has called 'a kind of absolute state of Do Not Disturb' – but all the same you belong to the curious community of the writing group, and you have responsibilities within it. After a while, you also begin to feel that you belong to a larger community of writers. Some of them, like Maurice Gee or Patricia Grace, actually visit the workshop, as do figures from the literary marketplace, from radio, film, television, magazine and book publishing. Some of them, like Ursula Le Guin and Grace Paley, live elsewhere; others, like Homer and Wallace Stevens, are dead. But everyone is somehow in the same big house of words. Maybe this, rather than mere self-absorption, is what the poet Richard Hugo means when he says that 'a creative writing class may be one of the last places you can go where your life still matters'.

A sense of community, if it is achieved, can be a key factor in whether students persist as writers. Whatever gets taught in workshops, I have never been much interested in describing it in terms of 'course objectives' or 'pedagogical outcomes'. It would be possible to teach the short story entirely in terms of technique: a workshop on beginnings, one on point of view, one on characterisation, one on dialogue, and so on. There are useful things to be learned, of course, and learning them can save a lot of time (sometimes years). It helps the budding poet to be told plainly how disastrous it can be to fill poems with adjectives, or with abstract language, or with dozens of '-ing' words (which in practice are just adjectives trying to sound a bit poetic). It helps an aspiring story writer to be warned off all those elegantly various verbs which signal direct speech. Contrary to what they used to tell us at high school, it is a very bad idea to write like this:

> 'Darling, I'm home!' called Odysseus cheerfully.
> 'Just a moment,' Penelope fluted from the bedroom.
> 'I hope there's plenty of beer in the house,' snorted Odysseus, picking his way past the loom. 'I've brought all the blokes back for a drink.'

A formal understanding of technique will only take you so far. As Flannery O'Connor (whose thoughts I sometimes distribute to the class) says: 'Discussing story-writing in terms of plot, character, and theme is like trying to describe the expression on a face by saying where the eyes, nose, and mouth are.'

So technical things matter – just as taking the right creative risks or acquiring the right work habits matter – and we deal with them as they come up, in relation to exercise or folio work. But they do not constitute a set of goals or course objectives. I suppose the course objectives appear in what students go on to write after they have taken the Victoria workshop – in poems, stories, novels and plays, in the works which the course itself may never have contemplated.

From the introduction to *Mutes & Earthquakes* (Victoria University Press, 1997)

MAURICE GEE'S *THE BIG SEASON*

The Big Season appeared in 1962 when Maurice Gee was thirty. It was his first published novel, though not his first attempt at writing one. Gee grew up in a household where writing was regarded as a natural activity. His grandfather, James Chapple, the model for George Plumb, had published two books. His mother, Lyndahl Chapple Gee, was a writer: one of her stories was anthologised in Frank Sargeson's collection, *Speaking for Ourselves*. Members of the wider family wrote too; there was an aunt who was a published poet. So it is not surprising that Gee should have begun his first novel at the age of seventeen, nor that, though he abandoned it, he kept on writing.

It was a long, dogged apprenticeship, as he has acknowledged: 'I wrote hard and I wrote badly.' His first short story appeared in 1955, and in the next few years he published several more in magazines like *Arena*, *Mate* and *Landfall*. In 1961 two of his stories were included in Hutchinson's showcase anthology, *New Authors Short Story One,* along with work by three other writers 'of outstanding quality and promise'. Hutchinson were plainly willing to back the quality and promise they had discerned in Gee's stories, for they brought out *The Big Season* a year later, and two years afterwards issued it again as an Arrow paperback. The paperback cover proclaimed and promised the 'raw, uninhibited story of a boy's growing-up in a rugby mad New Zealand town'. There is nothing especially apt about words like 'raw' and 'uninhibited'; but 'growing-up' is accurate enough, and there is no doubt about the rugby, or the rugby madness. Indeed, the season of the novel's title refers above all else to the rugby season; and the story is confined to the space of a single autumn and winter. (The novel which tells the story was much longer in the writing: about four years.)

Gee's short stories round about this period show a writer already familiar with his chief preoccupations. He was essentially a social realist, interested in sketching a range of New Zealand's sub-cultures, and concerned to do so as accurately as possible (most memorably, perhaps, in the horse-racing

Maurice Gee's *The Big Season*

world of 'The Losers'). At the same time, however, Gee used his stories to indicate some of the difficulties which dog close relationships, especially where those relationships (as in families) are subjected to the disabling pressures of convention and social expectation. And, he was interested in charting some of the ways in which communities suppress expressions of individuality and so bring their occasional non-conformists into line. Concerns of this sort turn up, more richly mixed, in *The Big Season*. The small-town setting supplies a backdrop for a carefully observed account of the world of rugby; yet it quickly becomes clear that rugby is well nigh incidental to the novel's larger concern, which is essentially (as Gee himself put it when interviewed as 1964 Burns Fellow at the University of Otago) an exploration of 'the pressures of a community telling on an individual'.

The community is Wainui, the individual is star rugby player Rob Andrews who, looking back, finds his home town a source of puzzlement and distress:

> ... tiny people would stand out like a child's cut-out figures on a painted background of shops and churches, domain and river, race-course and hills. And the events and people would make him grunt with annoyance, would puzzle him by becoming meaningless, would make him homesick and sorry.

Wainui is a version of Paeroa, where Gee worked as a secondary schoolteacher for a short time in the mid-'50s. He lived in a boarding-house a little like the one described in *The Big Season*; among the boarders there was even a professional burglar. But there is nothing particularly autobiographical about the novel, and certainly nothing at all *specific* about Wainui as a setting. Wainui is intended to be typical (domain and river, race-course and hills), very much a representative place.

Its values and priorities, which are those espoused by small-town New Zealand generally, are summed up by Arnie Fisher, a mild-mannered character whose epilepsy more or less guarantees his integrity as an outsider:

> Bob Scott kicked a goal in Auckland, the favourite was scratched in Wellington, the beer ran out in Christchurch, Christ was crucified in Dunedin. Get them graded in order of importance and I know which will come last every time.

The rugby-racing-and-beer ethos is attacked by Gee throughout *The Big Season*. He shows the narrow materialism of a society which is obsessed with possessions and status, which confuses success with winning (and celebrates the confusion on the rugby field), which does not have the capacity to distinguish between being respected on the one hand, and being respectable, on the other. The author's gaze is relentless, his hostility plain and implacable – perhaps too much so. Yet there is no doubting the stunted complacency which Gee points to; and he has hardly been alone among New Zealand writers in his determination to attend to it. There is a sly, ironic moment when he nods obliquely to the writer's role as a truth-teller by mentioning a horror film, *The House of Wax*, in which Rob and his girlfriend, Carol, witness the heroine breaking the villain's 'handsome mask to reveal the fire-ravaged face underneath'.

New Zealand rugby and its values have come much more closely under scrutiny since 1962, in life even more than in literature. Gee subjects rugby to very much the same sort of attention that it was to receive, some twenty years later, in Greg McGee's play *Foreskin's Lament* (1981). The movement of the authors' names – Gee to McGee – is a nice piece of serendipity. Both writers certainly *know* about rugby. (Neither invents a world for the purposes of disapproval.) Gee was never a junior All Black, as McGee was, but he played in the grades until the age of twenty-three and (like his character Rob Andrews) as a back. Also, both writers are less concerned with attacking a particular sporting code than with using rugby as a metaphor for New Zealand society in general. In both novel and play it is the team coach who makes the connection explicit. 'This is a team game, son,' says Tupper in *Foreskin's Lament*, 'and the town is the team.' In *The Big Season* it is Rob's father, Ray Andrews, who stresses the link: 'By withdrawing from the United team [Rob] had shown that he preferred a burglar, a brawler, a communist . . . not only to his father but to the town, to the world he had been brought up in, and all it stood for.' The word 'town' is a deceptive one – for it refuses to acknowledge the full variety of a community but refers instead to a dominant element within it: the merchant and professional classes, those who run shoe shops and stationers, who are lawyers, dentists, accountants and teachers. Rob himself points this out to his father in a moment of anger:

> The town . . . what do you mean by the town? What you really mean is you and all your cobbers. You want to use me and the rest of us; to keep some bloody stupid tin cup for you so you can all gather round it and pat yourselves on the back and say what a great little footballing town you live in. God, you're like a bunch of kids! Why don't you grow up?

Rob's question ('Why don't you grow up?') has special resonance. Rob has just turned twenty-one; the whole of the novel is structured about his own process of 'growing up'. The two paths his life might take are established in the prologue: will he be 'knocked into shape', wonders Bill Walters, or will he 'get away'? The stages by which Rob comes to reject family, team and town are the outward signs of his search for a fuller sense of purpose and identity than Wainui can supply. Nevertheless, the novel deals much more convincingly with Rob's relationship with the town than it does with his developing inner life – Rob is one of many loners and outcasts in New Zealand fiction, a sort of Angry Young Man Alone, as one reviewer wryly observed. Gee has commented several times on his belief in the essential loneliness of human beings. For example, he has written of his encounter, aged fourteen, with the works of Zane Grey, whose 'moments of clear cold sight' first focused such a feeling for him:

> With [Grey's] aid I was able to take my first long look at 'the human condition'. I saw that most human beings are lonely, that they lose what they most desire, that the passions that shake them produce cruelty more frequently than kindness.

Many years later Gee was pleased that what he remembered was not so much Zane Grey's happy endings as 'the sweaty hunted man on the dusty horse, heading into the badlands'. It is not a huge step from the Zane Grey cowboy hero ('alone under the huge sky, alone in the vast land, hunted, friendless, starving') to Rob Andrews, especially the Rob Andrews of the novel's climactic scene who takes his petition around the spectators at a rugby match, aware of the fruitlessness of what he is doing, and aware (particularly when he comes face to face with his father) of 'his sudden . . . solitariness, his outcast frightened state'. At the very end of *The Big Season* Rob leaves town rather like a western hero: 'The car lurched into the corner that carried the main street on to the highway north.' The means of locomotion has changed; but this seems quite close to the sweaty hunted man on the dusty horse.

Early reviewers of *The Big Season* were inclined to ask just where it was going. 'He is a hero without a cause,' wrote H. Winston Rhodes, 'a hero who becomes aware that the mean little people around him "haven't enough room in their minds"; but nevertheless an impotent hero'. It is certainly true that we do not know what will happen to Rob, what kind of a future he will have. But the novel takes him to the point where he can at least be guaranteed a future which will be his, and not the predictable existence promised by the community he decides to leave.

And there is the possibility that loss and solitude may be beneficial – if the alternative is Wainui: 'He felt deprived and lonely, but accepted this as inevitable, even felt some pleasure in it. It was what he had earned.' These are Rob's feelings after he has seen Bill Walters in a police cell. Rob is several times reminded that he has 'responsibilities' to his family and town but at this point in his life he shows he is capable of being responsible to and for himself. It is a mark of his growth that he comes to accept responsibility for his own actions and for the way in which they affect others. He acknowledges that he is to blame for what has happened to Bill Walters, that he has betrayed a friend; yet he is enlarged and made stronger by the recognition. (Responsibility, says a recent American poet, is to keep the ability to respond.) 'He did not want to escape anything. He wanted to see, feel, understand . . . he knew he was facing something that would alter and teach him.'

Other reviewers found the novel a bit solemn, and wished that Gee's attitude to his characters and action had been rather more satirical. This seems fair comment – although the moral earnestness of *The Big Season* is part of its quality of innocence, an innocence reflected as much in the too villainous personality of Rob's older brother, Don, as in the rather sentimental vision of mateship which 'encompasses the relationship between Rob, Bill Walters and Arnie. 'It was a young man's novel,' Gee has commented. 'A throwing down of the gauntlet, getting it out of your system, that sort of thing.'

It is easy enough to find weaknesses in *The Big Season*. Gee's characters are figures in a didactic scheme; they are sometimes capable of articulating the significance of their experience in ways which suit the author's moral design more than the requirements of verisimilitude. And because Rob is a kind of 'everyman' figure, other characters tend to be viewed mainly in their relationship to him, interacting little among themselves. Thus there is no very vivid sense of the independent life of the town. On occasion too, one catches glimpses of a young author trying out literary manoeuvres which must have seemed adventurous or well judged at the time, but do not now: the opening of Chapter 2, for example, with its managed and mannered exposition; or the impressionistic car chase around Auckland in Chapter 12. There are also moments when one is left wondering whether a cliche belongs to character or author: '. . . he tried to draw her into himself, pull her deep into the ache inside him that was as much loneliness as desire'.

There are strengths, of course, which Gee achieves so comfortably that one might easily take them for granted. The accuracy of the novel as a representation of small-town life in the '50s is worth stressing. Gee has an excellent ear for the way people talk (if their conversation is sometimes wooden, that is hardly his fault); and an excellent eye when it comes to observing the rituals of a Saturday night dance or a bar full of after-hours drinkers. There are some sharp ironies of circumstance and language, of the sort that characterise Gee's later work: calling the rugby team *United* is a nice stroke. The way Gee manages to give variety and movement to a rather thin story-line suggests someone who has no intention of being tied to a narrowly didactic purpose.

The episode which most fully vouchsafes Gee's quality as a writer is one in which Rob Andrews is essentially a spectator: the back-country pig-shooting expedition in Chapter 9. The episode has several functions. It varies the locations of the plot a little, but it is chiefly designed as part of Rob's moral and emotional education: he is faced plainly with the choice between team/town, on the one hand, and the fully human responsibilities of friendship, on the other. Rob's courage is tested in several ways; and further background and substance are given to Bill Walters, who is the catalyst for Rob's rebellion and growth.

Yet none of these things seem of consequence when set alongside the extraordinary figure of Bill Walters' father, an old man on a rundown farm, vindictive, uncouth, first seen walking out of the dusk in 'denim trousers and a singlet of washed-out pink'. His aggressive, coarse vitality is one of the memorable things in the novel, and the scene in which he plays cards against his son (one of several 'sporting' challenges which the story supplies) is one of the strongest individual episodes. Those who have read this chapter will not be at all surprised to learn that the fourteen-year-old boy who devoured Zane Grey went straight on to Dickens ('. . . the most enjoyable reading experience of my life. I never expect to have another like it. I'm not sure whether I swallowed him or he swallowed me.'). They will find it even less surprising that the author of *The Big Season*, the short-story writer 'of outstanding quality and promise', went on to write *Plumb*.

Introduction to reprint of *The Big Season* (Allen & Unwin, 1985)

GROWING POINTS OF TRUTH

George Plumb is a seeker after truth, a searcher for the light, and he sees his life as a sort of spiritual journey or latter-day pilgrim's progress. The novel he lends his name to is an account of that life, taking more or less the form of a memoir set down in the years immediately after World War II by an old man mentally preparing for death, not quite at home in the twentieth century (and a little proud of it, stubbornly clinging to his eartrumpet), whose significant memories reach back to the early 1890s and beyond. That's to say, *Plumb* takes the form of a journey through memory, as its narrator turns to reviewing his past. But it has also the shape of a journey in the novel's fictional present, as Plumb sets out from 'Peacehaven', the family home, to visit those of his adult children who live in Wellington.

While the journey to Wellington is central to the novel's action and meaning, and not merely a device to jog an old man's memory, it is the journey through the past which will initially catch the reader's attention. As Lawrence Jones has pointed out, New Zealanders seem to have an appetite for realism – and it isn't often we have the chance to read of a life which can boast among its 'highlights' trials for heresy and sedition. In outline (though outline only), George Plumb's life is that of Maurice Gee's grandfather, James Chapple, and Gee himself offered a sketch of it in his autobiographical essay, 'Beginnings' (*Islands 17*):

> ... He was not a great man but he was gifted and brave. My mother was the eleventh of his fourteen children. He began his religious career as a Salvationist. He and my grandmother met at an Army picnic. Then they entered the Presbyterian Church. He became a Home Missionary in Kumara on the West Coast, was ordained in 1901 and was minister in Eltham and at St Andrews, Timaru, until 1910. The years of his ministry were years of dispute and rebellion. He began to read in 'the wider bible of literature'. He joined the Socialist Party, and became a subscribing member of the Rationalist Press Association of London. In 1910 his Presbytery tried him for 'conduct at variance with the principles of the church'. He had taken the chair at a meeting of Joseph McCabe's. He resigned and became a Unitarian. Then the war came. He opposed it on religious and

political grounds. The police put a chain on the door of his hall. So he took his wife and children to California. (My mother grew thin there and pined for Timaru.) In 1917 America went into the war. The Chapples sailed back home and settled in Christchurch. And soon my grandfather was in Lyttelton jail. It was plainly seditious, the magistrate said, to say that children should not sing God Save the King. After his release the family migrated north. Tauranga first – *Dove Cottage*, then Henderson and *Peacehaven*. My grandfather was minister at the Unitarian Church in Ponsonby. He kept up his work for social justice and world revolution. He wrote his books and published them himself. He lectured from public platforms. My earliest memory of him is of a small bald-headed man shouting from a stage. Outside, my mother said, 'They were laughing at you.' He was deaf and had not heard. I never thought of him as a minister. We never went to church. He was retired by the time I knew him. I knew that at one stage of his life he had had mystical experiences. He believed in something called Cosmic Consciousness.

A life like this, given the kind of imaginative detail and circumstance with which Gee invests it, makes for fascinating reading, especially in the diverse issues and historical events it touches along the way. But as we read *Plumb*, we grow aware that it is the journey to Wellington which will give this life its achieved significance. For George Plumb does not view the past with pleasurable complacency; he continues to seek truth in the present. And in the present he means to 'gather in' his children: he is in search of understanding, reconciliation; implicitly, too, he intends a saying of farewells.

Wellington contains its surprises. Plumb learns that his memories of the past are not entirely accurate, or they have been selective: there were things he failed to notice at the time. It is Oliver – eldest and least favourite of his twelve children: a Supreme Court Judge efficiently dispensing the justice which once sent Plumb to prison for remarks about God Save the King – who emphasises the hardship suffered by the family while the father, after his resignation from the Presbyterian fold, continued to sit in his study 'doing brainwork'. 'You didn't have the slightest idea what went on. Meat and potatoes for you. The rest of us had porridge, even for tea. And all mother got was the scrapings out of the pot.' This is hardly to be believed, but is separately confirmed by a daughter, Felicity (another disappointment: she has converted to Roman Catholicism), who informs Plumb of the less easily borne social humiliations at the time of his imprisonment: malicious gossip among neighbours and friends, stones through the windows, excrement smeared on the front door.

Such exchanges make explicit some of the human damage which has followed from the courage of Plumb's public life. The facts about the past are modified for him even as he recalls them – and we are prompted to see that a very complex truth has been contemplated by the novel from the beginning. Even in the description of the birth of a second child during the early years in Kumara, there is some hint of how Plumb's relations with his family will go when, prevented by the midwife from retreating to his study for the duration of the labour, he is instead put to work holding baby Oliver. 'It was an easy birth,' he remarks, after mention of his small, unlooked-for burden. 'Edie cried out several times, but apologized later.' And a few years later, the family somewhat larger, we find Plumb describing his domestic life:

> I see myself cycling home from a pastoral visit, a small red-headed man, hair a little thin, hearing a little dulled; hot in my suit of grey and turnaround collar. People smile at me and call, 'Lovely weather, Mr Plumb.' I come to my gate, unsnap my trouser clips, put my bicycle in the shed. Children run to meet me from the garden, their fingers stained with weeding. They hang about my knees, and one, Emerson, climbs me like a tree and perches on my shoulders. Through an open window I hear my wife playing the piano. She allows herself a quarter of an hour each day. It is *The Rustle of Spring*. She welcomes me home with a gay tune. Kate clatters dishes in the kitchen. (Dear Kate, plump and bossy, more mistress to Edie than servant.) I go into the parlour, kiss my wife, and drink a cup of tea. I tell her about my day. Kate looks in, demands her in the kitchen, and she goes off with a smile of apology. I walk in the garden, examine the children's weeding, put the boys to stacking firewood. I eat a plum, think about my sermon for the next Sunday. And some neat turn of phrase drives me to my study, where I begin to write.
>
> An hour later Edie comes in with my dinner on a tray. I tell her the children have been very quiet and she grows pink at my compliment. I have got a lot done, I say, and I read her some of it. She approves; and goes out to eat her own meal. Later a child creeps in. They are always excited and nervous. This is Aladdin's cave. I hear her recite:
>
>> All wondering and eager-eyed, within her portico
>> I made my plea to Hostess Life, one morning long ago.
>
> I praise her and sit her down on a stool to read; and feel her kiss on my cheek when after half an hour she creeps out. I do not look up. I have found a new argument.
>
> Later I hear the sounds of children going to bed. There are tears, and I watch the door to see who will come in for punishment. It is Willis. He tells me he has been bad. He has drawn a moustache on Edith's doll. It is a small offence and I strike him only once with the cane. He says he is sorry and goes out smiling bravely. The house is quiet.

There is something good-natured, amusing even, about this routine. Plumb is a sort of comical Victorian patriarch, and there is a hint of the performance about his evening schedule of inspection and scholarly retreat, not to say a touch of self-satisfaction. But while there is plainly life in this household, it is hard to see that the father plays much part in it. In context, too, there is a nice irony, for even as Plumb gives his children (on a strictly rotational basis, one to an evening) a half-hour's physical proximity, he is preaching on Sundays against the iniquities of local parents who exploit and overwork their children, then 'send them off to school unfed, or with only a gulped plate of porridge'. All the same, we hardly notice Plumb's near-abdication from parenthood at this stage of the novel. He is presumably not unlike other fathers of his generation; and in any event our attention is fixed on more interesting things, his fight within the church.

But Plumb's defects as a parent are powerfully conveyed at the time he is serving his sentence in Lyttelton jail, and it is characteristic of Gee's human sympathies and narrative skill that they should be conveyed in a way which makes any question of 'judgement' irrelevant. A daughter, Rebecca, has been drowned at the beach. The event can only be reported to Plumb, and he reconstructs it in spare, moving prose:

> The day had been colder than usual. The sea was rough with small sharp waves, blown to spume on their tops. Matthew and Edie and John Willis sat on the sand, watching the children swim. Rebecca did not swim well. She was a thin child and felt the cold. Usually she was first out of the water. But she was excitable and the broken waves exhilarated her. She squealed with pleasure as they slapped against her face. When the others ran in no one noticed she had stayed behind.
>
> The cold must have caught her suddenly. She must have found herself too exhausted to swim. And she drowned silently while her brothers and sisters, wrapped in their towels, were walking up to lunch.
>
> Later everyone searched. John Willis found her, only a short way out. She was white and cold and dead. They tried for a long time but could not bring her back.
>
> Rebecca. Thirteen. A quiet child. Her hair was the darkest in our family. Her eyes were brown. She was good at her schoolwork and wrote little stories about wizards and princesses. I did not know her well, but she came sometimes saying no word, and put her cheek on my sleeve. That is the memory I keep of her.

Plumb has hardly known the child he has lost, and we are made quietly aware that the child has always been lost to him. His real isolation is not that of a man in prison, nor even that of the rebel who stands firm against an inhuman social and political order; it is the isolation of a man who is impossibly distant from those who are nearest to him.

One of the great strengths of George Plumb's character is the courage with which he eventually comes to face the truth about himself: what he has been, what he is. Towards the end of the novel he can observe: 'I have seen myself as the centre of the universe, around which everything revolves. My children surprise me with their independent lives.' And he has some awareness that the independence which disturbs him in his offspring stems as much from the initial distance between father and children as it does from those larger forces which shape human destinies. None of his children, though, is set at a greater distance than Alfred, who is banished from the household in a torrent of Biblical wrath after his father happens on him making love with a male friend under a quince tree in the orchard. The tree is chopped down, Alfred's name is not mentioned for more than twenty years. If it is easier to judge Plumb here, we are also persuaded to understand him. Moreover, the whole movement of his life is towards acceptance and inclusiveness. (It is no accident that one of his books should be called *The Growing Point of Truth*, nor that his last book – published at his own expense and bought by no one – should be a commentary on Whitman's *Song of Myself*.) And from another son, who lives in a dubious religious community in the Wairarapa, Plumb comes to learn acceptance. Robert, he discovers, makes no judgements on people. 'People were in nature. He did not question the shapes they had grown into.' Through Robert, Plumb learns to be human. 'I've been possessed', he tells his daughter on his return to Auckland, in one of the novel's few over-explicit moments. 'For twenty-five years. And after seeing Robert the madness has gone. Nothing human is strange to me any more. He showed me love.' And so Plumb attempts a reconciliation with his other, banished son. The meeting is hardly a success – yet despite its horrificness, it gives credibility and dignity to his words on the last page of the novel: 'I thought, I'm ready to die, or live, or understand, or love, or whatever it is. I'm glad of the good I've done, and sorry about the bad.' It is a moment of courage, and of benevolent calm.

Such an account of George Plumb's life is impossibly reductive, and fails to do justice to the complexity with which he is understood and rendered. Also, I have probably put the case *against* him more strongly than Gee does. But certainly the incontrovertible fact about him is the impossibility of separating what one dislikes in the man from what one admires. He is there complete. His virtues are considerable: courage, determination, integrity, energy; intelligence linked to an appetite for knowledge; an honesty in facing truths as they present themselves; a willingness to stand up and be counted even where he is the only one standing. These are rare qualities, worthy of respect; but they are inextricably joined to a rigidity which is essentially at odds with the domestic forms of human responsibility, a rigidity which is pointed up in a couplet penned by one of Plumb's friends:

> George Plumb, your name speaks true:
> It tells of deeps and of the straight line too.

It is this 'straight line' which leads Plumb to the real diminishments of his life: a son excommunicated, a loved wife exhausted as much by stoical support of her husband as by years of childbearing, children who are distant and 'disappointing'.

Plumb's tragedy – though tragedy isn't the right word for a life which is so full and, in many of its moments, blessed – is in many respects that of the man of principle. Before their marriage, when he and his future wife Edie are preparing to join the Presbyterian Church, she asks him if he thinks 'a person should put off doing something he believes is right because he knows it will hurt someone else'; to which Plumb's response is, 'I think as a general rule one must do what is right.' Plumb's sense of what is right shifts a good deal in the course of his lift; but both the manner and substance of his life follow from this belief in doing what is right. And a great many people *are* hurt, not least himself; for however admirable Plumb's principles, they too often prove incapable of adjustment to the human needs around him. In fact, they blind him to those needs. The deafness he develops in his middle years is both real and metaphorical – a cause of the distance between him and others, also a symptom of it.

From this point of view *Plumb is* a novel about a life whose private failures are inseparable from its public successes It is also a novel which invites us to consider and perhaps revise one of the more pervasive local myths: that which celebrates the outsider, the rebel, the nonconformist. (A comparison with one of Gee's early stories, 'Schooldays', which deals with the defiance of a schoolboy who refuses to have his hair cut, will suggest just how subtle and humane his understanding of the complex relations between individual and community has become.) In particular, George Plumb is an intellectual loner; and his story shows the limits of a life withdrawn from the quotidian. The place where he seeks to extend himself, his study, is the place he runs to when he can't cope – books are as much a resort from reality as a means of attaining it. And while the father closeted with his books is in one sense making one little room an everywhere, in human terms he is located nowhere – one can see the full ambiguity of the book-lined shed in *In My Father's Den* doubling as a place for storing garden poisons. One of the novel's gentler ironies is that Plumb's single moment of mystical illumination is a pure, *unsought* natural blessing, and comes, not in solitary contemplation of the light, but when he is surrounded by family and friends in the orchard at Peacehaven, marrying off one of his daughters to a real-estate agent.

Gee's control of the novel is masterly, especially given the range of its material and the research which lies behind it. The action spans four generations yet has the unity of focus of a single consciousness. It has, too, the satisfactions of its journeys: the near-circular shape of voyage and return, the completeness of a life seen whole as it proceeds through time. Time itself is a subject which has long fascinated Gee – the way in which the past informs the present, clarifying and complicating it, the way in which the present can draw out patterns of truth and significance from the past – and he has often forsaken the chronological plod in his fiction, uncovering layers of irony and surprise, revealing meanings which might otherwise be difficult to declare. In *Plumb* there is an intricate interweaving of past and present, after the manner of Joyce Cary's *To Be A Pilgrim*, a novel whose importance to his own Gee has publicly acknowledged.

The juxtaposition of past and present is particularly striking at the beginning of the book, where the old man – deaf, stubborn, a little doddery, capable of burning his hand on a hotplate because he is innocent of electricity – is placed directly against the young George Plumb, playing cricket, courting his wife, setting forth on his spiritual and intellectual odyssey. Thus the promise and expectation of the past are set sharply against the disappointments and emptiness to come; a world of possibility is seen in the hard light of a world of consequence. Even so, the description of Plumb's early years registers strongly, and is not displaced by what we know ensues. In New Zealand fiction there's in general a good deal of falling from grace and innocence, but the account of Plumb's younger years – particularly the days on the West Coast – is so forceful, with a joyful sense of spaciousness and crowdedness all at once, that it casts a warm, benevolent light through the rest of the novel. The losses of the present are made quite clear, but are somehow tempered by the *presentness* of what has gone. We are made aware of continuity as well as loss (indeed, while the present tense is occasionally used for passages from the past, it is never used for the relation of events in the novel's present); and in the course of the novel, past and present, the old man and the young, draw closer together, paralleling Plumb's own growing understanding of himself, overriding the distance between what was and what is.

Gee's contrapuntal time scheme thus works to insist on continuities, and it further allows the reader an ampler vision of things than is sometimes available to Plumb himself. We are encouraged to seek out connections between past and present. So, when the enraged Plumb, having found his son committing the sin of sodomy under the quince tree, has the tree cut down, it is the reader who glimpses the buried motives for this action. From Plumb's point of view it is a symbolic plucking out of that which offends; but the reader, alerted to the ways in which the past works its operations on the present, will recall from the early pages of the novel another quince tree, under which Plumb and his wife sat plotting their future life and happiness. This is a connection we are encouraged to make across great passages of text; but Gee's time scheme also allows for some strikingly direct juxtapositions, as for example when we 'cut' directly from a middle-aged Plumb in the dock, being tried for sedition, to an elderly Plumb in the Wellington Supreme Court, watching his son Oliver try a society adultery case.

Told by a less gifted writer, Plumb's story might easily have become one of those long, inert catalogues which never quite engage our real attention. But Gee has constructed a novel which is not only rich in content but is also very subtly paced. The short, flexible narrative sections, like Gee's sentences, expand or contract in response to the needs of character and event (the account of Rebecca's drowning quoted above is a single chapter), but there is space, too, for some nicely self-contained episodes which yet have their reverberations through the novel. These include the sexual adventures of a pegleg sailor son, the comic-heroic exploits of a son obsessed with aviation, known throughout Australia and New Zealand as the Sundowner of the Skies, and a fascinating discussion of women and marriage by men out on an intellectual ramble. Also, Gee doesn't waste a word. There's a precision about his use of language which can be wonderfully suggestive. The essential word in a remark quoted earlier ('Edie cried out several times, but apologised later') is a modest conjunction. In conversational passages, language is used with great skill to differentiate characters, to suggest the gap between generations. And only a second reading gives access to the charge which lurks behind many apparently innocent statements or passages quoted by Plumb from the Wider Bible of Literature. 'I would have all marriages cease to exist that are less happy than mine,' says Plumb during the discussion of women. 'For happiness is the end of marriage – that is the divine purpose of it. Happiness and children are the fruit. And a barren tree should be chopped out at the root.' And a few sentences later he comments: 'I did not spare my friends in the pursuit of an idea.'

I think some of the detail in Plumb is pushed a little too insistently towards the symbolic. I am suspicious, for example, of the number of references to eels and black water, which seem to be present mainly to suggest the darkness and violence which lurk below the surface of a 'civilised' mind. Likewise, there are rather too many plum trees and plum cakes in the novel, realistic enough, but there to indicate (or so I take it) the world of simple natural fruitfulness from which Plumb's 'straight line' removes him. Reservations like these, though, are the merest quibbles. They might seem more serious if Gee were telling the story omnisciently. But George Plumb is telling his own story – and as a preacher, quoter of texts and seeker after truth, it comes naturally to him to think in metaphor and symbol. It is he who explicitly attributes significance to his burned hand and its miraculous healing; and he who draws attention to his deafness, remarking in the novel's opening paragraph that he enjoys what he calls his 'aural blackness' – it sharpens his sense of otherness.

Because *Plumb* is told from one man's point of view, one might expect it to be a limited chronicle, at least in the variety of experience it is able to include. But it needs to be stressed that this is an extraordinarily rich and ample book, embracing both comedy and a deep, accepting sadness at the way things go. It offers, too, a curious sense of life at the edges, of a great variety of events taking place beyond its 270 pages. In the largest sense Plumb might be seen as a novel about the relation of the individual to history and social change – and certainly one senses that the historical *facts* are implicit here, that Gee uses only those which are appropriate to his needs but nevertheless knows them all. All the same, I'm reminded that Gee, writing in 'Beginnings', said that his first completed novel (one with a message) was 'no good', yet lived for him because of *the people* in it. *Plumb* lives in exactly this way. If Maurice Gee is able to complete the next two books of his proposed trilogy, and they come anywhere near this one, then New Zealand will have its most remarkable and intelligent piece of extended fiction. But *Plumb* is a magnificent achievement in its own right; and George Plumb is the most considerable character to have found a home in our literature.

Islands 25, 1979

SYMMES HOLE

Ian Wedde's *Symmes Hole* is a major novel about the Pacific – but is also one of those novels which are acclaimed and then lost from sight, at least in the marketplace. It came out in 1986, and has already become 'fast history', to borrow one of its own section titles. The book has a modest distribution outside New Zealand (Faber published it in the United Kingdom) and a sort of hidden existence on a few New Zealand university courses; yet it lacks a substantial readership – it is canonised but not widely read. Still, like the past which it partly records and partly invents, *Symmes Hole* has a submerged life which makes it a tenacious document and gives it great subversive power. It isn't going to go away.

'Fast History' indicates two areas of Wedde's attention. *Symmes Hole* is consciously a work of history – though the sort that exists when history is taken out of the hands of historians. The word 'fast' might easily enough refer to the pace and lyric dazzle of Wedde's prose. (Wedde is an extraordinarily gifted poet turned prose writer – cadence and tone, rather than storytelling power, make you turn from one page to the next.) But 'fast' refers to fast food – particularly the McDonald's empire – and points to ways in which Pacific history can be read in terms of American capitalism and the commodity mechanisms of the multinationals. There is a lot of food in *Symmes Hole*. *Symmes Hole* is about our relationship to the world which sustains us; it is a book about how to be healthy.

Wedde's novel takes place in present-day Wellington, New Zealand: a young man – a writer, a researcher – is making his way home from the Beehive (the name given to the country's parliamentary building). His research, which has become obsessive, involves Pacific history, particularly Pacific whaling history. He is also drunk, paranoid, in a marriage which will fail in the course of the book, and given to taking hallucinogens of one kind or another. The young researcher's story is counterpointed with the story of one of the objects of his research, the nineteenth-century whaler, James Heberley, who also came to the Pacific looking for a home. Heberley's home was one which looked promising – at least in the early nineteenth century before the process of managed colonisation got properly underway. The gap between the life which Heberley was beginning to make for himself in early New Zealand and the fast-food 1980s world which the researcher inhabits indicates the territory that Wedde seeks to explore.

Symmes Hole is full of quests and questing figures, driven by various kinds of appetite and desire. Herman Melville is here (indeed large chunks of the novel and the history it tells depend on the researcher's deranged belief that he himself *is* Melville); so are Robert Louis Stevenson, Mocha Dick, the mysteriously ubiquitous Doctor Long Ghost, Katherine Mansfield, and Jeremiah N. Reynolds, who last century financed an expedition to find Symmes Hole, the supposed south polar entrance to the Hollow Earth. The researcher's own quest ends in a New Zealand motorcamp where success and failure, beginning and end, manage an absolute overlap. The text ends with the image of a long jaw 'held up by a secret grin', and of a 'stroke-smitten eyelid [which] hangs in a perpetual wink' – a farewell reminder that serious topics don't preclude comedy and that history itself, while it is full of ghosts, is also, as the novel once or twice observes, 'a funny thing'.

Symmes Hole may be hard to come by outside New Zealand; but anyone seriously interested in Pacific Studies will have to read it alongside books by Stevenson, Melville and Wendt. Those who want to take things further will find Wedde's poetry a useful gloss on some of the novel's preoccupations. There are two important, related poems, 'Castaly' and 'Lonely & Afraid Up Here'. *Landfall* 167 prints an interesting note on the book by Wedde, written in response to a critical essay published in an earlier number. Wedde's most significant comments, however, are to be found in the lucid, mischievous 'Introduction' to *Symmes Hole*. This introduction is attributed to a mysterious Dr Keehua Roa (of the Social Anthropology Department of the University of West Hawai'i). Those who have read the book and have also looked up the words 'kehua' ('ghost') and 'roa' ('long') in something like the Williams *Dictionary of the Maori Language* will have some idea of just how much winking is going on in these pages.

New Literatures Review 20, 1989

KINDS OF CARING

In Frank Sargeson's *Sunset Village* there's a macabre little episode in the city morgue which includes, almost but not quite in passing, a nice image for the constraints society likes to impose on its members – the corpses are laid out on sliding racks, their big toes 'tied together so that feet might not fall apart'. Sunset Village isn't exactly a morgue but it seems very much a rehearsal space for some neat and final room where all the ends are tidied up. It's one of those pensioner complexes where the old are put into cold storage (out of sight, out of mind), the sort of place to which a 'concerned' society removes those it has not time or heart to be concerned with. The lucky pensioners have their own standardised flat-units, and a tenancy agreement which contains a number of heartless if predictable prohibitions: no pets, no overnight visitors of either sex, no planting of shrubs in the spacious lawns which separate dwelling from dwelling. The whole place is immaculate, a distressing example of what a community is capable of doing to the life within it, especially where that life is liable to be quirky, dirty, exuberant, just a shade embarrassing.

Still, appearances are only appearances – as this novella constantly insists – and Sargeson's book is a tragi-comic vision of exuberant life pushing hard against social prohibitions. It's clear very early on that few of Sargeson's villagers are anywhere near ready to have their toes tied together. Life remains very much a venture, official old age a statistic of very little account: or so it is said of Brixton Brake, in words that might describe the notions of many other villagers. Brixton himself spends a good deal of time in the Town Belt (a patch of messy vegetation where nature still contrives to take its course), providing homosexual favours to other aged gentlemen for small sums of money:

> . . . no pensioner could get by on the official money, so it was up to a man to see himself provided with something extra, although not by any means foolish or risky – robbery or violence or blackmail, they were out.

Not all the pensioners lead such outwardly venturesome lives. Brixton's occasional confidante Mrs Trigger seems the soul of commonsense and self-sufficient charity. A widow and retired nurse, she sits in her flat knitting, all the while keeping a watchful eye on the other inhabitants of the village. 'Appearances suggested somebody very formidable, a no-nonsense kind of widowed female of a certain age with a square jaw, grim features and a vast robust bosom.' However, as is revealed in a statement that has implications for rather more than Mrs Trigger's bosom, 'what was on view was not wholly to be depended upon'. In fact the secret life of Mrs Trigger's heart is altogether elsewhere, back in her days as a probationer nurse when she enjoyed a brief and whirlwind romance with another probationer –

> a pretty little prattling blonde, a powder-puff if ever there was one, who had fainted when required to remove and empty a bedpan: without her friend Amy's passionate support she would have become a sad loss to nursing.

Most of the pensioners pass their time watching each other, prying and gossiping. One whom Mrs Trigger watches most intently is Murray Piper, a former mental patient (also, we find, her brother) who supplies occasion for a kind of continuing debate in *Sunset Village* about the nature of sanity. One of his external features is a perpetual smile; and one of the small disturbing pleasures of this book is how often you find yourself smiling at event or character only to be reminded that a good number of the village's more bizarre residents spend much of their time smiling, and for a variety of unsettling reasons. (It's an engaging tale, in more ways than one.)

Another villager blessed with something of a smile is little Mr Hornley who, having lost his wife, has made what he calls 'the sensible decision to enlarge his heart and broaden out his energies and affections into caring for the whole of mankind in place of that one adored person'. A tall order, but at least he manages to be the village's 'most conspicuous do-good person'. He has worked as a mental hospital orderly and has become in retirement a kind of Welfare State on legs – delivering newspapers and milk throughout the village, administering first aid to those who happily accept it, and constructing with no sense of irony a garden gnome which outclasses all others. (This is Algy, a brightly attired ventriloquist's doll mounted on the seat of a tricycle; the delight of all members of the community – excepting Mrs Trigger – and to judge from fingerprints subject to the most alarming sorts of attention from his admirers.) Most importantly, though, Mr Hornley is the apostle of Caring.

> He did not quite say that everybody could without misgiving now throw away their Bibles – now that the sum of all the Past worthy of attention could be

expressed in the newly-emphasised word: but what he did say was that provided you dedicated yourself to Caring there was precious little else in life worthy of your time and attention.

Then there is Clementine who by common consent is (shades of the song!) a darling. Her great joy is that 'at a certain late age of her widowhood' she has been 'knocked all ways by an attachment'. With a comic discretion which fools no one, she conducts an affair with one John Whiteman, a large middle-aged van driver who delivers a never-ending stream of parcels to her flat. Naturally enough there is much interest in these parcels, but romantic encounters take place of an evening in the back of John Whiteman's van, parked in a local street. Still, if Clem's affair is offered as an amusing extravaganza, it is equally offered as a model of human care and pleasure against which much else in the book may be measured:

> But what Brixton would not have understood, was that no matter how unlikely, Clem and her John were lovers in the truest and most touching sense of the universal-saying – and that was to say that acts of love were more in the nature of pledges than ends in themselves. The pair were not stranger to 'all that sort of thing' (Clem after her child-bearing to a husband who had become a slave to the bottle and John with his terror of a teenage son, the unhappy little boy whose mother in the agony of a 'mood' had tried to expunge herself beneath the giant wheels of a passing road-bus); but neither, and equally, had known until now that the tender-hook ravages of hunger and thirst could be suspended without serious consequences, delayed and even assuaged by the ineffable joy of being within sound and sight of one who against all probability has taken up permanent lodgings in one's own heart.

It is after such a description of Clem and her John that Sargeson precipitates his plot. The lady is found sprawled on the floor beside her bed, a knife thrust deep in her back. Or so it seems. At any rate events grow quickly preposterous, in ways both predictable and unpredictable; and we learn a great deal more about the various characters. Most of them, it transpires, seem to have been acquainted in the past; one or two are even related. Clem, for instance, turns out to be Mrs Trigger's long-lost little powder-puff; and despite the efforts of two comic-cuts policemen (Tups and Ringer, a glorious pair) it is Mrs T., charged with reawakened passion, who tracks the killer down. Not that the killer is ever brought to justice, or not in the ninety-odd pages of *Sunset Village*. But then, the whodunnit is very much a pretext for games of hide-and-seek of a familiar Sargeson kind, and it gives nothing important away to say that the culprit turns out to be Mr Hornley, courtesy of his incompetent first-aid ministrations to a scratch on the deceased Clem's leg. It's apparent too, that Mr Hornley has done for a number of others in the neighbourhood in much the same fashion.

The point of this is plain enough. Caring, as Mr Hornley practises it, is the most dangerous virtue of all, for it is quite divorced from feeling. Clem is a woman killed by kindness, a kindness which is not so much well-meaning as self-regarding. Mr Hornley serves others in order to serve his sense of self; and his charity is directed not towards the few individuals for whom a single heart might truly care but towards a mass community where people cease to matter. Of course, there are other pictures of caring in the book. Mrs Trigger and Brixton, for instance, both begin as kind-hearted souls – although both are subsequently transformed by events which awake real feeling in them. (Brixton's transformation comes with his appearance in court on a charge of homosexual dealings in the Town Belt – the judge proving to be one of his partners in crime.) Yet their kindness, if on a less grand scale than Mr Hornley's, is different only in degree. Mrs Trigger's kindness is to knit garments for those who can afford the wool; Brixton's kindness, as practised in the Town Belt, has much to do with money. And if the sort of concern for others that Sargeson invites us to respect is clearly present in the love that Clem and John Whiteman have for one another, Caring à la Hornley makes short work of that (and no doubt passes on to care elsewhere, comfortably oblivious of the part it plays in human tragedy). The Welfare State, Sargeson seems to be suggesting, knows nothing of the welfare of the heart.

Yet it's not moral vision or extravagant characters (far less the semi-allegorical whodunnit) which supply *Sunset Village* with its chief and edifying pleasures. Rather it's the narrator, who – to borrow his description of Mrs Trigger and Brixton engaged in one of their public natters – is something of an exhibitionist, a theatrical type who enjoys putting on a show. His manner of delivery is one which some readers will have their problems with – witness the gentleman in the *New Statesman* who, on his urbane jaunt through the latest fiction releases, quoted a few choice phrases in order to suggest that Frank Sargeson must be 'seizing up'. Ah well, he has to be wrong, since one of the defects he finds in the book is that the narrative is stylistically indistinguishable from the passages of reported speech. Not so – one of the graces the book wears most easily (as you might expect with an author who has spent his life trying out other people's voices) is the sheer flexibility of the narrating voice, which can move comfortably from its own cadences to the gossipy tone of the village in general, and then shift to the distinctive idiom of any one of half a dozen different characters. And often Sargeson can give you several voices or perspectives at once, as if to insist that though his characters are a bit larger than life our knowledge of them will still be mediated in the complex ways that life demands. Thus, of Mrs Trigger: 'A knitting person, it was her great kindness to knit for anybody who could afford to buy the wool'; or of Murray Piper: 'Murray was a conservative-executive type, Chamber of Commerce, Rotary, all that sort of thing, a man who pulled his shirt cuffs down.' Much of the force of such character encapsulations lies in the way they keep several points of view in teasing balance.

In essence, the voice of *Sunset Village* is that of later Sargeson (*Joy of the Worm*, for instance, or *Man of England Now*) – but pitched up a little, a little more wordy and whimsical, as if some pustular eighteenth-century crank has been let loose in your own background. (And I suppose you can either attend in fascination or kick him off the property.) It's also a voice which, while it characterises others well enough, won't stand sufficiently still to be easily characterised itself. The narrator not only does amused and empathetic impersonations of his characters: in his own right he can be delicate, crude, sly, opinionated, discreet, melodramatic; and from time to time he is capable of mixing moral pronouncement with a quite startling lyricism. Above all, he is brimful of life: his voice – with its obsessive repetitions, its quirky circumlocutions, its tragic and comic hunches – frequently pushes *Sunset Village* toward the condition of poetry. (Indeed, poets like Browning, or even Whitman, spring to mind by way of comparison.) At any rate the book's chief triumph is one of tone: the character of the man telling the story is the chief centre of interest and source of values. As for the book's wide-eyed pretence of being a thriller, you could no more make a film of it than you could of *Paradise Lost*.

Interviewed in *Landfall* a few years ago, Sargeson found himself speaking of 'the spectre of old age, the end and dissolution of everything; the decay and the humiliations of age'. It's almost as if *Sunset Village* is a rejoinder to those remarks. No doubt one shouldn't confuse Frank Sargeson, writer, with his narrative frontman – but it's impossible not to be aware that Sargeson himself is an old man; and given that fact, the sheer vitality of his voice here makes this book not so much an analysis of senility and decay as a celebration of the human spirit whatever its physical age. *Sunset Village* shows life thriving in the face of mortality: there are two deaths in the course of the novel, neither of them to be taken too seriously.

It's tempting to compare the narrator of *Sunset Village* with the narrating voice of Kingsley Amis' *Ending Up*, another piece of fiction with a cast of pensioners. Amis' voice exists merely to serve a well-scripted plot: it's a dull and distant hum which stands well back so that the characters may reveal themselves as the failing unfortunates they are. There's no sympathy, no energy, only a kind of bland distaste. By contrast, Sargeson delights in his characters; and even when he opts for a vastly amused relationship with them – something a younger writer might not have dared to do – he never fails to take them seriously. In effect, he does what Kingsley Amis cannot – he makes himself part of his novel, and so part of its life. He makes you feel that humanity is worth attending to by the simple fact of attending well to it himself; and he insists that the world can be serious and entertaining all at once.

If *Sunset Village* has a weakness, it seems to me to come at the close, where the narrator does a rather anticlimactic vanishing act. The last paragraph gives a glimpse of Mrs Trigger and Brixton, after Brixton's trial has been sensationally abandoned:

> That evening there was much talk in the village: it was known by everyone that after a very unaccustomed arrival home the pair had spent the afternoon together in Mrs Trigger's flat: there had been the sound of much laughter, and bottles of beer had been seen on the window ledge.

Mrs Trigger and Brixton are certainly getting it all together, and no doubt discovering forms of caring they knew little of when the book began. But we are back with the vision of the village; fair enough, I suppose, but meantime the narrator, whose voice can be heard distantly, has sneaked off-stage. After all that's come before, it's something of a let-down. If the show has been good and the address a witty one, you want to demonstrate your appreciation in what is called the usual manner. It's a pity that Sargeson, or the character he performs so well, didn't see fit to take a few curtain-calls: at least the applause would have warranted some sort of formal farewell gesture.

Islands 21, 1977

THE POETRY FILE

Endings

> Don't throw your arms around me in that way:
>   I know that what you tell me is the truth—
>   yes I suppose I loved you in my youth
>   as boys do love their mothers, so they say,
>   but all that's gone from me this many a day:
>   I am a merciless cactus an uncouth
>   wild goat a jagged old spear the grim tooth
>   of a lone crag . . . Woman I cannot stay.
>
> Each one of us must do his work of doom
>   and I shall do it even in despite
>   of her who brought me in pain from her womb,
>   whose blood made me, who used to bring the light
>   and sit on the bed up in my little room
>   and tell me stories and tuck me up at night.

Poets are used to being asked how a poem gets started. But no one ever asks them about endings. Just how do you make a poem finish without simply tailing off? Or – even harder – how do you give a poem a sense of an ending without resorting to cheap flourishes or operatic thunder? Sermons and editorials sometimes lumber to a glib finale, but poems shouldn't.

This question of endings is quite different from the degree of formal complexity a poem possesses. A poem can be highly worked, but it should never sound *worked out*. Like the plots of high-class thrillers, the best poems mix, even confuse, inevitability and surprise as they move to their conclusions. You want to be mildly (or hugely) startled by the way they end, but also reassured. You gasp, then say, 'Of course!'

R.A.K. Mason's great sonnet, 'Footnote to John ii 4', begins as a piece of teenage rant. A boy is leaving home and his melodramatic fury seems to leave no room for second thoughts. The title refers us to Christ's rejection of his own mother – not necessarily to indicate that Christ is the speaker, but rather (I think) to suggest that we are about to meet a small, contemporary example of something which has happened many times before.

The brutal nature of the son's address is intensified in the self-description he offers in lines 5-8, where the sense of willed isolation is inseparable from a sort of gesturing sexual aggression. It's said that when James K. Baxter did a bit of part-time tutoring at Victoria University, he used to stun first-year students by the amount of phallic imagery he could find in Coleridge's *Ancient Mariner*. ('Consider that lighthouse, if you will, or that ship's mast. Now, what about the albatross?') He would have had a field day with Mason's poem.

There is certainly a kind of disturbed sexual bravado about those images of cactus, goat, spear, tooth, and crag. And the whole effect is reinforced by the way the boy addresses his mother. She is *woman* – set at an absolute distance, granted nothing special beyond the fact of her sex.

So far, so good. It all seems excessive and extreme, but clear enough.

At this point many sonnets, having announced a theme in their first eight lines (the octave), would use the last six (the sestet) to elaborate a conclusion. Mason, however, uses the sestet to contradict and complicate his poem's first eight lines. His end grows from his beginning, but it's also a surprise.

In fact, the gap you see on the page signals a crucial shift of meaning and perspective. The mother is about to become a 'her', not a 'you'; and where the first eight lines have been blustering public noises, the sestina turns to inner feelings.

If you were to try a simple paraphrase of the last six lines, you would end up with something like: 'I shall do what I must, despite my mother.' Yet the emotional meaning is far more mixed. It would take a long time to tease out all the resonances of Mason's ending. But one very obvious thing is the way that the speaker begins to use the language of a small child – so that by the final line we are more or less back in the world of the nursery: 'and tell me stories and tuck me up at night'.

So Mason's poem ends with words which inhabit the secure place the opening lines reject. Even so, the poem hasn't changed its mind. The speaker may yearn inwardly for the past, but he still means to walk out the door; and while the last line evokes childhood, its key phrases are nicely equivocal. Stories can be wonderfully reassuring, but the stories parents tell their children are not necessarily true ones; being tucked up may leave you

Endings

uncertain just where comfort ends and constraint begins.

'Footnote to John ii 4' is like many of R.A.K. Mason's best poems. It looks crude at first, heavy-handed and simple-minded; but it is actually delicate and subtle – a holding pen with complex stuff inside. It keeps several possible meanings in tension, without quite endorsing any single one of them. And it finds its way to a conclusion – a calm that gathers in the poem's equivocations – that it hardly imagined at the outset.

So back we go to the start. How on earth did the poem get from such a beginning to such an ending? But then, how could it not have? How amazing! But then, of course . . .

Uselessness

Poet's work

Grandfather
    advised me:
        Learn a trade

I learned
    to sit at desk
        and condense

No layoff
    from this
        condensery

This poem is by the American poet Lorine Niedecker (1903–70), and its intense, terse grace in some ways matches the essentially isolated life she spent in a cabin on an island on a lake in Wisconsin. When her writings were collected together in a posthumous volume, the last two lines of 'Poet's Work' were used as a title: *From This Condensery*.

Poetry is distinctively itself for all sorts of reasons but – in the twentieth century at least – the idea of *condensation* has been particularly important. Condensing is a sort of stylistic effect, which you see most often in brief, attentive notations like Lorine Niedecker's; though even a loose, extended, pseudo-epic like Ezra Pound's *Cantos* is crucially marked by moments of resonating concentration. However, it's harder to tell what else Niedecker is suggesting. Does she mean that poetry is a trade like any other? Or is it not a trade at all? Or is the poet's work a particular kind of trade – one where value and skill and time and effort bear absolutely no relation to commercial outcomes?

You certainly run into problems when you start trying to define what use the poet is to society. Shelley claimed that poetry was 'at once the centre and circumference of knowledge' and that poets were 'the unacknowledged legislators of the world'. In the post-religious West, so a recent version of the same argument runs, those seeking moral or spiritual guidance turn to the arts, and especially to poetry. My feeling is that they turn at least as frequently to psychotherapy. Indeed it's often said that poetry is essentially therapeutic. A poem can help its writer articulate and take charge of a set of difficult personal experiences; and it can help a reader in much the same way. As Tennyson put it, there's 'some use in measured comfort'. (But then it may just be a mixture of wishful thinking and sheer affectation to imagine that poetry does this sort of thing any better than, say, country and western music. Measured comfort comes in all shapes and sizes.)

There's still a general belief that poetry can intervene in the public world in significant and efficacious ways. This is clear enough from the threat that poets in the Soviet Union and Eastern Europe represented to their various governments after the second world war. Some argue that this is connected to the fact that poetry above all uses language. Language is the absolute dividing line between the human and animal worlds, and poetry – more than any other art form – uses all the resources that language offers. Words have meanings, and poetry keeps our words responsive and responsible – whatever our politicians have in mind.

But in the brave new world of the market economy, poetry is self-evidently useless. You can't measure poetry or 'grow' it; no one is going to float it on the stock market; you can't put it on television and sell the advertising space between the lines. If poetry actually intervenes in the world, its effects are remote and mysterious and intangible. Jim Bolger doesn't tremble in his bed when Allen Curnow publishes a new poem in *Sport*, though some of the ways in which he thinks about himself – even his new found Republicanism – may have been shaped by poems Curnow wrote forty or fifty years ago.

There's a wonderfully funny story, 'Career Move', by Martin Amis, in which film writers and poets are central figures. Sad, sensitive young men write their screenplays and send them off to literary magazines, endure the almost compulsory pain of rejection slips, and occasionally receive an acceptance and a derisory few dollars. Poets, on the other hand, are commercially astute, have wheeler-dealer agents, jet in and out of L.A., and spend their time developing projects with names like 'Sonnet', which after countless studio rewrites eventually open in cinemas across America.

The joke is deft and devastating: Amis' story reverses the realities we know, where writers in the world of film and television have wealth but not much in the way of integrity or self-respect, while poets have shabby, unsuccessful careers but nevertheless a sort of perverse job satisfaction. For of course, as Lorine Niedecker suggests, poets can't stop doing what they do: there's 'no layoff / from this condensery'. Equally, and in a further sense of Niedecker's phrase, poets can't be made redundant: the corporate sector can contract or collapse, but poets have total job security.

W.H. Auden took poetry's uselessness for granted. As a youngish poet lamenting the death of William Butler Yeats, he asserted that 'poetry makes nothing happen'; twenty-five years later he said the same thing, better, in his 1964 elegy for Louis MacNeice, 'The Cave of Making'. 'After all,' he wrote, 'it's rather a privilege / amid the affluent traffic / to serve this unpopular art' – for the fact that poetry is unpopular is finally what guarantees its worth. Poetry can't – like music – be turned into 'background noise for study'. It can't – like a piece of contemporary art – be 'hung as a status trophy by rising executives'. And it can't

>   ... be 'done' like Venice
> or abridged like Tolstoy, but stubbornly still insists upon
>   being read or ignored

Short Cuts

Goodbye

If you are still alive when you read this,
close your eyes. I am
under their lids, growing black.

Saint Geraud

The author's name sounds mystical, but in fact this tiny poem was written by the American Bill Knott (b. 1940), who published his first book, *The Naomi Poems: Corpse and Beans*, in 1966 under the pseudonym 'Saint Geraud (1940–1966)'. Saint Geraud does not appear in my handy *Penguin Dictionary of Saints*.

Whatever the author's name, the poem itself seems quite straightforward – there are no difficult words, no sophisticated allusions to Dante. Yet the more you look at it, the more mysterious it becomes; the poem's meaning is not quite as transparent as the nineteen individual words it is made of. In fact, it's quite hard to say exactly what 'Goodbye' means. Perhaps the poem is a small suicide note – or so the title might suggest. But the whole thing is full of paradoxes and contradictions. Even the last two words seem at odds with one another: 'growing' suggests something which is coming into being, while 'black' suggests some sort of opposite process – a darkening of clarity and vision. More obvious, and rather silly, but certainly a problem once you notice it, is the question of how you proceed if you do as the poem tells you. How can you read the last sentence with your eyes closed?

The poem seems to get its deepest power from the connection it sets up between the speaker and the reader, between the I and the you. You find yourself holding a copy of *Quote Unquote*, reading the poem, and, yes, still alive, thank you. In other words, you accept the poem as a piece of personal address. But having done so, you are then committed to accommodating the strong, even threatening, sense of relationship which the poem ends with. Somehow the poem, or the voice it speaks in, has involved you, got inside you, and begun adjusting the way in which you look out at the world. A good deal of the poem's meaning lies in how it treats you.

There would be other ways, and lengthier ones, of talking about 'Goodbye'. But my point is simply that short poems often 'mean' far more than their length. In the very best of them, less is infinitely more. There is a particular kind of short poem, the epigram, which in its wit and symmetry and rhyming force, can sum things up with wonderful deftness. For example Alexander Pope's eighteenth-century 'Epigram Engraved on the Collar of a Dog which I Gave to His Royal Highness', whose title is exactly as long as its text:

> I am his Highness' Dog at Kew:
> Pray tell me, sir, whose dog are you?

The epigram sorts its subject out with a kind of ruthless panache; there's no room for argument. But the sort of short poems I have in mind are less complete and definite. They look accessible but are always keeping something back; they say that the thing which looked simple is actually complex and mysterious. I am thinking of poems like Wordsworth's Lucy poems or Blake's 'The Sick Rose', or this anonymous cry from the early sixteenth-century:

> Westron winde, when will thou blow,
> The smalle raine downe can raine?
> Christ if my love were in my armes,
> And I in my bed againe.

Such poems involve the reader in their imaginative life; they never spell things out. If they are longer-lasting, it is because they are more like music than muzak – they go on giving us work to do. Or as Robert Bly puts it, they are poems where 'the poet takes the reader to the edge of a cliff, as a mother eagle takes its nestling, and then drops him. Readers with a strong imagination enjoy it, and discover they can fly. The others fall down to the rocks where they are killed instantly.'

The most popular short poem form in the West is the Japanese haiku – a three-line poem usually of seventeen syllables (five, seven, five) which should contain a reference to a season. The form thrives locally (the New Zealand Poetry Society has published the *New Zealand Haiku Anthology*) and has also adapted comfortably to the new technologies. There's a software programme called Haiku Master which can help you write them, a haiku magazine on the Internet called *Dogwood Blossoms*, and an electronic discussion group called The Shiki Internet Haiku Salon which is based at Matsuyama University in Japan. The haiku is on the move; or it is, as one of the Shiki poets, David McMurray, puts it

> Reaching for you
> Far across the Milky Way
> Keyboard fingertips

If the danger with epigrams is the ease with which a clever rhyme can pass itself off as a telling idea, the danger with haiku is that a few autumnal mood words will often do perfunctory duty for a poem. For what it's worth, my favourite short poem – indeed the shortest poem I know – is by Aram Saroyan. Once you have seen it (or it has got you in its sights), you can gaze for a long, long time:

> eyeye

Underground Poetry

Sonnet: On His Blindness

When I consider how my light is spent,
Ere half my days, in this dark world and wide,
And that one talent which is death to hide,
Lodged with me useless, though my soul more bent
To serve therewith my maker, and present
My true account, lest he returning chide,
Doth God exact day-labour, light denied?
I fondly ask; but Patience to prevent
That murmur, soon replies, God doth not need
Either man's work or his own gifts, who best
Bear his mild yoke, they serve him best, his state
Is kingly. Thousands at his bidding speed
And post o'er land and ocean without rest:
They also serve who only stand and wait.

John Milton (1608–74)

In the world of poetry, a word like 'underground' can sometimes conjure up images of dangerously subversive texts circulating somewhere out of sight, beyond the gaze of political authorities or arbiters of taste. Sometimes it just means bad performance poetry. But the meaning has begun to shift. If you travel on the London Underground these days, while you're slowly adjusting to the grim silence in the carriage, you might glance up and see John Milton's great sonnet. Yes, there it is, 'On His Blindness' – among the advertisements for alcohol and insurance companies and mouthwash.

Poems have been travelling on the Underground for about eight years now. London Transport provides 4000 free advertising spaces, and covers all production costs for the poetry posters which fill them. Three times a year a fresh set of six posters goes up – about 130 since the inception of the project.

There are marketing spin-offs: the posters can be bought over the counter or by subscription, while the anthology *Poems on the Underground* managed to sell over 50,000 copies within a year of publication. The whole project has been good PR for London Transport; and even better news for poetry.

The idea has been spreading. Poems now ride around on public transport systems all over the globe: Dublin, Stockholm, Paris, New York, San

Underground Poetry

Francisco, Sydney, Melbourne. It might be worth taking bets on which New Zealand cities, if any, will follow suit.

The one European city which has had trouble (I'm told) is Glasgow, where Edwin Morgan was commissioned to supply work for the inauguration of a revamped Underground system. The authorities decided against using his poems, no doubt because of stuff like this:

This Subway Piranhas

Did anyone tell you
that in each subway train
there is one special seat
with a small hole in it
and underneath the seat
is a tank of piranha-fish
which have not been fed
for quite some time . . .

Poetry's underground London life is just part of a larger renaissance in poetry in the United Kingdom. Books and anthologies are big business there at the moment. And a nationwide promotion of twenty 'New Generation' poets, partly funded by the Arts Council, gets underway in May.

But poetry is also finding its way into the British media in much more everyday ways. No one quite knows why, but the major newspapers are falling over themselves to print poems. Every weekday the *Independent* prints a poem by a contemporary writer. Other major newspapers – like the *Guardian* and one of two of the quality Sundays – print a weekly poem.

And on the airwaves poetry has a life well beyond Radio 3 (the equivalent to Concert FM). BBC's Radio 4 (like our National Radio) has a regular late-night poetry programme, 'Stanza' – which sometimes discusses poetry; and sometimes broadcasts edited recordings of platform readings. Even Radio 1 (a sort of ZB/ZM equivalent) is about to start broadcasting poems – dropping them in from time to time amid the pop music.

In New Zealand television is the medium which has been most hostile to poetry. In Britain, however, it too has gone poetic. Some astonishing films have been made over the last few years by the director Peter Symes, working with a range of poets, but most notably with the Yorkshire writer Tony Harrison. And late in 1993 BBC2's newsroom had poets like Fleur

Adcock and Roger McGough in the studio, writing verse commentaries on lead stories of the day. The poems were read on screen, inter-cut with news footage of the events they dealt with.

Meantime a friend just back from the US reports a recent initiative there. She checked into her hotel somewhere in New Hampshire and found on the bedside table a book – not the Gideon Bible but a fat anthology, *Six American Poets*. A note explained that it had been placed there by the American Poetry and Literacy Project. She could leave it for the next guest to enjoy. But if she would like to take it away, then the hotel could let her have it for a single dollar.

Thus poems are alive and well and back on the street. The thought that you might bump into them in the ordinary life you lead – in hotel bedrooms or on the local bus or on the television news – is pretty encouraging. Certainly if John Milton, Sappho and Spike Milligan are all rumbling around the London Underground together, something's going on.

LARKIN AT SIXTY

Kingsley Amis recalls Philip Larkin telling him that he had once found in a writers' manual, 'a list of names not to be given to serious characters'. One of the names on the list was 'Larkin'. At the time (April 1941), Amis himself thought the name a trifle comic; and no doubt it might still seem so – a bit of a lark, perhaps, or maybe a cross between a songbird and a rather straitlaced larrikin – were it not for the fact that 'Larkin' is now defined by a body of extraordinary poems, the same poems which have called forth the birthday tributes gathered in *Larkin at Sixty*.

Larkin at Sixty is edited by Anthony Thwaite, who worries out loud about the range of his twenty or so contributors. 'Not everyone who should be here is here. I originally had lined up an American, a Russian, a Pakistani and a woman ("minority enthusiasts", one can hear someone saying); but illness, silence, disappearance and diffidence eliminated them, I am sorry to say.' It is hard to sympathise with this for a number of reasons, but one reason is that twenty contributions is pretty good going – enough to give an impression of substance, but not so excessive that the whole thing runs the risk of looking immodest. Immodesty might not be especially well received at a Larkin celebration.

Three of the pieces elicited by Thwaite are poems (Peter Porter, Sir John Betjeman, Gavin Ewart). A few others are devoted to Larkin's poems (Christopher Ricks and – impressively – Seamus Heaney, who writes of the 'melody of intelligence' which he finds in Larkin's work). Most essays, however, take the form of anecdotal homage. Homage is probably the right word, for Larkin seems to generate in those who know him both affection and respect, with a good deal of overlap between the two. The poems themselves have the capacity to generate such feelings in their readers. That is part of the point of an often very funny essay by Alan Bennett, who has never met Larkin but who has for him, purely on account of the poems, immense affection. He feigns surprise at the occasion ('Apparently he is sixty, but when was he anything else? He has made a habit of being sixty . . .') and suggests that this collection of essays might be thought of as 'the literary equivalent of an electric toaster presented by the divisional manager at an awkward ceremony in the staff canteen, and in the firm's time too'.

Most of the essays are founded on personal acquaintance. There is a piece by Noel Hughes on the schoolboy Larkin ('popular with the boys because he mocked the staff, and with the staff because he was invariably polite to them'), while Kingsley Amis writes about the Oxford undergraduate. (Oxford in the 1940s seems to have been a training ground for crusty anti-modernists of the most self-conscious sort.) There are essays on Larkin the librarian, Larkin the jazz critic, Larkin the anthologist, Larkin the novelist; and several interesting essays by those who have published his poems.

The piece by Charles Monteith, Larkin's editor at Faber and Faber, is especially fine. Monteith manages to strike a personal note, without at the same time obstructing our view of the poet. He quotes from Larkin's various missives over a long period: postcard squibs, occasional limericks, and gloomy self-mockeries of the sort occasioned by the prospective publication of Larkin's jazz reviews, *All What Jazz* – 'I think the best line you can take is that you are promoting a freak publication ... Treat it like a book by T.S. Eliot on all-in wrestling.' There are eloquent, acute descriptions of the work of Barbara Pym (Larkin had wanted Faber to reissue her novels), which suggest a good deal about the qualities to be found in Larkin's own writing; and some intriguing judgements – for example, that Louis Armstrong 'was an enormously important cultural figure in our century, more important than Picasso in my opinion but certainly quite comparable in stature ...'

Monteith refers in passing to Larkin's notorious dislike of 'Abroad', and recalls his description of the Greek drink retsina as, 'that interesting wine which tastes of cricket bats'. It isn't hard to find Larkin's Little Englandism disturbing, for it sometimes seems to be part and parcel of a larger stance which assumes, almost as a matter of course, that most kinds of human behaviour and aspiration are likely to be phoney or ill-considered. But Larkin's inward, backward gaze should not be lightly dismissed. He is important in England in something like the way Frank Sargeson has been important in New Zealand. Like Sargeson, he stayed at home to some point. He has preferred to be minor and provincial – attending with integrity and with a kind of controlled intensity to what is local; and in the course of attending to what is local, he has acquired an authenticity of voice which has come to seem absolutely major, important to us all.

Larkin's books travel Abroad, even if he prefers not to. As second-year students at the University of Otago, a friend and I found ourselves studying his poetry, including the satirical piece called 'Naturally the Foundation Will Bear Your Expenses', the first stanza of which – despite our triumphant spotting of a Biblical allusion in the last two lines – seemed quite incomprehensible:

> Hurrying to catch my Comet
> One dark November day,
> Which soon would snatch me from it
> To the sunshine of Bombay,
> I pondered pages Berkeley
> Not three weeks since had heard,
> Perceiving Chatto darkly
> Through the mirror of the Third.

We sent a letter off to Larkin – or my friend did. Larkin wrote back. The poem was intended, he said, 'to portray a professional literary lecturer flying to Bombay where he intends to deliver a talk which three weeks ago he gave in Berkeley (California), and which he now thinks he might well publish as part of a collection with the British publishers Chatto & Windus, after giving it yet again on the Third Programme of the BBC'.

There must have been more to the letter than that, but I never copied it out: perhaps I was mainly concerned with passing an exam. But whatever ritual courtesies there may have been at the beginning and end of Philip Larkin's letter, the very act of sending it was a considerable kindness, and one which seems to be characteristic of him. Crustiness, by definition, is only skin deep. Certainly his courtesy is emphasised by several contributors to Larkin at Sixty; so is his honesty. Perhaps these are peculiarly English virtues – at any rate, they make Larkin a peculiarly English poet. Given the fact that courtesy and honesty have been effectively screened out of New Zealanders' mental landscape in the last few years, virtually by act of government, Larkin is likely to seem to us rather more 'old-fashioned' than he actually is.

Courtesy and honesty are agreeable enough qualities in themselves but make for a formidable combination when they are mixed together in a poet's work: they get involved in 'awkward' tonal contradictions; they try to throw each other off the page. A good deal of what is compelling in Larkin's major poems ('Church Going', for example, or 'The Whitsun Weddings') comes from the way in which the honesty of gaze and the courtesy of address tug gently but persistently against each other. This may be why Larkin's feelings, including what is sometimes called his pessimism, are often far more interesting than those expressed by more openly confessional poets.

Larkin has been giving birthday presents lately, as well as getting them. By my count he has published only three poems in the last five years. The most recent one is a piece of self-styled but amiably stylish 'doggerel' – couplets addressed to Charles Causley on the occasion of his sixty-fifth birthday.

> Dear CHARLES, My Muse, asleep or dead
> Offers this doggerel instead
> To carry from the frozen North
> Warm greetings for the twenty-fourth
> Of lucky August, best of months
> For us, as for that Roman once –
> For you're a Leo, same as me
> (Isn't it comforting to be
> So lordly, selfish, vital, strong?
> Or do you think they've got it wrong?),
> And may its golden hours portend
> As many years for you to spend.
>
> One of the sadder things, I think,
> Is how our birthdays slowly sink:
> Presents and parties disappear,
> The cards grow fewer year by year,
> Till, when one reaches sixty-five,
> How many care we're still alive?
> Ah, CHARLES, be reassured! For you
> Make lasting friends with all you do,
> And all you write; your truth and sense
> We count on as a sure defence
> Against the trendy and the mad,
> The feeble and the downright bad . . .

Larkin speaks there in ways which are friendly, generous and just: I hope he knows that what he admires in Charles Causley, his own readers admire in him.

Review of *Larkin at Sixty*, ed. Anthony Thwaite (Faber, 1982) *Listener*, 1982.

NOT UNTRUE, NOT UNKIND

The Life of Philip Larkin

> They fuck you up, your mum and dad.
>   They may not mean to, but they do.
> They fill you with the faults they had
>   And add some extra, just for you.

These are probably Philip Larkin's best-known lines. Even novelists have been known to quote them from memory. No wonder Larkin himself once observed, in his glum, professionally self-deprecating manner, that the poem would be his own 'Lake Isle of Innisfree' – 'I fully expect to hear it recited by a thousand girl guides before I die.'

As it turns out Larkin's mum and dad were a pretty devastating mixture. The father, Sydney, was Treasurer of the city of Coventry – passionate about books, but remote, solitary, intolerant. He admired fascist Germany, and even kept a small statue of Hitler on his mantelpiece which saluted if you pushed a button. He was, in his son's words, 'the sort of person that democracy didn't suit'. Eva, his wife, became a monotonous complaining figure, full of limitation and defeat, partly because Sydney saw her as little more than a domestic acquisition. Certainly his parents' marriage left Larkin with two convictions: 'that human beings should not live together, and that children should be taken from their parents at an early age'. Like many of his pronouncements, the joke was deadly serious.

Larkin recalled his childhood as a 'forgotten boredom', which may explain why he himself preferred to begin reading biographies 'halfway through, when the chap's grown up and it becomes interesting'. Fortunately Andrew Motion starts at the start, giving us not only Larkin's childhood and youth but also his years at Oxford where he was a bit of a dandy (cerise trousers and a bowtie) and a failure with women. He read D.H. Lawrence devotedly every day, and wrote prolifically, even producing under the pseudonym Brunette Coleman a pair of lesbian novellas – schoolgirls and lust and a number of tremulous spankings.

Eventually, of course, he became 'Philip Larkin' – the bachelor, the librarian, the poet of muted disappointments. Andrew Motion manages to make Larkin's life more interesting than this, and far more dignified than the list of interests in the index (which include jazz, smoking, pornography, cars and cricket) might suggest; and he shows how consciously Larkin constructed the image of himself as the poet of deprivation. His most impressive achievement is to uncover the emotional plot of Larkin's life, which he traces through a range of friendships and (more specifically) through Larkin's relationships with women.

Larkin professed not to approve of women, but his inner world was defined far more by them than by the rather embarrassing fourth-form noises he made about sex to one or two friends like Kingsley Amis. And even while he wrote poems about romantic disillusion, about missing out on everything, he was leading an intense life of sexual and emotional entanglements. For a time, fairly late in his life, he was involved with three women at once, maintaining his long-term relationship with Monica Jones alongside his courtship of Maeve Brennan, while also embarking on a fairly pragmatic affair with his secretary. He avoided the conventional commitments of marriage well enough, but he wasn't by any means a Mr Bleaney.

Andrew Motion charts these complex allegiances, evasions and desires in a way that is both clear-eyed and – I think this is the word – courteous. He also suggests that the most important woman in Larkin's life was his mother, Eva. The son complained about his mother constantly (especially after his father's death), took her for holidays (which he then complained about), and wrote to her regularly. 'Difficult and limiting as she was,' says Motion, '[she] produced the mental weather in which his poems prospered, and many of his best were either triggered by her or actually about her.'

Motion's subtitle, 'A Writer's Life', means what it says, and while his accounts of Larkin's poems sometimes have a dutiful lit crit atmosphere to them, he does show how deeply personal Larkin's verse was. Though they lack specific details, the poems always had their origins in powerful emotions and the intense particulars of experience. What might have been, in other writers, confessional revelations became, in Larkin's utterance, patterns of feeling to which all of us assent.

Or perhaps not all of us. For whatever else Larkin was, he was also – we now learn – full of reactionary gripes and hatreds. He grizzled about blacks, women, children, the working classes, Christmas; and made adoring noises about Mrs Thatcher and the Queen Mother. Andrew Motion's task was thus extraordinarily difficult: to reveal the 'real' Philip Larkin, without simply defending or attacking the man behind the poems.

My feeling is that he has managed pretty well. He is good on all sorts of things – how Larkin's life and poetry swung between romantic and cynical impulses, how closely related the poet's modesty was to laziness and self-regard. He lets us see Larkin's moments of love and generosity, yet sets against them the prejudices and weaknesses. He charts the poet's late decline – into a bald, deaf, overweight grouch, frightened of death, depressed and alcoholic – with an exacting yet sympathetic clarity.

Of course, Larkin could make most of these points perfectly well himself. 'So now we face 1982,' he wrote to Kingsley Amis, 'sixteen stone six, gargantuanly paunched, helplessly addicted to alcohol, tired of livin' and scared of dyin', world-famous unable-to-write poet, well you know the rest.' What I miss in this biography is that liveliness of voice – and especially the rich variety of tones it adopts in Larkin's *Selected Letters*.

For Andrew Motion's is a judicious, reasonable chronicle whose scrupulous patience comes, perhaps inevitably, at the expense of narrative pace and flair: we never turn the pages with excitement. We turn them with trust, though. Motion has caught Larkin's life, with all its contradictions, in words which – to borrow the poet's own phrasing – are 'at once true and kind, / Or not untrue and not unkind.'

Review of *Philip Larkin: A Writer's Life* by Andrew Motion (Faber, 1993) *Listener*, 1993

WHO IS SYLVIA?

The Life of Sylvia Plath

It is nearly thirty years since Sylvia Plath put her head in the gas oven of the London flat where Yeats once lived, and in that time she has been transformed into the legend she only half-created in her poems. Death made her larger than life, and the voyeurism of the living has guaranteed her a place in a distressingly glamorous tradition.

Plath belongs to a self-destructive generation of American writers. Her *Ariel* poems, said Robert Lowell approvingly, play Russian roulette with six cartridges in the chamber; while another suicidal compatriot, Anne Sexton, penned a poem of envy ('Thief! – / how did you crawl into, / crawl down alone / into the death I wanted so badly and for so long . . .?'). And of course Plath is simply one name on an even longer list of Romantic suicides and early deaths – Chatterton, van Gogh, Katherine Mansfield, James Dean, Marilyn Monroe, Janis Joplin . . .

Most of us know that Plath took her own life. Probably fewer have read the poems she wrote. Students at university and senior high school study her work – and not only because the poet's fate makes them and their teachers gasp. Many feminist teachers and readers see Plath not as a Romantic cot-case but as a piece of telling evidence. So this is how a male world exacts vengeance on talented women . . . The Sylvia such readers claim to know is a persecuted sister, driven to a death from which she might have been saved by the feminism she just failed to coincide with. In the words of one (male) critic, by her suicide Plath 'simply enacted the fate of women's words in a patriarchal culture.'

Who knows what the truth might be – except that it can hardly be so simple. Biographical enquiries until now have tended to take up a position somewhere along the highway between Romantic Suicide and Patriarchal Victim. By either account, Plath is the straight-A student obsessed with success, worshipping the trinkets of middle-class America, yet cripplingly damaged by the loss of her father, who died when she was eight – and doomed finally by the collapse of the marriage she railed against in the black vowels of her poem 'Daddy'. The gap between surface accomplishment and how things felt inside was just too big – it opened wide and Plath went down the middle. Did she jump or was she pushed?

Compared with earlier biographers, Anne Stevenson – who thinks Plath jumped – has had what amounts to the blessing of the poet's estate. A prefatory note says that contributions to the text by Olwyn Hughes (Plath's sister-in-law and literary agent to the estate) have made *Bitter Fame* 'almost a work of dual authorship'. This is almost a team biography, then, and in fact the team has more members: appended to Stevenson's text are three memoirs by friends of Ted Hughes and Sylvia Plath. These give a curious effect, for they have already been paraphrased and quoted in the main body of the book. It is rather like hearing witnesses at an inquest give their evidence twice.

Dido Merwin contributes a particularly spiteful memoir; but she also expresses the animating spirit of this new biography when she remarks that, 'nobody I know was prepared to say a word as long as Sylvia's children were growing up, with the result that her hagiographers got a head start of two decades plus in which to shape their apotheosis, which snowballed onward and upward virtually unchallenged'.

Biographers are said to be especially prone to the disease of admiration. Well, there are no such worries here. The Plath of *Bitter Fame* is a thoroughly appalling person: irrational, demanding, self-absorbed; complaining and paranoid; ambitious and hypocritical; full of envy yet empty of conscience. The dust-jacket promises a book which will be 'authoritative': 'as complete, balanced, and objectively written as the facts allow'. But any balance here is a matter of redress. Where earlier biographies put a case *for* Plath, this one puts the case *against* her.

Stevenson writes intelligent, accessible prose – but perhaps because so many of the central facts of Plath's life are well enough known, she shows little narrative flair. The story she tells is made out of paragraphs, not events. There are 358 pages of text. Only fifty-eight are given to the first twenty-two years of Plath's life, while 300 are devoted to the next eight years. It is as if Stevenson accepts the conventional accounts of the younger Plath, and that it is only after Ted Hughes comes on the scene that the lengthy, detailed business of revising received opinion must begin.

Hughes agreed to check *Bitter Fame* for errors of fact, but he declined to be interviewed. Perhaps that is why so many of the book's voices seem to take his part. But as an actor in the tale, he seems to be absent – except as a patient, long-suffering man doing his best in near-to-impossible circumstances. As an emotional presence, someone who has feelings and behaves in certain ways, he is off-stage. Thus *Bitter Fame* vindicates him, yet leaves him out of the picture. You would hardly gather, for example, that it was Hughes' affair with Assia Wevill which lay behind the collapse of the marriage – whether as a symptom or a cause hardly matters. The affair is referred to, but you might easily finish the book thinking the whole thing was a silly idea of Sylvia's.

We are in the land of gossip here, of course, a place where Hughes, along with his children, has had to live out much of his life. Yet Hollywood gossip is probably what most of us want – something to match the cover blurb on the American paperback of Plath's novel *The Bell Jar*: 'The heartbreaking story of a talented young woman who descends into madness.' Perhaps one of these days we will have the Spielberg movie, co-scripted by Anne Rice and Stephen King, with someone like Robin Morgan retained as feminist consultant to make the enterprise politically sound.

Meantime, the Plath industry goes on thriving. There are still plenty of scholars and critics keen to say, as A. Alvarez did in 1965, that Plath's death seemed 'in a way, inevitable, even justified, like some final unwritten poem'. It ought to be time for the reviewer to say piously that we should now leave Plath in peace and turn back to the poems – to the cold serenities of a world where Lady Lazarus eats men like air, the black telephone's off at the root and the squeal of brakes might just be a birth cry. But the poems and the life belong to one another, and both are subject to the facts of the poet's death. That is why Anne Stevenson's well-informed and quietly partisan book is both a major event and – whether we seek a compassionate, inward view of Sylvia Plath or simply an exercise in judicious balance – a major disappointment.

Review of *Bitter Fame: A Life of Sylvia Plath* by Anne Stevenson (Viking, 1989) *Listener*, 1989

THE GOVERNMENT OF THE TONGUE

Ever since as a young, aspiring poet Seamus Heaney gave himself the pen-name Incertus, he has been forging his verse out of the processes of doubt and uncertainty. Like many poets he has been concerned about the proper relationship of the poet to the world: poem after poem – from 'Digging', which opens his first book, *Death of a Naturalist*, to 'Riddle', which closes *The Haw Lantern* – has made its ostensible subject into some kind of metaphor for the process of writing. Of course, the function of poetry has been one of the great subjects of poetry over the last couple of hundred years – and in the hands of bad poets it is a preoccupation which can seem both enormously self-regarding and needlessly arcane. But it is a subject which can never be entirely inward, certainly not solipsistic, because it depends on a constant inspection of the connections between internal and external states. How does humankind use language to realise and articulate its sense of self? How does it govern and construct the world in which it comes to consciousness? In the hands of someone like Heaney whose inner and outer worlds incorporate the fact of being Irish in a time of Troubles, these questions of the powers and duties of poetry are real and pressing: everyday matters, uneasy mental baggage which is easily kept in mind.

A few years ago Heaney reviewed Italo Calvino's *Mr Palomar* – a sequence of prose observations of a figure who is himself named after an observatory. This is how he described the title character:

> Mr Palomar is a lens employed by his author in order to inspect the phenomena of the world, but the lens is apt to turn into a mirror which reflects the hesitations and self-corrections of Mr Palomar's own reflecting mind. The book consists of a graduated sequence of descriptions and speculations in which the protagonist confronts the problem of discovering his place in the world and of watching these discoveries dissolve under his habitual intellectual scrutiny.

The review of *Mr Palomar* is not included in Heaney's new book of essays and lectures, *The Government of the Tongue*, yet it describes the procedures of these essays just as accurately as it seems to describe what goes on in many of Heaney's poems. *The Government of the Tongue* explores – hesitatingly, with many passages of self-correction – a range of positions in the old debate between art and life, between Ariel and Prospero, between *dulce* and *utile*. In order to give the debate immediacy, Heaney proposes ('more melodramatically') the terms Song and Suffering, and begins with an anecdote which dramatises the tension which all these essays variously take up. In 1972 Heaney went with his friend, the singer David Hammond, to a Belfast recording studio, to make a tape of songs and poems for another friend in Michigan. As they travelled to the studio, there were explosions in the city; they could hear the sound of ambulances and fire engines. And there was news of casualties:

> It was music against which the music of the guitar that David unpacked made little impression. So little, indeed, that the very notion of beginning to sing at that moment when others were beginning to suffer seemed like an offence against their suffering.

Heaney and Hammond abandoned the recording session: 'to have sung and said the poems in those conditions would have been a culpable indulgence.'

In retrospect, the self-correcting Heaney is less certain that he and Hammond made the right decision. 'Why should the joyful affirmation of music and poetry ever constitute an affront to life?' He cites Chekhov, drinking cognac on the prison island of Sakhalin – 'unabashed by the suffering which surrounds him because unflinchingly responsible to it.' He thinks that lyric poetry, unlike various forms of narrative, is in a special situation here. The lyric poem is part of history, but also exists alongside history. It deals in transcendent moments, it lifts free of circumstance, has about it 'an element of the untrammelled'. Inevitably the poet – whether it is David Hammond refusing to sing or Chekhov with his cognac, 'savouring a fume of intoxication and a waft of luxury in the stink of oppression and the music of cruelty' – will be touched by embarrassment, for 'he exercises his free gift in the presence of the unfree and the unhurt'. 'This is the reason,' thinks Heaney, 'that, psychologically, the lyric poet feels the need for justification in a world that is notably hampered and deprived.'

Presumably the act of writing essays about poetry, for Heaney anyway, springs from that need for justification. Certainly the writers he attends to in *The Government of the Tongue* tend to be those who have registered a similar set of preoccupations. So he admires, grudgingly, the First World War poet Wilfrid Owen, who sponsored an art 'which seems to rebuke beauty in favour of truth', but reserves far greater admiration for the Russian poet Osip Mandelstam, a victim of Stalinism who died because he believed in unconstrained utterance. 'Mandelstam died because he could not repress his urge to sing in his own way.' Heaney prefers Mandelstam to Owen – partly because he sees the poets of the Soviet Union and Eastern bloc as analogous to the poets in Northern Ireland, partly because the deepest part of him also believes that the act of poetry must be 'free, self-governing, self-seeking', although he is clear that the value of the poems that are made will depend crucially on the sort of responsibilities the poet acknowledges between moments of creation. But most of all Heaney admires poets who are aware that problems exist: and as a critic he turns frequently to poets who have made their poetry out of problems.

Thus he writes a tribute to Philip Larkin which indicates those moments of release and vision which rise above the usual glum good manners of Larkin's verse. But he also celebrates in Larkin what he calls 'the melody of intelligence', an effect he glosses as the 'encounter between a compassionate, unfoolable mind and its own predicaments'. Heaney admires the West Indian poet Derek Walcott for finding 'a language woven out of dialect and literature, neither folksy nor condescending, a singular idiom evolved out of one man's inherited divisions and obsessions'. He commends Miroslav Holub's 'high-spirited distrust'; Holub's poetry has all the worn-down truth-to-life of the disillusioned man, but it also has a contrary and heartening vision of a possible good based upon optimism about decencies and impulses in the usual life'. Zbigniew Herbert is both tender-minded and tough-minded – there is a 'division within the poet, deriving from the co-existence within his own deepest self of two conflicting strains'.

This idea that poetry lives among the contraries and does best when it agrees to acknowledge them runs through the work of all the poets Heaney admires, and through his own work. All of these essays – whether they are about Sylvia Plath, W.H. Auden, Osip Mandelstam or Patrick Kavanagh – are (*pace* Mr Palomar) passages of self-inspection, self-interrogation. And Heaney is an excellent scrutineer, wonderfully alert to the specifics of particular passages of text. He himself is a dab hand at the sort of 'impressionistic and text-centred' criticism for which he admires Geoffrey Grigson – it may not be 'up-to-date in its idiom', but he admires it, he says, because 'it is so closely allied, as an act of reading, to what happens during the poet's act of writing'.

The essay here which has the strongest implications for Heaney's own practice as a poet – at least for the directions he is currently testing – is

'The Impact of Translation'. In it Heaney suggests that poets in English have begun to gaze East, prompted by the translations of Eastern European verse which have appeared over the last twenty years: poets in English are beginning 'to concede that the locus of greatness is shifting away from their language'. It is not the poets of England and America but those of Russia and Eastern Europe who have become heroic names:

> They are the ones who have toed the line, not just the verse line but the line where courage is tested, where to stand by what you write is to have to stand your ground and take the consequences. For these poets, the mood of writing is the indicative mood and for that reason they constitute a shadow-challenge to poets who dwell in the conditional, the indeterminate mood which has grown so characteristic of so much of the poetry one has grown used to reading in the journals and new books, particularly in the United States.

What Heaney seems to admire most is, as he puts it, 'the faith in art itself which becomes manifest in the extreme conditions'. And he thinks that 'contemporary English poetry has become aware of the insular and eccentric nature of English experience in all the literal and extended meanings of those adjectives'. Born in the North of Ireland, speaking English, growing up 'in between', he wishes to situate himself imaginatively among the Eastern Europeans. He does not quite say that Belfast is a suburb of Warsaw – but he constantly refers to the poets of Eastern Europe with a sense of kinship. One of the challenges they face, he thinks, is 'to survive amphibiously, in the realm of "the times" and the realm of their moral and artistic self-respect, a challenge immediately recognizable to anyone who has lived with the awful and demeaning facts of Northern Ireland's history over the last couple of decades'.

The 'amphibian' techniques that characterise Eastern bloc poetry turn up in Heaney's own new volume of poems, *The Haw Lantern*. About a third of the book consists of anecdotal poems which have been carefully scattered through the text. These have the qualities of parable, allegory. Fable-titles like 'From the Republic of Conscience', 'From the Land of the Unspoken' or 'From the Frontier of Writing' interrupt and destabilise other poems which are more or less continuous with Heaney's earlier work. The repeated 'From' of their titles suggests communication from a far-off place; and it also suggests a process of translation ('from the Russian'; 'from the original Greek'). The idea of translation is important in Eastern European poetry – political commentaries are obliged to be coded, oblique, as so many of Heaney's own verse commentaries on Irish politics have been. Thus, when

Heaney writes, 'We lived deep in a land of optative moods, / under high, banked clouds of resignation', he is presumably talking about his own community – the Ireland in which he grew up. And when he talks later in the same poem ('From the Canton of Expectation') of a 'change of mood', of 'a grammar / of imperatives, the new age of demands', of the banishing of the conditional, of his own yearning for someone 'who stood his ground in the indicative', he is using the language of language-teaching to talk about the recent history of Northern Ireland. The conditional / indicative metaphor, of course, indicates to what extent these poems are written out of the preoccupations which produced essays like 'The Impact of Translation'.

The austerity of some of these new poems also betrays Heaney's unease with his own lyric charm – an unease which had been earlier signalled in one of the *Station Island* poems, in which the shade of his dead cousin Colum McCartney charged him with using poetry as a device to make reality pretty:

> You confused evasion and artistic tact.
> . . . you whitewashed ugliness and drew
> the lovely blinds of the *Purgatorio*
> and saccharined my death with morning dew.

Heaney's Eastern European poems probably don't indicate the way his poetry will develop, but they represent a response to the challenge of the times, and to the challenge of his own success. They show a poet still prompted by doubts about his own activity, still concerned to change and grow.

The elegiac strain has been important in Heaney's work from the beginning – the living mourning the dead, also the older man regretting the loss of younger versions of himself. At the heart of *The Haw Lantern* is a short sequence of sonnets, 'Clearances', written in memory of the poet's mother. They are fine poems, predicated like all of Heaney's work on the belief that the ordinary is valuable. The sequence sits at the centre of the collection and all the other poems seem to flow towards it, or away from it. And while these sonnets are deeply personal, they are continuous in language and idea with the essays of *The Government of the Tongue*. One sonnet even echoes the title of the book of essays:

> Fear of affectation made her affect
> Inadequacy whenever it came to
> Pronouncing words 'beyond her'. *Bertold Brek*.
> She'd manage something hampered and askew

> Every time, as if she might betray
> The hampered and inadequate by too
> Well-adjusted a vocabulary.
> With more challenge than pride, she'd tell me, 'You
> Know all them things'. So I governed my tongue
> In front of her, a genuinely well-
> adjusted adequate betrayal
> Of what I knew better. I'd *naw* and *aye*
> And decently relapse into the wrong
> Grammar which kept us allied and at bay.

Language has both personal and political implications for Heaney – it is tied up with power, with territory and betrayal, with the presence or absence of community. In his work a 'metafictional' pleasure in language as a medium mixes with the political and cultural implications of what it means to be Irish yet speak and write in English.

Seamus Heaney is one of the directors of the Field Day Theatre Company, a group of artists and intellectuals who believe that 'the political crisis in the North and its reverberations in the Republic [have] made the necessity of a reappraisal of Ireland's political and cultural situation explicit and urgent'. They have mounted a range of theatre productions (their first was Brian Friel's *Translations*, an extraordinary play about languages and colonialism which, to my knowledge, has been completely ignored by theatre directors in New Zealand). They also publish a pamphlet series. One, a poem by Seamus Heaney was addressed as 'An Open Letter' to the editors of the recent *Penguin Book of Contemporary British Verse*, who had given him pride of place in the new poetic dispensation. He objected to the adjective 'British':

> You'll understand I draw the line
> At being robbed of what is mine,
> My *patria*, my deep design
>   To be at home
> In my own place and dwell within
>   Its proper name –

Another Northern Irish poet, Tom Paulin, also a director of Field Day, is the author of a pamphlet called *A New Look at the Language Question*. He begins by questioning the ideas of 'evolution' and 'purity' which have conditioned some thinking about language, and makes the straightforward proposition that the history of a language 'is often a story of possession and

The Government of the Tongue

dispossession, territorial struggle and the establishment or imposition of a culture'.

Paulin discusses dictionaries and the ways in which they institutionalise a sense of community or nationhood. He thinks that the Oxford English dictionary is perceived as 'both book and sacred natural object, one of the guardians of the nation's soul'. More practically, he thinks it is 'the chief lexicon of a language which can be more accurately described as "British English"'. In Paulin's own lexicon, 'British' English does not include 'Irish' English. His interests and commitments lie with the dialect of the North; he talks of the language being at present in a state of near anarchy:

> Spoken Irish English exists in a number of provincial and local forms, but because no scholar has as yet compiled a *Dictionary of Irish English* many words are literally homeless. They live in the careless richness of speech, but they rarely appear in print. When they do, many readers are unable to understand them and have no dictionary where they can discover their meaning. The language therefore lives freely and spontaneously as speech, but it lacks any institutional existence and so is impoverished as a literary medium.

Paulin wants to support his native tongue, to raise the popular conception of it, in a phrase he quotes from G.B. Thomson, 'above the level of the after-dinner story'. But there are problems for the writer wishing to use Irish English as a literary medium, who 'must either explain dialect words tediously in a glossary or restrict his audience at each particular "dialectical" moment'.

This is a problem which also confers a sense of power – as Maori (and occasionally Pakeha) writers will know. Paulin offers a nice description of the strength of small language communities. The use of dialect, he says, creates

> a form of closed, secret communication with readers who come from the same region. This will express something very near to a familial relationship because every family has its hoard of relished words which express its members' sense of kinship. These words act as a kind of secret sign and serve to exclude the outside world. They constitute a dialect of endearment within the wider dialect.

These concerns carry over into Paulin's practice as a poet. He has published four books of poetry (all with Faber). The first two were generally reviewed as the work of a somewhat dour writer who mixed real accomplishment with considerable promise. A reviewer of his second book told him in the *Times Literary Supplement* that he must develop, 'even if it means trying out ways of producing non-poetry . . . of acquiring kinds of exploratory looseness, flexibility, solvent instability that may harden into a new kind of style'. Whether or not these comments meant anything to Paulin, his next two books, *Liberty Tree* and the recently published *Fivemiletown*, do experiment with an exploratory looseness, largely by making room for the homeless language of Northern Ireland.

The result is that Standard English is no longer the language of Paulin's poems. Sometimes it is simply a matter of orthography – 'eejit' must be 'idiot', for example. But phrase after phrase reads as if it has been plucked off the streets of Belfast: 'a formal slegging', 'that lunk July', 'for a geg', 'a creashy lane', 'dew brish on the grass', 'a stramash', 'this wick decade', 'dwammy sick', and so on. If a *Dictionary of Irish English* is ever put together, the compilers are going to be very grateful to Tom Paulin's poems. Meantime, Paulin's political-cum-linguistic programme makes for difficult poetry – local dialect and a formidable range of intellectual reference conspire to leave most of us (I would guess) feeling like outsiders. Something endearing is going on, but the reader is left unembraced. It is not even clear that there is a solid, settled world in Paulin's poems that one might try to learn about and enter. The poems in *Fivemiletown* breathe both the air of the streets and the academy – an admirable thing – but there is a willed, restless, dissident air about them; they want to be at home in too many places at once.

Paulin's recent *Faber Book of Political Verse* is another dissident piece of work – yet its idiosyncracies make for an ineffective challenge to the status quo. It isn't hard to share Paulin's disapproval of those who think that 'poems exist in a timeless vacuum or a soundproof museum, and that poets are gifted with an ability to hold themselves above history, rather like skylarks or weather satellites'. Nor is it hard to sympathise with his desire to avoid what he once called 'the dithering middle-ground' between such a view of poetry and its opposite extreme, which sees literature solely as a vehicle for hard-line political propaganda. This anthology represents Paulin's attempt to occupy the middle-ground without dithering, and perhaps it is the wish not to dither that gives his introduction such a sense of combat. Part of his general belligerence springs from a buried argument that he seems to be conducting with Craig Raine, his editor at Faber and Faber, and he is also trying to 'boost' a Puritan/Republican tradition at the expense of a Monarchist/Anglican one (with some attempts at even-handedness). The whole enterprise certainly has atmosphere – Paulin is like a very intelligent drunk going the rounds at a party, looking for trouble and able to turn the smallest chance remark into grounds for a fist-fight.

The editorial selection is a strange one – though intended, I think, to be fairly ecumenical. Paulin wants to accommodate what he believes to be valuable from 'English Literature' (hence lots of Milton, and all of Dryden's *Absalom and Achitophel*) yet at the same time offer a challenge to the idea of the English canon in its conventional definitions. But his inclusions reveal a vision which is largely Eurocentric. His sense of US poetry, despite his inclusion of two blues pieces, is curiously 'English': a couple of e.e. cummings poems, for example, but nothing by William Carlos Williams; a poem by Elizabeth Bishop, nothing by Adrienne Rich. There is also a parochial quality here. Why, in an anthology of *political* verse should Derek Mahon be represented by three poems, when Bertolt Brecht and Tony Harrison have only one poem each and poets like Edwin Morgan and James Fenton are nowhere to be seen?

One could go on quibbling about the selections from Europe and America, but the gaps in Paulin's anthology are more obvious if one looks a little further around the world. There is nothing here from Asia or Africa; nothing from the America that lies north and south of the United States – except for one poem by Pablo Neruda; nothing from any of the 'new literatures' in English. Paulin may have looked and found nothing to admire, of course; but I think the absences in his anthology betray a narrow and, in its way, sectarian vision.

Like Seamus Heaney, Tom Paulin particularly values the poets of Eastern Europe. There, he says, 'the poet has a special responsibility both to art and society . . . and this responsibility is single and indivisible'. Such poets remind us 'that in certain societies to write poetry is to act socially, not to turn one's back on contingency'. It is hard to know exactly what the lessons are for Western writers, however – writers may need to be tested, but no one is likely to emigrate to Eastern Europe or Iran for the sake of their art. Ironically, a poet like Mandelstam is a political poet by virtue of his refusal to write political poetry. If he had lived in Sweden, his four poems might never have found their way into Paulin's anthology. Skylarks and weather satellites can live dangerously, too.

Many British and American poets have been reading and translating the poets of Eastern Europe – but the sense of kinship which Northern Irish poets have recently asserted is an uneasy one. The points of correspondence seem clear, and the reach beyond insularity is admirable; but perhaps there is also something less healthy going on: a need to be part of 'a modern martyrology' (Heaney's phrase), which will be different from yet continuous with the mythologies of sacrifice and heroism fixed in the

Irish consciousness by Yeats. It all seems a little like Sylvia Plath comparing her private sufferings to those of the Jews at Auschwitz and Dachau – excessive, glamorous. Heaney and Paulin come from a distressed and beleaguered place; but while they deal with harder realities than some other writers, they also live more comfortable lives than the poets of the Warsaw bloc. They are both, from choice, partial exiles from the North: Paulin teaches at an English university, Heaney commutes between Dublin and the East Coast of the USA. Their separations from the place they might call home are not, like those of Kundera or Brodsky or Milosz, absolute.

There is no doubt, though, that the example of Eastern Europe has become a real imaginative pressure in the work of a number of Northern Irish poets. Here is Paulin's fine 'local' version of a poem by Anna Akhmatova. (The poem springs from Akhmatova's visit to Osip and Nadezda Mandelstam in Voronezh, the place of their exile.) The fact that the poem appears as a translation in the *Faber Book of Political Verse* while in *Fivemiletown* it is reprinted, in effect, as Paulin's own work means that it can also represent the ambivalent, admiring gaze which the poets of Northern Ireland have begun to cast towards the East.

> VORONEZH
> You walk on permafrost
> in these streets.
> The town's silly and heavy
> like a glass paperweight
> stuck on a desk –
> a wide steel one
> glib as this pavement.
> I trimp on ice,
> the sledges skitter and slip.
> Crows are crowding the poplars,
> and St Peter's of Voronezh
> is an acidgreen dome
> fizzing in the flecked light.
> The earth's stout as a bell –
> it hums like that battle
> on the Field of Snipes.
> Lord let each poplar
> take the shape of a wine-glass
> and I'll make it ring

The Government of the Tongue

as though the priest's wed us.
But that tin lamp
on the poet's table
was watched last night –
Judas and the Word
are stalking each other
through this scroggy town
where every line has three stresses
and only the one word, *dark*.

Review of *The Government of the Tongue* (Faber & Faber, 1988) and *The Haw Lantern* (Faber & Faber, 1987) by Seamus Heaney; *Fivemiletown*, by Tom Paulin (Faber & Faber, 1987); *The Faber Book of Political Verse*, ed. Tom Paulin (Faber & Faber, 1986). *Landfall* 170, 1989

REAL HOT AIR

The back cover of *The Penguin Book of Contemporary British Poetry* tells us that we have just picked up 'a brilliant new landmark in anthologies of modern poetry'. Blurbs will be blurbs, but this one seems more than usually extravagant, and a good deal less accurate than the image on the front cover of the book, which is a quasi-abstract landscape painting with not a hint of a landmark in sight. What is depicted is the shadow of a hot-air balloon: this seems to be glimpsed from the vantage of the balloon itself, so that while the shadow is static, we are presumably meant to imagine it travelling along at the same pace as the eye which gazes down towards it. The shadow is cast across a thoroughly flat surface – a stretch of hessian-toned sand, an expanse of blue ocean – whose colours are serene and pastel, pleased by one another's presence. The whole image is tactful, agreeable, stylishly well-mannered, like much of the poetry inside the anthology, and, like rather less of the poetry inside the anthology, the cover picture also suggests a sort of limited transcendence – the imagination observing its own processes and interventions, the mind in flight (maybe) recording its own quiet markings on reality.

A less generous way of reading the cover might be to complain that we aren't offered a real balloon but only the shadow of one. There isn't even real hot air. But then, hot air is precisely what this anthology refuses to have to do with. It stares determinedly, coolly, back down the last two decades at A. Alvarez's *The New Poetry* (1962); and the editors, Blake Morrison and Andrew Motion, have gone some distance out of their way to insist, in the course of their introduction, that the work Alvarez assembled is now the old poetry.

It has been the old poetry for a while. It was already well into middle age back in 1972, when the *Review* ran a symposium on 'The State of Poetry' which asked contributors to indicate, among other things, any developments they hoped for in the next ten years. Clive James hadn't at the time quite perfected his line in one-liners, but one of the things he imagined was

'Alvarez, attired as a crow', who would, he posited, leap from the top of the Matterhorn 'and in the few seconds before he reaches terminal velocity write all there is to be written about Ted Hughes'. The new Penguin anthology is here to tell us that Alvarez's ideas reached terminal velocity years ago and that there is no point in sending out a search party.

The risk-taking poetry of extremism has gone then: poets as different as Charles Tomlinson and James Fenton have penned verses attacking Alvarez, and no self-respecting, well-informed young poet in Margaret Thatcher's Britain is likely to come down with a touch of the William Blakes. (What did happen to the Children of Albion, anyway?) The one thing which the poets in *The Penguin Book of Contemporary British Poetry* have in common is that they represent none of the things which Alvarez advocated: '[they are] not inhabitants of their own lives so much as intrigued observers, not victims but onlookers, not poets working in a confessional white heat but dramatists and story-tellers.'

Very well – here are twenty poets who are like each other because they are not like something else. They are not confessional poets; nor, fortunately, are they editorialists-in-verse, a more common British condition. Blake Morrison and Andrew Motion claim rather more than this, of course. They believe that 'a decisive shift of sensibility' has occurred, that 'a body of work has been created which demands, for its appreciation, a reformation of poetic taste'. Their anthology, they say, is 'didactic as well as representative', and is designed to educate the new reading public.

But are they right? Should they be trusted? They sound trustworthy and judicious in their introduction – but somehow they make assertions about this new sensibility which manage to seem more convenient than true. These poets, we are told, 'have developed a degree of ludic and literary self-consciousness reminiscent of the modernists'; or they have exchanged 'the received idea of the poet as the-person-next-door, or knowing insider, for the attitude of the anthropologist or alien invader or remembering exile'. Quietly paced statements like these, especially in their fuller context, come across as modest, unexceptionable attempts to acknowledge the full range of tendencies in the poetry under review and to locate them safely somewhere in recent history. But the result is that everything has been unnaturally tidied up: the poets are assembled under a single flag whose several colours, although no willed efforts have been made to conceal them, can hardly be made out for all the flapping in the winds of change.

In fact there is much more variety in this anthology than the editors allow. Six of the poets come from Ulster, but as individuals are no more like each other (Muldoon and Mahon?) than they ought to be. Several poets have backgrounds which are provincial and working-class: they write about roots and cultural displacement, but so differently that it is hardly realistic to suggest that they share a point of view. Nevertheless, the editors firmly link a pair of these poets, Douglas Dunn and Tony Harrison, and write about them in a way which is accurate but heavily loaded: they are both 'sharply conscious of a background and upbringing which sets them at an angle to the cultural establishment'. That *at an angle* conveniently signals a perspective which can also be carried across to the Martians – almost as if no gap has to be crossed in the process at all. There are several Martians here, in particular Craig Raine, Christopher Reid and David Sweetman. There are also the purveyors of fantasy, wit, serious whimsy (James Fenton, Paul Muldoon). A different cross-section would discover a large number of writers, different in their emphases, who owe something of their tone of voice to Philip Larkin; yet there are others who have listened hard to Robert Lowell or W.H. Auden. Then there are the women, five in all (who perhaps represent a statistical gesture: there is certainly no *women's* poetry here, of the kind that other English-speaking places can supply). Or there is a poet like Jeffrey Wainwright, who seems to have history, as a poetic territory, almost entirely to himself. And so on.

It wouldn't be hard to show that British poetry is even more various than the inclusions in this anthology indicate. (One recent part of it which is most obviously missing is the strain anthologised at the back of Carcanet's *British Poetry Since 1970.*) Still, the point to stress here is that the voices included in the new Penguin anthology are at least as interesting for their differences as they are for their similarities. Alvarez (who, for all his dogmatism, admitted into *The New Poetry* a number of writers whose work he disapproved of) was able to make a composite poem out of passages from eight *New Lines* contributors – the idea being both to display and reprove those qualities he did not care for. It is possible to imagine a composite Martian poem, but not so easy to see a composite piece being constructed out of all the kinds of poet in the Morrison–Motion anthology or even from the work by the five poets who seem to me to be the most interesting: Seamus Heaney, Tony Harrison, Craig Raine, James Fenton and Tom Paulin.

Heaney and Harrison are already very considerable figures. Heaney is probably a major one. Morrison and Motion think him the most important new poet of the last fifteen years and have 'very deliberately' placed him first in the anthology, printing twenty pieces by him and sneaking another, 'The Grauballe Man', into their introduction. There is thus enough of

Heaney's work represented to convey some sense of those 'interlace' effects which are so compelling in any sustained reading of his five published volumes and which make his many, small separate poems accumulate towards a single *work*. There's something a little odd, however, about the sequence of Heaney's poems in the Penguin: they more or less follow the orderings of the original books, but not quite. For example, the order of 'Anahorish' and 'Broagh', both poems about language and territory, is reversed – nothing is lost by this, but it is hard to see what has been gained. More strikingly, 'The Tollund Man' has been removed from the company of other *Wintering Out* pieces and transported forward to join a group of bog-people poems from *North*. This makes sense, perhaps; yet a damage has been done to the larger weave of Heaney's work in that the poem no longer anticipates a future journey and epiphany ('Some day I will go to Aarhus') but seems to have had the experience granted to it already. (Incidentally, *does* the Tollund Man's stained face repose at Aarhus? Isn't Heaney planning a visit to the wrong museum?)

Alvarez has written disapprovingly of Heaney's 'beautiful minor poetry', judging that his interests lie mainly with 'the seductions of fine language, the verbal showman's sleights of hand'. There is truth in this, though it is an ungenerous half-truth. Many of Heaney's poems use language as if it possesses a tactile quality, like potter's clay – so that on the page the poems look as if they might be textured wallpaper; you feel that you could run your fingertips across a passage of text and touch raised surfaces. This is a considerable pleasure in itself, but with poems like 'Broagh' and 'Anahorish' in mind, Morrison and Motion are able to make the further point (really in answer to Alvarez) that Heaney relishes language 'as something that embodies politics, history and locality, as well as having its own delectability'.

This is well said, and might be said equally of Tony Harrison, except that delectability would be a bit genteel for the bruising relationship he has with words and which his words in turn have with the world they handle. Like Heaney he is strongly aware of language as physical substance; and is just as much aware of it as something which codes into itself a variety of cultural assumptions, with the result that it is constantly engaged in 'making up' the reality it is made from. A number of his poems read like fights between 'civilised' and 'vernacular' forms of discourse. This sense of aggression inhabits even the most tender and moving of his poems ('Long Distance', 'Book Ends'), while the spark and directness of his feelings make you wonder if he hasn't strayed out of *The New Poetry* after all. The people in Harrison's poems seem much more real than those in Heaney's – as if

Harrison feels a need to attempt confrontation and contemplation in the one breath, while Heaney, despite his ability to register process, is chiefly concerned to record the aftermath of contemplation. There is certainly an *oomph* about Harrison's work which sets him off from almost everyone else in the Penguin anthology, and which gives him more in common (to be parochial for a moment) with such otherwise different poets as Ian Wedde or John Tranter.

'A Martian Sends a Postcard Home' leads off the selection from Craig Raine's work – another rearrangement which makes an editorial point, since poems of earlier composition are placed after it. Raine has become enormously influential in the last few years; it even seems possible to speak of a 'school', although some British reviewers react as if something much worse, like the invasion of the bodysnatchers, is taking place. Raine writes a lot of poems which describe his own habits of mind, and his Martian speaker is an artist-figure who misconceives ordinary reality in ways which defamiliarise it, thus making it fresh and interesting again. His misconceptions are metaphorical, and there are many moments of alert, exuberant metaphor in Raine's work. Yet the overall effect isn't exuberant, or cheerful. 'Flying to Belfast, 1977' is a poem which offers pleasure in the surprising, apparently frivolous comparisons it offers:

> It was possible to laugh
> as the engines whistled to the boil,
>
> and wonder what the clouds looked like –
> shovelled snow, Apple Charlotte,
>
> Tufty Tails . . . I enjoyed
> the Irish Sea, the ships were faults
>
> in a dark expanse of linen.
> And then Belfast below, a radio
>
> with its back ripped off,
> among the agricultural abstract
>
> of the fields . . .

But while the poem talks of laughter, it makes no place for it.

I suppose 'Flying to Belfast' is not so much sad as menacing – yet a powerful sadness inhabits Raine's best poems and seems to have more to do with his image-making procedures than with the situations he attends to. Raine's images are essentially local effects, and any longer poem by him tends to be a sequence of linked local effects. Thus 'A Martian Sends a Postcard Home' could probably be a little shorter or a little longer and be none the better or none the worse for it. Normally to say this of a poem would be to offer a calculated insult. In Raine's case it isn't so – the source of his sadness, it seems to me, has to do with the way in which each new piece of a poem effectively abandons the piece before it. That's to say, his poems build displacement into their structures: they move forward in discrete couplet and triplet units, they offer small bright pleasures and ask us to pass on quickly. Simile and metaphor insist on the links between things, but in a Raine poem the sheer number of them leaves you feeling that individual images have been brought into line only to be dismissed. It is a disconcerting effect for the reader, who is made to undergo a concentrated, slightly mannered, experience of loss. The effect reminds me of the train journey in Philip Larkin's 'Whitsun Weddings' poem, where the passengers who are taken on board at each stop somehow bring with them the sadness of what is left behind as train and poem press ahead – things glimpsed through the window ('A hothouse flashed uniquely') and girls on station platforms 'posed irresolutely, watching us go, / As if out on the end of an event / Waving goodbye / To something that survived it.' All of Raine's bright surprises bring with them sadness and diminishment.

Not that Martian techniques of themselves guarantee good poems. There are plenty of recent British poets who supply evidence of that, and Raine himself is sometimes a victim of his own techniques. A piece like 'In the Mortuary' comes across as sentimental and portentous, a poem which *uses* its subject when it presumably means to be exact and human. 'Laying a Lawn' is tenderness gone wrong; Raine's small daughter is set apart, made solitary, removed from her relationship with her father rather than drawn into the ambit of his affection. Yet poems like 'In the Kalahari Desert' and 'Flying to Belfast, 1977' are superb creations, and quite enough in themselves to justify the Martian invasion.

James Fenton is a rarity among English poets – someone who is happy to be cryptic, who will withhold information or even pretend to have information solely in order to be seen not to be making it available. His poems mean to baffle (I imagine), and that is part of how they mean; they go for pastiche, too. Fenton is a *bricoleur* who can sound silly and serious, friendly and a bit dangerous, all at once. 'A German Requiem' is one of the best things in the book. Like Fenton, Tom Paulin has been influenced by Auden, but he has a tougher, more earnest surface and hammers away at the difficult relationship between the self-delighting tendencies of art and the implacable worlds of politics, society, religion. His poems have an extraordinarily confident movement – syntax and cadence never seem to doubt themselves. Recently he has been developing a rather cranky way with diction – his words seem remote, indifferent, interested in their own devices, yet are caught up into rhythms which demand of them some sort of full emotional engagement. Many of his poems ought to be bad but aren't. (Oddly, his 'Iniskeel Parish Church' has here been turned into 'Davros Parish Church', with its first few lines revised. Someone should tell the congregation.)

There are other good poets in *The Penguin Book of Contemporary British Poetry*. Fleur Adcock, Medbh McGuckian and Paul Muldoon are among those I enjoyed particularly, while Douglas Dunn and Derek Mahon are thought well of by so many people that I must be missing something. All the same, a good many of the poets in the anthology are perfectly able and perfectly expendable. It would be an easy thing to drop ten and replace them with ten more from the twenty or thirty others who are waiting in line. The anthology would be none the worse for it, though its introduction might seem more partial.

The Penguin Book of Contemporary British Poetry is one sign of life in a world which is already various and lively. But it is hardly, as its editors think, the harbinger of a whole new sensibility. The Martians' importance lies not in their alien theology but in the fact that Craig Raine is a particularly good poet; and some of the claims for a renewed interest in anecdote and narrative sound like special pleading or wishful thinking. In fact, despite the playfulness and wit of a few of these poets, and the ways in which some of them relish language and the movements of the imagination, the world recorded here remains the place of gentility and quiet commonsense which Alvarez objected to. And what is offered as having 'something of the spirit of postmodernism' looks much more like the patient introspection which Wordsworth engaged in, what Seamus Heaney has written of as 'the revelation of the self to the self'.

So here is an anthology which contains many good poems and a few fine poets but is not the brilliant new landmark it half believes itself to be. The prospect, alas, if this new Penguin has its way or achieves the sort of influence its introduction seeks, is not a new excitement but a literature where insubstantiality is raised to a fine art. (I adapt this last phrase from

Real Hot Air

Blake Morrison, who has used it of the work of his co-editor, Andrew Motion.) If that happens, British poets will be left to choke, not on hot air but on the Tennysonian mists. In such a climate it will not matter much whether the shadow of the balloon has made a mark or an impact – for the balloon itself, with all its passengers, will sail away and come to earth elsewhere.

Helix No 17, 1984

THE POETRY FILE

Prose Poems

Saltimbanques

At the centre of that parade, together with a dancing child, there is a man who lifts weights. His arms are tattooed in blue and are lifted to the skies, in testimony to their useless strength.

The child dances delicately, in tights several sizes too large for him; he is even lighter than the little balls on which he struggles to keep his balance. When he holds out his money cup, nobody gives anything for fear of filling it with too heavy a weight. He is so thin.

This is a prose poem by Pierre Reverdy (1889–1960). The prose poem – which of course revels in the contradictions of its title – is something which, many people say, doesn't exist. But enough writers are producing works they call prose poems to make you feel that something's going on.

The form is essentially a French creation. Cadenced and 'poetical' prose exists in most languages – just think of the King James Bible. But in nineteenth-century France there seems to have been a fierce reaction against the extraordinarily dogmatic rules of versification insisted on by the French Academy (that same purifying body which still worries about the corrupting effects of foreign loan words). Rather than move to the flexibilities of free verse, a number of French writers abandoned the verse line altogether.

Poets like Baudelaire and Rimbaud developed the form most influentially. The title Rimbaud gave to his own work, *Illuminations*, hints at the painterly quality which a prose poem sometimes possesses. Reverdy's poem, for example, is like a painting in a specific way, for it alludes to work from the so-called Pink Period of Picasso; but in a more general way it is painterly, for it manages to insist on its own moment, its status as lyric, at the same time as it implies a narrative. Where is the parade going? Who is

Prose Poems

watching it go by? What will happen when the child stops dancing? Can he stop? Will this very piece of writing let him?

Some of the world's major writers – Rilke, Gertrude Stein, Pablo Neruda, Borges – have tried their hand at prose poems. Even T.S. Eliot produced a short piece, 'Hysteria', at about the time he was writing 'Prufrock'. And because of the influence of French modernism, prose poems have been enormously important in twentieth-century Japan, where they are called *sanbushi*.

The prose poem has a very doubtful life in England – perhaps because surrealism (to which the form has links) never caught on there, perhaps because poetry in English was never as inflexible as poetry in other languages. Geoffrey Hill's *Mercian Hymns* comes to mind as a significant attempt at the genre; and in Ireland writers like Seamus Heaney have dabbled in the form.

In New Zealand, too, prose poems are few and far between. They tend to turn up occasionally inside poetry sequences, as in Vincent O'Sullivan's *Butcher* poems, or in hybrid texts like Dinah Hawken's *Small Stories of Devotion*. Richard von Sturmer has produced some very interesting work. One or two of Janet Frame's stories read to me like prose poems, and there's a whole novel, Gregory O'Brien's *Diesel Mystic*, which (I reckon) is secretly a set of prose poems.

It's in the United States that the prose poem has had most of its life in the English language, among such writers as Robert Bly, John Ashbery, and Charles Simic. The Americans even have a specialist magazine (*The Prose Poem: An International Journal* – edited from the English Department, Providence College, Providence, RI 02918, USA). Charles Simic won the Pulitzer Prize a few years ago for his remarkable book of prose poems, *The World Doesn't End*, and he himself has written a brief essay, 'The Poetry of Village Idiots', which stresses both the genre's contradictory lyric/narrative impulses and also the importance of the comic spirit, which he sees as the form's 'true Muse':

> Playful and irreverent treatment of every subject is usually the custom. In order to free poetry of its mannerisms and its ticks, the prose poem must not take itself too seriously. Impossible to write, illegitimate in the view of so many poets and critics, it must remain a pariah and an object of ridicule to survive.

Simic's own work often has a quality of fable and fairy tale, another common characteristic of the form. Here's one of his untitled pieces from *The World Doesn't End*:

I am the last Napoleonic soldier. It's almost two hundred years later and I am still retreating from Moscow. The road is lined with white birch trees and the mud comes up to my knees. The one-eyed woman wants to sell me a chicken, and I don't even have any clothes on.

The Germans are going one way; I am going the other. The Russians are going still another way and waving good-by. I have a ceremonial saber. I use it to cut my hair, which is four feet long.

My own favourite writer of prose poems is the dedicatedly eccentric Scotsman, Ivor Cutler. Now he can be seriously strange:

Large and Puffy

She beckoned me with a finger. It was large and puffy, like a cheap white pillow.
No, Betty, that finger puts me off and you know it.
It was my night for sex and I was hot and irritable. Betty's white finger was the last straw.
I moved into the brown verandah and sat listening to the heavy rain, but in vain.
Betty would have to wait.

Charm

Wen

1
Wen, wen, little wen

here you shall not timber
nor have abode

but journey north to the hills
& your miserable brother

he will lay a leaf at your head

Charm

2
Under the haunch of the wolf
under the wing of the eagle
under the claw of the eagle
may you sicken forever

lessened like coal on the hearth, burning
like mud on the wall, scraped down

lessened like water, low in the pail
staining the air

3
Be small as a linseed-grain
eaten by worms

& smaller than a worm's hip-bone
dragged under till you are nothing

When Sam Hunt talks about poetry he sometimes speaks of 'charm, charge and chant'. Cunning alliteration. But by charm he doesn't mean a poem's ability to be agreeable and attractive – like some sort of verbal picnic spot. He means the stronger, more ancient sense of the word: charm as magic talisman or spell or incantation. In fact, if I look up my rather elderly edition of the *Shorter Oxford Dictionary*, the first entry under *charm* is perfectly clear about it: 'The chanting of a verse having magic power'.

'Wen' is a loose translation of an Anglo-Saxon charm – an ancient medical prescription designed to rid the body of warts. You don't need tablets from the chemist for a fine complexion, just the magic of powerful words. This charm keeps company with a range of other Old English texts: there are charms for a sudden stitch, for delayed birth, for the theft of cattle, for journeys, for a swarm of bees.

Poetry still operates on the rather primitive assumption that language – especially when stylised and cadenced and repetitive – can intervene magically in the real world. You can see it in some of the great Romantic poems, like Shelley's 'Ode to the West Wind', which is probably the greatest (and longest) piece of magical incantation in English. And ideas of magic survive in the notion that poets are somehow *inspired*. At the point where a poem is made, poets are possessed and powerful, and their humble earth-bound listeners fill with fear. Coleridge caught this at the end of 'Kubla

Khan' when he imagined the terrified audience of a poem recoiling awe-struck from its divinely inspired maker:

> And all should cry, Beware! Beware!
> His flashing eyes, his floating hair!
> Weave a circle round him thrice,
> And close your eyes with holy dread,
> For he on honey-dew hath fed,
> And drunk the milk of Paradise.

And then there's the way many poets *read* their poems. Like Tennyson or Yeats or James K. Baxter, Sam Hunt is in a long line of poets as priests and prophets. He often presents himself as a court jester and troubadour, but he is as much shaman as showman. When he says a poem aloud he *chants* it – intoning rhythmically – as if declaiming a spell, as if some other voice is speaking through him, as if the words of the poem are somehow coming into being at the moment of utterance.

But the poem as charm survives in far more humble guises. The verse messages inside some of the Christmas cards you recently sent and received are forms of verbal magic. Probably 'good cheer' was there, rhyming in a tired, familiar way with 'new year'. But the message would have been clear enough, and would have implicitly endorsed a belief in the power of words to make the future turn out well. Even the Valentine's Day card is making a come-back – another poetic device to make the world behave the way you'd like it to.

Charms tend to take the shape of commands, usually a sequence of them. The words are busy impelling the change they want to bring about. Probably the most familiar modern-day charms are recipes – spells of wondrous transformation. My favourite poetry charm is Gary Snyder's 1964 poem 'How to Make Stew in the Pinacate Desert'. It's too long to quote in full, but it tells you where and how to buy the ingredients, how to build the fire and do the cooking:

> Throw in the beef shank meat,
> And stir it while it fries hot,
> lots of ash and sizzle – singe your brow

Finally, having like any good spell brought something astonishing into being, the poem tells you exactly what to do next: 'Dish it up and eat it with a spoon, sitting on a poncho in the dark.'

Finders Keepers

The Old Masters

The old masters
Were not so nervous as we are.

VELASQUEZ: He must have felt
And willed all that he did.

COROT: The quality of mind
That makes you paint as you do is what counts.

MANET: Notice the meaning of every change.
HOGARTH: The head of a fish girl.

Here is a sketch by Leonardo da Vinci.
I enter this sketch

And I see him at work and in trouble
And I meet him there.

Who owns this poem? It's printed in a book by Annie Dillard, *Mornings Like This* (1995); but, like all the poems which surround it, its words were penned by someone else. The poet found it somewhere.

In the case of 'The Old Masters', the words are Robert Henri's, and they appear in a 1929 volume, *The Art Spirit*, which was compiled by his student Margery A. Ryerson. Presumably she took notes, as attentive students do. What Annie Dillard has done is to take those words and make them into a poem. We know the words make a poem because they come in lines and stanzas. The lines and the stanzas and – most importantly – the title are Dillard's; everything else is Henri's.

Well, not quite everything. The invisible bits – selection and ordering – are also Annie Dillard's. She may not have invented her text, but she has still composed it. 'The poems are original as poems; their themes and their ordering are invented. Their sentences are not. Their sentences come from the books named. I lifted them. Sometimes I dropped extra words; I never added a word.'

In this case Dillard has composed a poem about art which moves deliberately from the abruptness of its opening examples to the slow expansiveness of the two final couplets, which sketch a process of engagement in which viewer and artist meet on equal terms within the world of da Vinci's sketch. The poem says something about the way in which a great work of art encourages and welcomes, and does not condescend. It also says something about the power and role of the viewer.

Dillard's book is full of poems made out of words from other places. She has found her poems in medical texts, and grammar books, in van Gogh's letters, in an instructional leaflet on how to use watercolours. There is a two-page poem called 'Deathbeds', which is made up of lines from Edward Le Comte's compilation, *Dictionary of Last Words*. Another poem is composed out of the index of first lines from the *Penguin Book of Irish Poetry*.

Found poetry is no doubt modelled on the visual arts. It is the verbal equivalent of the *objet trouvé*, or of collage work. Some of Ezra Pound's *Cantos* seem to be made almost entirely out of other texts. Even T.S. Eliot's *The Waste Land* is full of fragmentary texts from other places. And Eliot himself has said that immature poets imitate, while mature poets steal: 'Bad poets deface what they take, and good poets make it into something better, or at least something different.'

The process of transformation is crucial. As Annie Dillard remarks of her own work, 'the original authors' intentions were usually first to go'. A text changes when its context changes, and often the process with found poems is that material is taken from quite banal contexts, and given fresh interest through being presented as a poem. Turning a piece of prose into a poem takes advantage of the way in which our culture – rightly or wrongly – still falls to its knees in the presence of Poetry. We still associate wisdom with poems, and the found poem invites us to look for wisdom in the ordinary world. 'Notice this,' says the poem. 'Pay attention.' There is also the pleasure of two competing sets of meanings, for the new text never entirely abandons the old text.

Found poems can be dug up in all sorts of places. The American David Antin has made a poem out of a text describing the codes of flag behaviour, while nearer to home James Brown has made a wonderful piece out of the words you meet when you use a Cashpoint machine. And here is a short piece by Michael Mintrom, one of that dangerous breed of New Zealand poets who have worked for Treasury. Mintrom found his words in a book called *Youth in Crisis*, and made his poem out of a selection of possible answers to a multiple-choice questionnaire. In the process he transformed a stale, pseudo-scientific document into something much more moving:

Finders Keepers

Borstal Girls

I am a hopeless case
a girl with a
very bad centre
a borstal trainee
bored stiff, a girl who is
feeling lonely

Life goes on and on
is a bore
is slack
is a big hassle

My mother
she's all right
I love her, but I can't show it

I'd like most
to go home
to try and behave myself
to be free

Secretly I want to wake up and
know the right thing to do
wish I could experience
life over again
would like to be dead
hate life
wish I hadn't got into trouble

Titles

1571

How slow the Wind –
how slow the sea –
how late their Feathers be!

DOUBTFUL SOUNDS

The nineteenth-century American poet Emily Dickinson is one of literature's most famous recluses – by the end of her life a sort of white-robed ghostly presence in her own house. Like most of her work, this mysterious three-line poem has no title other than the number given it by a later editor. The missing title is easily enough explained, though: in her own lifetime almost none of Emily Dickinson's poems was published. The reading public insists on titles; but Emily Dickinson never had a reading public. People knew she wrote, of course, but even her sister Lavinia, sorting out Emily's effects after her death, was astonished to find something like 1800 poems tucked away in the bedroom.

In April 1862 Dickinson sent some of her poems to Thomas Wentworth Higginson, a worthy man of letters who had published a magazine article giving advice and encouragement to young writers.

> Mr Higginson,
>
> Are you too deeply occupied to say if my Verse is alive?
> The Mind is so near itself – it cannot see, distinctly – and I have none to ask –
> Should you think it breathed – and had you the leisure to tell me, I should feel quick gratitude –

The poet didn't sign her name. Instead, she wrote it in pencil on a card, then slipped this into a smaller envelope which she placed inside the letter.

Higginson must have sent a puzzled but encouraging reply, for ten days later there is another letter from Dickinson, thanking him 'for the surgery' – and offering strange snippets of information about herself. Near the letter's end she mentions two editors who 'came to my Father's house, this winter – and asked me for my Mind – and when I asked them "Why," they said I was penurious – and they would use it for the World –'

The two editors must have wanted to publish Emily Dickinson's poems, and she must have decided to refuse permission. It's not hard to see why. On the rare occasions her poems did get into print, they were thoroughly mangled. Grammar and punctuation were corrected, scansion and rhyme schemes repaired, agreeable titles added. The result was a distinctive voice made polite and conventional, poems botched and blanded out. (The process still goes on – if you find yourself reading Emily Dickinson's work in a text *without* strange dashes and capital letters, then you aren't reading the poems she wrote.)

We can admire Emily Dickinson's decision to reject the marketplace and maintain what she called her 'Barefoot-Rank'. But if she had decided to let her work be published, would she have seriously considered poem 1571? It's perfectly conceivable that she never thought of it as a poem: the lines may have been jottings, notes for future reference.

However, at some point, a battle over titles would probably have begun. 'But Miss Dickinson,' her publisher might have said, 'our readers like titles. They *need* them. Titles make them feel secure. Why, think of Mr Milton's *Paradise Lost*. Titles are like signposts: they point the reader in the right direction.'

My bet is that Emily Dickinson would have stuck to her guns, insisting that to give a poem a title is to rob it of its mystery before it has even begun – like offering the answer to a riddle before you pose the question. She might, just possibly, have resorted to the sometimes desperate, sometimes cute, measure other writers have tried, and settled for 'Poem' – a title which simply invites the reader to pay attention, since something unusual is about to follow. But 1800 poems called 'Poem' . . .

Still, suppose the publisher had had his way. We think that Emily Dickinson wrote this poem in 1883 about three years before her death. What if she had called it 'Growing Old'? Would the title make the poem more interesting, or less?

Much less interesting, I reckon. It would be quite at odds with the poem's sense of awe at the way time passes – an awe which is there in the word 'how' which generates each line, and in the exclamation mark which ends things, so that the text sits on the page like a slow-motion gasp, three quiet intakes of breath. Put 'Growing Old' at the top, and the lines immediately look soggy and complacent.

But anything is possible. What if Dickinson had called her poem 'The Waves?' Or 'The Brides?' Or even 'Gulls over Rangitoto'?

Titles can be the trickiest things in poems: too much information and your readers have lost their imaginative freedom; too little and they can be frightened to go on. Emily Dickinson clearly settles for as much mystery as possible. If we read her poems, we can expect to work: she offers exclamations, not explanations. Or, as she puts it in another short poem, also without a title:

> The Riddle we can guess
> We speedily despise –
> Not anything is stale so long
> As Yesterday's surprise –

EVENTS AS PEOPLE

Notes on Private Gardens

NOW ON SALE (BUT HURRY!) / Over 30 N.Z. Women Poets / A Milestone in Poetry Publishing in New Zealand / Illustrated throughout.

1

Triumphal noises, and the publisher's advertisement goes some way towards justifying the reluctance of poets like Janet Frame and Ruth Dallas to join the party. Riemke Ensing tells us in her introduction to *Private Gardens* that Janet Frame asked if a companion volume by New Zealand men was envisaged. Ensing takes the point, but adds by way of reply that: 'a collection of women poets seems . . . no more arbitrary than a collection of, say, *Young* New Zealand poets, or *Recent* New Zealand poets, or *Georgian* poets, or poetry *between the wars* – as arbitrary in fact as *any* collection whose taste and slant must inevitably present the editor's choice and point of view'. The dash betrays a large and sneaky leap in argument; and it's necessary to say that the collections Ensing cites are based on groupings by period or generation. Something more comparable might be the anthology of verse by merchant seamen recently published in London; or any one of the many women's anthologies which have appeared in other countries. That said, however, it's a pity that Frame and Dallas decided not to contribute. Any path through the forest is worth having; and the absence of poets like these severely limits the anthology in range and quality.

This particular path is carefully protected and hedged about. Riemke Ensing's introduction is interesting: direct and open – but somehow preoccupied with anticipating objections to a book of poems by women. And while Vincent O'Sullivan's 'Afterword' is well worth reading – it's sensitive and accurate to the poetry it describes, and quite without condescension – it inevitably smacks of a Good Housekeeping Seal of

Approval. Indeed, there's a sense of protective worry about the whole book. The poetry is well wrapped up, not quite allowed to speak for itself. Forty of the 160 pages contain no poetry at all. There are introduction and afterword, photographs (mood pieces to accompany poems and pictures of the contributors themselves), notes on their poetry by Fleur Adcock and Gloria Rawlinson, and ten pages of 'Biographical Notes (not necessarily in alphabetical order)' [sic]. Perhaps there are commercial considerations somewhere here, an awareness that the market for women writers as a 'minority' group is a large one – a good deal larger than the market for verse – and that many of those who fork out their money are likely to want something more than poetry in return. It will be a pity, though, if *Private Gardens* doesn't reach beyond the market it seems to be chasing, if it isn't read by men as well as by women – and more for the sake of the writers than the readers. The American poet, Adrienne Rich, may be right when she says that women writers have always been inhibited by the fact of writing to be 'overheard' by men; but the ladies have always been well within earshot too, and the real danger which attends on anthologies like this one is that they may lead their contributors to believe that the only responsive audience they can expect will be composed exclusively of women.

2

Of Riemke Ensing's thirty-five poets, some – like Fleur Adcock and Gloria Rawlinson – are already well known from anthologies; others are more or less unknown. In between are those who easily command attention but whose reputations are comparatively recent: poets like Christina Beer, Lauris Edmond, Rachel McAlpine, Jan Kemp, Elizabeth Smither. It comes as a surprise that there's little explicit feminism in the anthology. Of the names above, only McAlpine approaches anything resembling a feminist stance, and even then not in the poems which represent her here. Yet most of these poets must owe the fact that they are writing well, *and* being published, to the women's movement – which suggests that, in literature at least, we should not hold its jazzier publicists against it.

The poets I miss from the anthology, besides Frame and Dallas, are those omitted by the editor because their work was 'readily available in most New Zealand anthologies' and because she wished to concern herself 'only with living poets'. Hence no Ursula Bethell, no Robin Hyde, no Eileen Duggan – poets who would have lent the collection a substance it lacks, who would also have offered some interesting comparisons. Two poets I'm particularly pleased to encounter are Mary Stanley and Hilaire Kirkland.

Mary Stanley offers the book some of the authority that the absent poets might have provided. To my knowledge, her work hasn't been anthologised since Chapman and Bennett's *An Anthology of New Zealand Verse* (1956); her one book, *Starveling Year*, appeared in 1953. Riemke Ensing performs a valuable service in making her poetry available again. She does even greater service in including work by Hilaire Kirkland. Kirkland died in 1975, leaving behind a handful of poems, mostly published in student magazines while she was a student at the University of Otago. Her voice is sharp, astringent, with a tight-lipped emotional force which recalls R.A.K. Mason. Two of her poems were reprinted posthumously in *Islands* 15; *Private Gardens* prints four more. Here is another (from the Universities' *Literary Yearbook 1964*), plus a plea for someone to bring all her poems together:

Observations 1

arranged on the opposite porch is a male
waist-coated and posing to catch my eye
you are far too unsubtle for such as I
dear sir, who prefer whipped cream and spice with pudding

besides you've a paunch and I've done with loving.

I've too sick a humour to take the veil
salvation oh lord's not in praying but work
till a board-hard bed in a prickling dark
of half-heard taxi wheels and footsteps hesitating

and a clock not kisses to wake me in the morning.

that girl with the cat-yellow ponytail
sixteen and slim and (thank you) quite ready
swaying my street like a sailor's lady
plucks and shreds he-loves-me leaves in passing

so what. I did that once myself when walking . . .

3

Rosemary Seymour, writing in *Outrigger* 6 about an earlier *Outrigger* gathering of women's poetry, complained that most of the contributions were, 'timeless and placeless; . . . derivative, polite and resigned'. She was presumably in search of poets who found and communicated 'power, security, love and excitement in sisterhood'. There aren't such poets here; nor are there compelling public or political voices, as the title implicitly acknowledges. But there is not much, either, of the timeless and placeless variety. True, the weakest poets are least easy when they attempt to move from the specifics of a situation to a plane of generalisation: some take to a Baxterish intoning; a few live almost entirely in the realms of abstraction. But the best poets stick to – or at least clearly start from – the world they know and move about in. Thus, in a broad sense, the most rewarding poems in *Private Gardens* are domestic: they concern themselves with ties of emotion, with people and with places. The people are liable to be lovers or immediate family; the places, houses. Mary Stanley's poem, 'The Wife Speaks', was written over twenty years ago, but the voice we hear might be speaking on behalf of many of the writers in Ensing's collection:

> A house designs
> my day an artifact
> of care to set the hands
> of clocks, and hours are round
> with asking eyes. Night puts
> an ear on silence where
> a child may cry. I close
> my books and know events
> are people, and all roads
> everywhere walk home
> women and men, to take
> history under their roofs.

This is hardly house-bound. The poem reveals an accurate recording eye, and one which sees beyond deceptive old mythologies (made by fathers?) to the real details of human loss. Events are people – the poem continues, and concludes, with these lines:

> I see Icarus fall
> out of the sky, beside
> my door, not beautiful,
> envy of angels, but feathered
> for a bloody death.

Stanley's wife speaks for contributors to *Private Gardens* in yet another way. Her eye is steadfastly fixed on what is painful and distressing; many other poets have the same kind of gaze. When joy appears in their poems, it is usually provisional, under threat behind the scenes. 'If most of these writers have a common Muse,' writes Vincent O'Sullivan, 'her name is Hecate. Reports on her terrain are brought back in poem after poem.'

4

In her note on poetry, Gloria Rawlinson quotes from an English review of Robin Hyde's poetry which congratulates Mr Hyde on his 'boisterous pugnacity':

> His first wish is to let off steam. This he does in a 'Heigh-ho and away we go' fashion. He has the vigour and weight of a forward in a rugger scrum, and if his language is not so commonplace and explosive it is none the less realistic and sometimes more strenuous than the occasion demands. From his poem 'Woman' I imagine Mr Hyde has played mixed rugger.

Gloria Rawlinson is writing about the dangers of group judgements, and there could hardly be a better way of making her point. Yet an anthology like *Private Gardens* positively invites judgement of the group within it, so let me risk a couple – both of which would need qualifications if faced with the work of individual contributors.

First, there is a depressing lack of range in the book as a whole. This is inevitably tied to the strengths of the best poets, who naturally enough speak from their experience of the world. But somehow the *collective* experience in the book is a limited one. There is a mediating world of objects somewhere between the emotional details of our lives and the abstractions which we then construct; and it is a world which poetry has to take account of. We would probably find it in an anthology of male poets; we would certainly find it in one which mixed male and female together. But it is not apparent in *Private Gardens*, at least in its possible variety. 'Life is full of all kinds of wonderful crap. Splendid confusion. Poetry should be able to take it all in' (Erica Jong).

The second point is related. There is a strangely cerebral atmosphere in *Private Gardens*. Again Mary Stanley's poem will do duty: it is essentially a comment on experience, carefully thought and wrought. Hence a short poem, like this untitled piece by Jan Kemp, can surprise and delight merely by being different, by offering something which works as pure experience, moving from past to present in the moment it takes to be read:

It was your face.
It was shy.
We walked.
It was your head.
It was lit with sun.
I unbuckled your belt.
Hush, don't speak,
the yellow flowers are bursting.

Sadly, few of the poems in *Private Gardens* offer such immediate life. I have the impression that for most poets here the intellect controls the act of writing, mapping out the territory for a poem, defining the path to be taken. 'Hush, the poets are thinking!' The imagination is hardly missing – it is invited to supply occasional metaphors. But it is only there to make the poems poetic, it is not allowed to make the poems. To stop the ramble, and as an extreme but concrete instance of what I most miss in *Private Gardens*, here is a poem by an Oruaiti schoolgirl, from Elwyn S. Richardson's *In the Early World*:

The Tea

The tea makes you funny as can be
It is a hush tea; it goes for you
Hush a bye on the tree top,
Goodnight tea.
Makes yourself as good as gold,
The gold.
The gold is a wonderful thing;
It is a happy gold.
Gold go to sleep.
He bites all the little dogs' feet.

Review of *Private Gardens: An Anthology of New Zealand Women Poets*, ed. Riemke Ensing (Caveman, 1977) *Islands* 19, 1977

SMITHEREENS

Elizabeth Smither's poems always manage to look quiet and well ordered on the page, wedded to the patient symmetries of line and stanza. Yet the moment you begin to read them, they dart away, throwing out striking images and aphorisms, moments of wild ellipsis. What looked stable, starts to quake.

> *Stubble Fields*
>
> In some stubble fields an indentation
> Perhaps a small swamp dried in summer
> Traces a faint black imperfect sowing
> Like a panda's eye.
>
> Fields that contain these small infelicities
> Are more beautiful than the perfect
> Skinhead fields they emulate
> More individual, with a love-bite.

It is easy enough to feel mildly lost at the end. How does that tiny preposition *with* work, in the poem's last line? Are love-bites equivalent to small infelicities? Are the poems Smither approves of somehow like love-bites? (And how far should we pursue that idea?) And, anyway, how does the last line connect with the one before it? It seems almost to be a point of honour with Smither not to use punctuation marks at the ends of lines. But this poem would be instantly more accessible if a friendly dash followed the word *emulate*.

Probably the truth is that the poem exists for the extraordinary image of the panda's eye. That is why 'Stubble Fields' is worth bothering with, and perhaps why Elizabeth Smither wrote it. All the same, the poem's general idea accounts not only for its own behaviour but also for much of Smither's work. Her poems are full of indentations and faint, imperfect sowings. If they often mix the clear and the cryptic, if brilliant moments are succeeded by rather ordinary ones, that is a matter of choice. The word *imperfect* challenges perfection; the love-bite flickers on the lovely neck.

'Stubble Fields' also seems true to Smither's work in the way that words like *swamp*, *field*, *panda*, and *skinhead* resonate with different cultural burdens. The poem sets up a series of arm's length collisions between items which have their own backgrounds. Smither has another poem in this new book about postcards on a wall. Edouard Manet balances on Mrs James Cook's bonnet, Dickens' house sits next to the Delphi charioteer. The point is not simply the pleasure of juxtaposition – it is the way in which such details transform each other through mutual awareness. 'Details when you list them can cross borders / Into the next postcard . . .'

I wonder if it has ever occurred to Elizabeth Smither to call one of her books *Smithereens*? Her best poems are always little, postcard length, and the poems in this book behave very like the postcards she describes. They wave to one another, open doors and climb through windows. Even a long Smither poem is really a collection of short ones, all paying some kind of attention to one another.

A Pattern of Marching is published to coincide with the *Listener* Women's Book Festival, but Smither belongs to none of the currently empowered schools of wimmin's poetry. If I were seeking signs of kinship with other women writers, I would look to poets like Emily Dickinson, Stevie Smith, and the wonderful Josephine Miles. They are all poets whose work darts in and out of aphorism, and who work on a small canvas which turns out to have no edges at all (or only edges you can fall from), who produce riddling fragments instead of epics, who, in a single breath, can move from the whimsical to the serious, from the satirical to the mystical; who adopt a pedantic manner to address situations they are frequently at the mercy of. Their poems record the cryptic, imperfect world; and while they can be fey or arcane, they can also go suddenly, ruthlessly, to the heart of things. The only other New Zealand poet I can think of with these qualities is Janet Frame.

Elizabeth Smither's is a hit-or-miss art, as her reviewers like to point out. It seems to me that her hits get more and more interesting. Like Emily Dickinson, she is intriguing but wearying in bulk; but – also like Dickinson – a ruthlessly winnowed selection of her verse would surely be dazzling. Meantime, *A Pattern of Marching* has several poems which will march straight into the anthologies. My picks would include 'A Cortège of Daughters', 'The French Translation' and 'The Muse (for women poets)'. Smither has said in an interview that she wants her poems 'to go on into an area that's outside the end'. 'The Muse', which lifts out of the world of second-hand romance into a moment of real transcendence, gives a glimpse of how that sort of thing can happen.

> I often think of him
> As secretly booked into the Algonquin
> And sending up the bellboy
> With flowers and a knowing grin.
>
> 'The gent's anonymous.' His tip
> Outdoes yours for information.
> Coming down the lift is rosy
> And what is this light about the page?

Review of *A Pattern of Marching,* by Elizabeth Smither (Auckland University Press, 1989)
Listener, 1990

STRANGER AT THE RANCHSLIDER

Elizabeth Smither says somewhere that there's no middle ground with James K. Baxter: either you're swept away or you're not. Well, I'm sometimes swept away, and sometimes not; and sometimes I'm swept away a little bit, swept away up to a point. Anyway, that's the position from which these comments come.

I imagine everyone here will have wondered, just for a moment anyway, what Baxter himself would have made of this gathering. My guess is that he would have disapproved – probably in memorable phrases – but that he would also have glowed (or even gloated) inwardly. Of course, Baxter made rather a fetish of disparaging the university world. I remember seeing a letter which he wrote to a friend of mine who had sent him some poems as a schoolboy. It was clear, Baxter wrote, that my friend had already glimpsed the double-bladed axe of sex and death: he was a real poet all right. But the one thing that might knock him off course would be a university education. Stay away from the place. Leave school and enter the world, not the sterile halls of academia.

In an essay in the Otago University *Review* in 1968, not long before he left Dunedin and his family on the journey that would eventually take him to Jerusalem, Baxter wrote:

> Then there is the matter of higher education. When I see various hopeful people swarming like spermatozoa in the concrete vagina of the University, it does not make me feel particularly hopeful. I have the sense that anything that is going to happen is going to happen somewhere else.

And so on. Yet Baxter had an enormously productive relationship with New Zealand universities. He got himself a degree – starting at Otago and finishing, after celebrated difficulties with Anglo-Saxon, at Victoria. Student newspapers and literary magazines were significant outlets for his poems and pronouncements. He taught and lectured at most of the country's universities. He had two remarkable years as Burns Fellow at Otago, and the *Jerusalem Sonnets* were first published by the Bibliography Room here. And of course as a teenager Baxter once wrote 'A Song for Otago University' – of which, more later.

I was a student at Otago in the years that Baxter was Burns Fellow. I met him once or twice, but not in any way that would have mattered much to him. Which is another way of saying that I was extremely aware of Baxter, and Baxter not at all aware of me. We did both belong to a poetry group, which met in different members' houses. A range of aspiring writers like me, and a few real ones like Charles Brasch and Iain Lonie, gathered once a month to discuss one another's poems. Baxter must have attended two or three times. I don't think the meetings much interested him. He came along to support his daughter Hilary, who was herself beginning to write poetry. I remember one member of the group, after Hilary had read a poem, commenting that he could see mountains crouching like tigers behind her lines. And I distinctly remember the mixture of annoyance and pleasure on Baxter's face. There are two other things I recall. The first was Baxter commenting that one of my poems, 'A Death in the Family', was 'a beauty'. (That wasn't at all hard to remember! Baxter was a very generous and encouraging figure in his dealings with other poets.) The second was a fascinating disquisition on the use of couplets, which included the observation that, in his experience, lines fell into alternating masculine and feminine endings almost as a matter of course.

I was, of course, a member of Baxter's various audiences. I remember him in the old university staff club giving his talk about 'Henley Pub', later published as 'The Virgin and the Temptress'. This was at an Arts Faculty Students' Association weekend organised by Kevin Cunningham. At the time his commentary on his own poem struck me as astonishingly strange and silly – mostly because of a high seriousness that I couldn't really cope with. Yet I was also totally devastated by his ability on the same occasion to recite from memory whole poems by Yeats ('Easter, 1916' and 'Sailing to Byzantium'). He lectured to English courses, too, but what he said hasn't remained with me. I do remember a mild sense of occasion – Alan Horsman in the back row of the library lecture theatre crying, 'Speak up, Jim!' as the low, enunciating drone went on; and the odd phrase has stuck – 'drinking gin by day and benzedrine by night' got into my head. But that was it, really.

In fact I was never wholly convinced by Baxter. It was partly that I had grown up in the world he romanticised. My parents were publicans, and hotel bars and serious alcoholics were the day-to-day world as I knew it in the Crown Hotel on the corner of Rattray and MacLaggan Streets. It never struck me as a particularly *glamorous* place to be. Nor was I convinced that Baxter's celebrated ear for the vernacular was much good. His world of alcoholics and social derelicts seemed to me neither accurate reportage, nor even a dramatic intensification of the real. It and its phrasings just seemed like a romantic invention – the sort of stuff you might try to shock your parents with. But equally I was a pretty cautious, tentative and inhibited person. And Baxter struck me as a dangerous figure – someone who was partly responsible for the human problems to which he ministered. By day he offered the excitements of liberation to students on the university campus, then in the evenings counselled the same students in his basement room in the Moran Building. I probably assert all this in retrospect; but even at the time there was an obvious contradiction between his preaching of free love and his views on the evils of contraception.

I grew up listening to *The Goon Show*, to Peter Sellers' records, to *Beyond the Fringe*. When I was in my last year at Otago Boys' High School (1963), I went to an evening of satire in the museum auditorium, called *Yes or No as the Mood Takes Us* – a show which was modelled on and had even nicked its name from *Beyond the Fringe*, and in which Jocelyn Harris, one of the conveners of this conference, played a leading part. I imagined that I would find at Otago a campus full of high sophisticated wit and wicked satirical humour. The nearest I got to this as a student was co-editing *Capping Book* – which was not, as it turned out, very near.

I think what I am saying is that – though I wanted to write poetry – I was temperamentally at odds with Baxter. He was an enchanter figure, and I had been partly shaped by various forms of disenchantment. He was the first person I had come across for whom being a poet was a vocation. He lived the part and played the part. He came from a background of great moral and physical courage and of intellectual power and distinction. A deep confidence inhabited all that he said and did. I felt much less sure of myself – or less sure of my right to feel sure, especially in the matter of poetry.

The Baxter that we talk about now is a mythological figure of his own creation. I ran a quick survey on a second-year tutorial group at Victoria University last week. None of them could name a *single* one of Baxter's poems, though one student had studied his work at school. But they had all heard of him. One had friends who sometimes went to Jerusalem to visit his grave.

We could find that depressing, I suppose. Not a single poem among them? Yet the remarkable thing is that, twenty years after his death, Baxter is still a familiar name. His afterlife has been extraordinary. There are a huge number of poems (many of them elegies) about him; he turns up in short stories and novels, in memoirs and autobiographies, in plays, in paintings and photographs, in film, in songs. There's at least one street which bears his name.

And Baxter has had a fruitful existence in the poetry of others. As Gregory O'Brien has shown in a recent issue of *Sport*, his work has been a powerful influence on younger New Zealand writers – on poets as different as Dinah Hawken and Robert Sullivan, for example, both of whom began writing long after Baxter's death. And those who admire his poetry come from around the world. Poets like the English/Cornish poet Charles Causley, the American Galway Kinnell and the Australian Peter Porter admire his work immensely.

Part of Baxter's afterlife has to do with his death. And this brings me to the title of my talk. I speak partly as someone who recently supervised a postgraduate thesis (by an Indonesian Buddhist) on 'Death in the Poetry of James K. Baxter' – but any casual skim through Baxter's poems would show how much a sense of mortality informs his various utterances. 'Man is a walking grave. That is where I start from.' Anyway, let me play you an interpretation of Baxter's death. The death occurred in 1972; the song, by Ross Mullins and the Snaps, was written and recorded just last year:

Stranger at the Ranchslider

Lights go on in Lockwood Ridge
It's been another day of drudgery
Barry pours himself a beer
While Sharon's cooking up the tea
The paper didn't come tonight
Must be a new boy on the street
And there's a stranger at the ranchslider
Face as pale as a sheet,

No it's not another market researcher
No it's not the Rawleigh's man
There's a stranger at the ranchslider
Knocking with a trembling hand

Stranger at the Ranchslider

Sharon sips her semi-dry
She's had a bad day trying to humour the boss
She's worried 'bout the mortgage
That's another bridge they'll have to cross
TV's blaring in the lounge
They're showing replays of the test
And there's a stranger at the ranchslider
Clinging to his chest

No it's not another market researcher
No it's not the Rawleigh's man
There's a stranger at the ranchslider
Knocking with a trembling hand

No one brought the washing off the line
It's out there flapping in the wind.
And old Meiklejohn across the road
Is staring through the slats of his venetian blinds

The dinner's in the warming drawer
And the pots are piled up in the sink
Barry's got no *Star* to read
Now the TV's going on the blink
Sharon sets the table
With wedding present cutlery
And there's a stranger at the ranchslider
With long hair and a rosary

No it's not another market researcher
No it's not the Rawleigh's man
There's a stranger at the ranchslider
Come to die on your divan
Come to die on your divan

That song represents a view of Baxter which is pretty general, one that he helped to construct and would probably be well pleased with. In it Baxter is figured as the unsettling and tragic victim of the loveless society which rejected him, which let him die because it could not cope with the terrible insights and challenges his work contained. You can find a milder form of the same judgement in a notice on the wall of the church at Jerusalem, which talks about Baxter's belief in arohanui, the love of the many, and about nga mokai, the fatherless flock whom he accepted the duty of shepherding. It then says: 'For these precepts he lived intensely and ultimately died.'

The strongest articulation of Baxter as a sacrificial outcast figure came in Paul Maunder's play, *Hemi: the Life and Times of a Great New Zealand Poet*. At the end of that play we witness Baxter in a suburban Auckland street; he is afflicted by a heart attack, knocks on what seems like a high wall, and is refused admission by the heartless secular Calvinists behind the wall – so that he dies, there on the street, there on the stage, before our eyes. I remember being at this play with Bill Oliver, who had recently written his very fine (and just re-issued) biography of Baxter. Bill remonstrated mildly with Paul Maunder as we were leaving, for we know – or Bill certainly knew – that when Baxter sought help, he was taken in, and a doctor was called. Paul Maunder answered that the events we had seen on stage, though he agreed they were not literally true, were nevertheless symbolically true.

Well, that is the Baxter myth, and we know that he wrote it himself. 'Organised society,' he once said, 'can offer little more than a plush coffin to the man who has for a while stood outside it.' Or: 'The sense of having been pounded all over with a club by invisible adversaries . . . has been with me as long as I can remember.' Or: 'I think that various factors combined early to give me a sense of difference, of a gap . . . between myself and other people.' And that climate of alienation is also the climate of his poems:

> *High Country Weather*
>
> Alone we are born
>   And die alone;
> Yet see the red-gold cirrus
>   Over snow-mountain shine.
>
> Upon the upland road
>   Ride easy stranger:
> Surrender to the sky
>   Your heart of anger.

Yet it is possible to be disappointed that Baxter chose to see himself as alone, as a stranger, as a victim. In the International Year of the Family, I find myself preferring the man whom Jean Tuwhare heard say as he was dying, 'I have a wife and children in Wellington.' I prefer the man who was finally taken after his death to Jerusalem by his wife and his children and his good friend Colin Durning.

I made my first visit to Jerusalem two weekends ago. We walked up to the grave through rain and mud, and stood before it, watched through a mesh fence by the largest pig I think I have ever seen. We were eventually joined by a restless, aggressive young man, who had a dog with him. 'Donation!' he yelled. 'This is private land, you have to make a donation. Five bucks a head!' Thus has the poet who so publicly embraced poverty become part of the market economy. We asked the young man if others came very often to the grave. 'Not much,' he said. 'A bit in summer.' But two others had arrived at the grave before we left. They were also asked for a donation.

Baxter's grave was producing a nice mixed crop: onion weed and a fuchsia bush. There was a jam jar beside the headstone, with five or six recently picked daffodils in it – bright yellow trumpets – and in the jam jar there was also what looked like a long letter written in blue ballpoint. I didn't take out the letter and read it. But I assume the letter was to Baxter. It strikes me as perfectly possible that a serious devotional cult will grow up around him in the next twenty years. The next gathering that deals with James K. Baxter may well find itself putting the prophet before the poet. I can't say that I will be eager to attend.

I have an uncorrected proof copy of Baxter's 1966 collection, *Pig Island Letters*. On the cover are stamped the words: SECRET AND CONFIDENTIAL. All of us like to have authors with whom we have a secret and confidential relationship. But Baxter invented himself so publicly, so completely, that there's not much space for that secret author to come to life in. I do, though, want to indicate something of the Baxter that I like and would like to see more of; also the Baxter that I like and wish there had been more of.

The Baxter I am thinking of is the rather anarchic man who has a fair share of mischief and vigorous reproof, who writes 'A Small Ode on Mixed Flatting', who talks with God in the *Jerusalem Sonnets* and accepts God's returning laughter, who enjoys the ridiculous spectacle of himself in pyjamas on a suburban street just before dawn, just as much the undignified old fool as the tomcat for which he's searching – the man a senior police officer described as 'crafty', a 'likeable rogue'. This Baxter is shrewd, sometimes fraudulent, dangerous and likeable – more like a trickster god than an Old Testament prophet.

I don't mean the Baxter who wrote obscene or bawdy verse – in fact the bawdy verse by Baxter which I've seen is a bit embarrassing, trying very hard to shock the world in which he came to consciousness. Here, though, is a piece of his obscene verse as an illustration of what I mean. This is the final verse, a sort of chorus, from his 'Ballade of Cunt'. The voice you hear is Baxter's own, recorded in Wellington in the early '50s:

> O cunt, cradle of our beginnings,
> O cunt, gate, grave and billabong,
> O cunt that plays on my gonad-strings,
> Cunt is the measure of my song!

Well, we won't go on to the 'Ballade of the Sailor's Dong'. What I want to say, though, is that there's nothing especially striking about using the word 'cunt'; and certainly nothing unusual about the references to 'gate' and 'grave' and 'cradle of our beginnings'. But what is wonderful there is the use of the word 'billabong'. That seems to me to be a brilliantly sly, rhyming intervention in the text; it marks something that is true to Baxter's whole mode of being, and it's there in much else that he wrote. Here is another example of what I mean – a Dunedin document from 1968.

> TO WHOM IT MAY CONCERN
> I have known Miss Priscilla McQueen for several years through my association with the English Department of the University of Otago. I know her to be capable, hard-working and able to mix well with different groups of people. Her personal honesty is perhaps her most notable characteristic. I would not hesitate to recommend her as an applicant for any job at all that was within her wide range of possibilities.
> James K. Baxter
> Catholic Education Officer
> Moran Buildings
> Octagon
> Dunedin
> 14/10/1968

That was written when Cilla McQueen was applying for work at Cherry Farm. Baxter gave her another testimonial, though, 'chortling', as Cilla put it to me in a recent note, as he passed it over. *This* is the Baxter I like!

> TO WHOM IT MAY CONCERN
> I remember vividly Miss Priscilla McQueen's impersonation of an Arab mare in a brothel scene in a particular play by Jean Genet. It was not only her acting ability that impressed me – it was perhaps most of all the suggestion of multiple erotic possibilities which she extracted from this role. Some people are by nature

limpets and some by nature nautiluses. It is my opinion that Miss McQueen belongs to the latter category. Few men between the ages of nine and ninety could spend long in her company without experiencing an erection. When these qualities are (as in her case) combined with a vigorous and slightly anarchic intelligence the results may be explosive. Because of her superb figure it would be distracting for other employees if she had a job where she were obliged to appear at work in the nude; and since women universally dislike other women who are beautiful, I doubt if she should become either a nun or a waitress. There is no perfect answer to this kind of problem.

J.K.B.

Well, I said that was the Baxter I liked. But it would be nearer the truth to say that the Baxter I like is the man who wrote both of those documents in presumably the same moment: the convict self alongside the respectable, church-going family man – the man without perfect answers.

So the Baxter I care for is a figure of contradiction. In the end I don't have much affection for the pitched-up, seamless voice and certainties of the early poems. Like many readers, I prefer the later work, the sequences like *Pig Island Letters* or *Jerusalem Sonnets*, where the messy, contradictory nature of the poet's own circumstances informs everything that he says. The other thing I like about such poems – especially the *Jerusalem Sonnets* – is that they come in the form of a letter: whatever is on his mind, Baxter is talking to another person. He's in conversation, not alone and clutching at his chest beyond the ranchslider.

I believe that there's a collection of Baxter's prose writings soon to be published by Oxford. But the book I most look forward to is a selected letters. Baxter's was a vast life and there is a vast correspondence to match it. There are the early letters to Noel Ginn. There are the '50s male-bloke letters, there are letters to aspiring poets and to Cardinals, there are engagingly professional letters to *School Journal* contributors, and others to close friends and family: parents, wife, children. Some letters are very intimate indeed; some – like the verse letters – are written to be overheard. As a set of letters to the world, they show extraordinary diversity, great intelligence and sympathy and generosity, wonderful humour. In them you meet a man who is fully alive in his own contradictions, a *social* being caught up in a huge network of human relationships.

One other surprise I had at Jerusalem was to learn that in death Baxter has company. I had imagined a lonely grave in a paddock. I'm not sure why I had this mental image. But others I've spoken to have carried the same picture in their minds; ultimately it must have been Baxter who painted and framed it in his life and work. In fact Baxter is in a small urupa; there are seven or eight graves in the upper section of the graveyard, and Baxter's grave, Hemi's grave, is now one of three in the lower section. He is about twenty paces from a house where people live. He isn't, in the end, alone.

I want to end by playing you a musical rendition of James K. Baxter's 'A Song for Otago University', a text he wrote before ranchsliders had been invented. The setting – unlikely as it may seem – is by Douglas Lilburn. All loyal members of the University of Otago are welcome to sing along. I'm playing this partly because I know that Baxter's shade, should it be hovering about this place, would be infuriated and delighted in equal measure. As I said earlier, I'm sure his feelings about this conference would be equally mixed, and I look forward to its proceedings immensely.

A Song for Otago University

Among these hills our fathers came.
By strength of eye and hand alone
They built: and murmur loud as flame
Their voices from enduring stone.

Forget not those whom Scotland bred
Above whose bones our cities stand.
Forget not them! Nor the unknown dead
Whose broken veins flow through our land.

As streams in wildernesses rise
And green the desolate shingle plain:
So under windy southern skies
Peace flowered and wisdom shall remain.

The generations rouse and pass
Like failing birds to well of night;
Or like the wind-sown summer grass
Now tall, now withered in our sight.

But our sons' sons alike shall find
Perpetual though nations cease,
Within these walls the quiet mind,
The storm – unshaken rose of peace.

EVENTS AND EDITORIALS

Baxter's Collected Poems

James Bertram said some time ago that Baxter's *Collected Poems* would contain only about a quarter of the verse he left. There are about 620 pages of text in the published volume, and if that makes Baxter our most prolific poet, we can probably feel sure that the quality of his work comes somewhere near its quantity, from the sheer amount of critical activity it has generated. There are already four or five books about Baxter, plus scores of briefer commentaries. Some of this material is extremely good, some is pure Baxteriology. It will not give offence to those who have written well about Baxter if I say that the most suggestive and revealing remarks about his poetry are probably still his own. Many of those remarks are in Frank McKay's *James K. Baxter as Critic*, into which you can dip almost at will and come up with attractive formulations of Baxter's sense of himself as a poet. Attempting to reconcile two roles which he fears may be at odds with each other, those of Robert Burns Fellow and New Zealand writer, he will call himself, with a sort of gloating humility, 'a donkey who is able from time to time to excrete gold'. And then there are all those encapsulations which seem tailor-made for chapter headings or journal articles – the poet as a cell of good living in a corrupt society, the poet as the sore thumb of the tribe.

Baxter was given to phrase-making and to parable (which, for him, was effectively a narrative form of making experience into phrases) and this made memorable a large proportion of anything he wrote, whether in verse or prose. Being memorable is no guarantee of anything, of course, least of all truthfulness of observation or feeling, and Baxter is sometimes guilty of aphorisms splashed with not much more than colour. But often in his critical writing, as in much of his later verse, the phrase-maker slides off into the wings and one meets a man who is plain about his procedures and, moreover, enviably clear sighted about the nature of his own gift:

> The problem for me in the forties and fifties was to get rid of the mere echo language in my poems, the twists of phrase (and so of thought also) that belonged by right to Hardy or Yeats or Dylan Thomas or Louis MacNeice. I have been from the start a very imitative writer. Not a bad thing in itself, if one already has some deep particular experience for a particular poem to grow from – I am not inventive in the making of new stanza-forms, and so take them regularly from other people – but the habit is dangerous when the experience behind one's own poem is weak or trivial.

Baxter got Yeats' rhetoric off well enough, though it never really squared with his own inborn sense of experience. Hardy was probably the poet most suited to his temperament, weighted as it was with a compassionate gloom which sought out appropriate occasions, most often landscapes, which might prompt it to expression. And that gloom, which Baxter was well aware of, carried over into many of the early poems of Catholicism. It was as if that faith enabled his feelings to seem less self-willed, giving a sort of external authority to ways in which he already felt about the world; giving him too, as has been said of Robert Lowell, a convenient and splendidly decorative position from which to launch attacks on the troops of Calvin. In the 'light' verse which Baxter sometimes used for such attacks, the gloom became a sharp invigorating anger. When he wrote poems like 'A Rope for Harry Fat' or 'A Small Ode on Mixed Flatting', echo language was hardly a relevant consideration. The tradition in which such poems have a place is so much a compound of anonymous voices, each voice local in its detail but somehow approximating every other, that the poems' feats of imitation seem wholly appropriate. Whether by way of Yeats or Hardy or Burns, the closer Baxter approached that larger composite voice, the more individual integrity his own voice seemed to have.

Or perhaps one might say that, for the skilled writer of satirical or ballad verse, there is no substantial difference between imitating models and absorbing them. It isn't hard, anywhere in the body of Baxter's poetry, to find him engaged in imitation; but eventually he moves through imitation and absorbs his influences. In his later work the process of absorption seems complete. One can still observe affinities (Lawrence Durrell is probably behind the unrhymed couplets of the *Jerusalem Sonnets*), but there is nothing like the devout, frantic mimicry of 'Guy Fawkes Night', a poem from 1962, which begins with a touch of Dylan Thomas, then turns quickly into a vehicle for the rhetorical and mythological grandeurs of early Lowell:

I saw the freckled children burn their guy
In dry November by the reddened waves
That wash the doorsteps of the dead. Our graves
Are tinder. Look, the sacking falls apart,
The straw will catch as the leopard flames jump high
And grip the squib-plugged heart
Of the poor guy. The dead who have no names
Are shouting, Miserere! from the flames,
The sheep of Calvin, clipped for Judgement Day;
Poseidon hammers on their house of clay,

Laird, bullock-driver, wife in stiff black gown
And kitchen hussy. In the scrubwood pyre
They suffer, Lady. Hoist them from the fire
And give them water – water for that old
Worm-eaten Adam with an iron crown,
An Odin of the sheepfold
My great-granduncle set upon a gatepost
To guard his dying mana. Through the Host
They climb to God. Your Child laughs on my tongue
Among the trampled hay and cattle dung.

The transformation by the time one comes to Baxter's last poems is extraordinary. Here, for example, is 'Haere Ra', written only seven years after 'Guy Fawkes Night' and published for the first time in the *Collected Poems*:

Farewell to Hiruharama –
The green hills and the river fog
Cradling the convent and the Maori houses –

The peach tree at my door is broken, sister,
It carried too much fruit,
It hangs now by a bent strip of bark –

But better that way than the grey moss
Cloaking the branch like an old man's beard;
We are broken by the Love of the Many

And then we are at peace
Like the fog, like the river, like a roofless house
That lets the sun stream in because it cannot help it.

'Haere Ra' might or might not find its way into a 'Selected Poems', but by comparison with 'Guy Fawkes Night' it represents a scaling down which is a wonderful scaling up. The settled peace of the poem is fully at one with the settled voice we hear. That is part of its authority. Even the similes on which the poem rides are ordinary, not deployed on behalf of extravagant discoveries or effects. True, they are part of a process of revelation – for the poem is a quiet coming-to-terms with the resonances of its title – but they are there because they have come into view, objects from the poem's real landscape. The eye sweeps slowly round and sees them, and the poem accommodates itself to what is seen. This is very much the voice of the Jerusalem poems, attending closely, quietly, to the self's experience, yet somehow, at key moments, quite empty of self. I suppose that here again Baxter is approaching another anonymous-voiced tradition, that of verse mysticism. Certainly the poem shares a curious effect with a number of the Jerusalem writings – as if it has been translated from another language, and might stand free of the niceties of language altogether.

Vincent O'Sullivan, at the end of his excellent monograph on Baxter, talks of Baxter's work as, 'the most complete delineation yet of a New Zealand mind'. O'Sullivan means much more than the mere matter of 'influence'. But Baxter's problems with 'echo language', and his transcending of those problems, might be allowed to stand for a development in the larger New Zealand consciousness – a growth from dependence on a world of models to a state of authentic self-possession, a self-possession which accepts but is not bound to models, which doesn't need to make them an issue. It may be hard to think of Baxter as the child born in a marvellous year to whom Allen Curnow once looked forward – but at the end, however much he was the poet of the Fall, he seemed to be standing upright all the same.

The first part of a longer review of James K. Baxter's *Collected Poems*, *Islands* 31–32, 1981

NEW JERUSALEM SONNETS

I
John, it's hot in here. I promised once,
Colin I think, from my grave at length

A muddy spring of poems would gush out,
A kind of poor man's Taieri you might say,

A tide to float the incubus of flesh.
Heresy, man! It is the eel,

That mortal worm who swallows stones
(Or so Aquinas told me) is the body

All our words inhabit. A poem first resembles
Darkness, John, and then the void.

I remember we talked at Brighton,
In a rented boat. Not wishing to disturb

The couples in the lupins,
We kept the paddles going.

II
You had been reading Lowell.
Upstream we shared *kai* – a limp communion

That the young come last to –
Under the quarried breast of Saddle Hill.

Man, they want to amputate our hearts
And then our balls. We suffer

DOUBTFUL SOUNDS

The maenads of the state each morning.
Dressing for breakfast, rolling a joint

For the *kuia* whose heart also bleeds,
We have to feel their nails

Hauling us like junkies down to the clink:
A concrete bed, John, the last embrace.

Up the creek, you told me about your book,
A prayer to crush the nothings.

III
I fancy Hatana made the weeds
That clogged the rudder of our boat.

Barefoot, you pocketed your notebook – then
Wading into the mud as thick as

The porridge of our Presbyterian fathers,
You shoved us clear. Man, I needed you that day.

There is mud here too, John,
Te Whiro's brew, the kind that bears us up –

I think it is a lining for the stomach
When the grog of life is cut.

The problem is emptiness.
It is like the act of kind,

Requiring our nakedness and loss
Before life fills us, casting us adrift.

IV
We hitched the painter to a stump
Of rotten totara. I felt then it resembled

Some *tuakana* who once bent to the river
Till the water swallowed him –

New Jerusalem Sonnets

Well, hollowness in the belly, maybe wind –
You put your shoes and socks back on.

Up Saddle Hill we tasted cloud – everything
Carries a habitual moisture – I suppose

It oils the wheels of conversation.
We sat in tussock, just under the left nipple,

And looked over a brackish sea
Where kelp streamed to the horizon

Like a drowning bird – call it the soul –
You asked me to call you Hoani.

V
The journey down, John, is the worst.
The feet are a kind of condition –

They want to carry us under the earth,
Not over it. Sometimes I think

They'll drop off from too much work,
Like a good man's balls.

These days I find the body
Is a place of shelter, the *whenua*

where nothing matters – even a problem
With the bladder being a pain you share.

But it is steps which worry me mostly –
I have to watch them in polite company

Or I'll be glued to the spot.
Walking away, man, is an illegitimate pleasure.

DOUBTFUL SOUNDS

VI
The fires of wrath, John! Sometimes I think
My poems speak from the bronze arse-pipe

Of the bull that the Romans roasted slaves in –
The yobbos in the amphitheatre

Could be relied upon to applaud politely
When the groans subsided –

Man, how can you take the *via crucis*
And still be humble?

That day we skipped stones over
The broad belly of Hua –

I thought of Muldoon working the thumbscrews,
And wanted to be a stone pissing off to the horizon,

With a good death in a cool element.
You skipped the best stone.

Written with Brent Southgate. *Spleen*, 1973

DOUBTFUL SOUNDS

The Poems of Denis Glover

> When Tom and Elizabeth took the farm
> The bracken made their bed,
> And *Quardle oodle ardle wardle doodle*
> The magpies said.

It's hardly surprising that New Zealand's best-known line of poetry – *Quardle oodle ardle wardle doodle* – should be so determinedly unpoetic. New Zealanders admire doggedness and reticence, and Denis Glover's magpies don't sing: they say. They offer the plain, unmusical facts of the matter. After listening to the refrain a number of times, however, you begin to feel that the magpies are also searching for the conventional harmonies of birdsong – perhaps even for a well-worn verb. Surely this poem is trying to *warble*? Denis Glover's work as a poet, nearly fifty years of it, continually voices a tension between two kinds of articulation: lyric utterance, on the one hand, and on the other the gurgling, gargling sounds of fact and disenchantment. On page after page, he doodles as he warbles – or the other way about.

'The Magpies' is the single New Zealand poem to have achieved a kind of 'classic' status. It interests children as much as adults; and it has a life well beyond the anthology pages – in a range of musical settings, in paintings, and in the theatre. Like the best sacred texts, it also has its own myth of origin. Allen Curnow has recalled (*New Zealand Herald*, 29 July 1987) that Glover composed the poem while driving to visit him at Leithfield, north of Christchurch:

> Glover . . . got out of his little tiny baby Austin in the middle of a wild nor'wester to have a pee by the roadside. There were magpies squawking everywhere. And when Denis arrived and came to the door of the bach he didn't say anything at all except 'quardle oodle ardle wardle doodle' – just like that.

DOUBTFUL SOUNDS

Indeed, 'The Magpies' is now so familiar that an alternative account of its origin has been confidently offered by the television comedy show, *Skitz*. In a sketch written by Dave Armstrong, we are shown the increasingly tipsy poet in the throes of composition, testing and rejecting a range of conventional farmyard noises:

> When Tom and Elizabeth took the farm
> The bracken made their bed,
> And *Arf arf arf arf arf arf*
> The sheepdog said.

A number of animals later, he roars: 'Would you magpies shut up! Quardle oodle ardle wardle doodle all bloody day! I'm trying to write a poem here ...' – at which point a look of slow triumph crosses his face, for indeed a great poem has suddenly found its destined form. The joke has to do with the way in which mundane reality forces itself upon the vision of the inspired poet – which of course simply endorses the poem's point.

It would be wrong to think that Denis Glover's magpies are somehow migrants from a world beyond the poem. More than the inarticulate figures of Tom and Elizabeth, who are known to us only by what they do – or, worse, by what happens to them – the magpies and their stubborn, impure music are essential elements in the poem's own voice. The poem doesn't so much record magpie sounds as utter them; and you can hear magpie noises of one sort or another throughout Glover's poetry. They are there in his sardonic, satirical verses, those constant asides which mock the silliness of the respectable. They are there in his determination to deflate romantic ideals – 'Lili, emotion leaves me quite dismayed,' he wrote, famously, to the pianist Lili Kraus; 'If I'm on fire I call the fire-brigade.' Or you find them in the way his poems, especially in the years before and during the war, borrow the voices of others: Yeats especially, some of the Georgians, '30s poets like Auden and Day Lewis and MacNeice; even the Ezra Pound of *Lustra*.

> My enthusiasm for the tall tree
> and the moon sliding swiftly over the rooves
> knew no restraint.
> Alas there was no-one to tell of it.
>
> And now you are come at last
> you insist on prattling away about the scenery.

That Poundian observation comes from *Thistledown*, a pamphlet of three poems published in 1935. Its narrative is standard in Glover's work: the enthusiastic declaration no sooner made than displaced. Condemnation of prattling, along with a sneaking regard for it, will be a repeated note over the years. But what seems wrong in this case (and Glover, who was a good judge of his work, never reprinted the poem) is the sense of finality; there is no room left for argument.

Denis Glover is never entirely convincing when he aims for absolute statement. A boxer-poet, he is much more impressive when dancing his way through many rounds for a points victory than trying for a single knockout blow. Critics sometimes express disappointment that Glover produced no big poems which seem absolutely central – as if his work was finally no more than a series of interjections made in a world where more sustained and powerful voices were doing all the talking. But very often it is that quality of interjection – of flexibility, of moment-by-moment responsiveness – which guarantees his poetry's interest. Cumulatively, all the thoughts and afterthoughts and footnotes and asides offer a formal scope and tonal range which make Glover's work far more rewarding than that of tidier poets. In some ways, a 'well-made' poem like 'The Magpies' gives a thoroughly false impression of what he was best at.

The title of another poem, 'Thoughts on Cremation', acknowledges something about Glover's procedures. We are not going to meet a single thought, or a considered conclusion. Rather, what follows will be random jottings, shifting perspectives and registers – nothing too fully *managed*. The poem begins with the formal inversions of ritual lament:

> Not like a fallen feather
> Is he laid away under the high
> Rooflessness of sky . . .

then in section IV a conversational quatrain gets tossed in:

> Would he be done yet, Bill?
> Asked the assistant-stoker.
> – Better give him another minute or two:
> He was a big joker.

while VIII, the final section, which is not quite a conclusion, offers another tone again:

> Have no misgiving
> The man to the mourner said;
> Let us look to the living,
> And earth will look to the dead.

'Thoughts on Cremation' first appeared in *Recent Poems*, the 1941 volume which also introduced 'The Magpies'. (*Recent Poems* was a formidable anthology; as well as a selection of Glover's poems, it included work by Allen Curnow, R.A.K. Mason and A.R.D. Fairburn.) When Glover reprinted the poem in his first major verse collection, *The Wind and the Sand* (1945), he included only sections I, VII and VIII. The poem was reduced to its purely respectable moments. Glover must have decided that, without its variety, without the lowerings into apparent bad taste, his poem had lost an essential part of its character, and he reinstated the full text in *Enter without Knocking*, the 1964 selected poems.

The comic and facetious elements in Glover (which he sometimes herded into separate books with names like *Poetry Harbinger* or *Sharp Edge Up*) are quite as important as the serious and solemn; or, to put it another way, they are part of how he is serious. His versions of reality usually come with their own subversions readily to hand. For a poet who writes with so much formal craft, he can seem astonishingly uneven and casual. Of course, unpredictability is part of the general enterprise – at the end of *The Arraignment of Paris*, Glover compares himself to a rugby football in the way he bounces – and by turns he can be serious and flippant, urgent and off-hand, sentimental and heartless, inspired and banal. Like some other New Zealand poets – Elizabeth Smither and Hone Tuwhare come to mind – his poetry welcomes incongruity, can seem as pleased with the squib as the skyrocket. In Glover's case this may be related to the anarchic temperament which contemporaries like Charles Brasch thought they glimpsed in him. But it also puts him in the company of poets like William Blake or Stevie Smith, or one or two of Shakespeare's fools.

Thus it makes sense that his poetry should be filled with weather, and with a view of human experience as something primarily composed of the shifting weathers of time and change. In 'Stage Setting'; 'the band / Is played by the wind,' the sun is a spotlight, and we can see 'in the side-stalls the sea / Moving restlessly':

> And the plot, the plot?
> – How you and I
> Were unhutched and crawled
> And learned to be.
>
> Then what?
> – To grow old, and die.

One notices what will be a persistent interest in age and death. Like James K. Baxter, Glover could use his verse as a way of being old before his time; he had not turned thirty when he wrote 'Stage Setting'; was only twenty-three or twenty-four when he wrote the earlier 'Epitaph'.

But 'learned to be' is the interesting phrase in that passage. Within their stage settings – of weather and mountains and sea – Denis Glover's poems are quietly instructive: they show us how we might learn to lead our lives. Their various characters and personae, among whom one counts the love-struck poet himself, are present as simple exemplars of how to exist in the world.

'Learning to be' does not mean evasion or retreat. Sometimes figures like Harry or Arawata Bill are construed merely as recluses and loners, men whose rural existence represents an evasion of the social and political worlds, with all their bustle and hurry. ('Let the world hurry by, / I'll not hurry, / Sings Harry.') The natural world may be a simple place, but it too is marked by the processes of time and change; the real evader is the person who settles into a contented complacency which seeks to shut change out. The man who settles for the world of fences – 'And the sea never disturbed / Him fat as a barrel' ('Song') – represents a fairly general failure. As William Blake wrote, 'Do what you will, this life's a fiction / And is made up of Contradiction.' In Glover's work, change and contradiction govern all human affairs. And his most typical poems are those that make change not just part of their subject matter but part of their very behaviour.

The linked, diary-like poems of *To a Particular Woman* are a good example of this. The sequence feels its way forward, coming into being – learning to be – by being true to its word, to the contradictory circumstances and feelings it describes:

> Embrace victory or defeat
> Without pride or rancour,
> Taking what turns up
> Wary of elation, seeking no solution

> That can be predicted or designed . . .
> ('For Myself and a Particular Woman')

To a Particular Woman charts – and the language is often nautical – the course of a love affair of late middle age (the poet would have been approaching sixty when the events that he records took place). The title of the sequence suggests the distinctiveness, the particularity, of the loved one; but it suggests, too, a woman who can be particular in her demands and expectations, whose moments of welcome and reciprocity include a clear sense of what she will and will not put up with. She is desired, but hardly fixed in place – so that the poems addressed to her are full of risk and loss, brief contentments, moments of hope and bafflement and regret, and an occasional cranky elation which is never silly enough to take itself for granted. Glover may have spent much of his time making jokes about love poetry, but he writes about mature love here, with all its twists and turns, to-ings and fro-ings, and tenacious sense of miracle. The opening poem, 'Home is the Sailor', closes with a moment of transformation, where a pebbled shore becomes something more remarkable. Discovery becomes revelation:

> On that sure-traced
> Miraculous psephite shore
> You stood,
> Waiting to be embraced.

There's nothing embarrassed there – or embarrassing. But it is typical of Glover that the conventional conclusion should arrive at the outset: the questing lover has found his loved one in the very first poem. The real love poetry, the true adventuring, will happen hereafter.

The voice we hear in *To a Particular Woman* is clearly the poet's own: like Yeats, he is 'walking naked'. But, also like Yeats, many of his more extended enterprises involve the use of a mask – historical figures such as Arawata Bill and Mick Stimpson, or the imagined Harry. These gave the poet ways of expressing obliquely what he felt, without obliging him to answer in person for his feelings or opinions. Perhaps Glover's most obvious mask was donned in 1952 for a single, short poem which gave him an ironic screen for a piece of sermonising. 'Polonius' Advice to a Poet' is exactly what it calls itself – with the implied proviso that Polonius's willingness (in Shakespeare's *Hamlet*) to offer advice didn't do *him* a great deal of good. This Polonius's views on love poetry are often used to gloss Glover's anxieties about the public statement of intimate feelings:

> Love-poems if you like. But keep them short.
> It's all *vieux jeu*, unless you're crude and stark.
> She won't, we needn't, read them. Sport,
> Tell her you love her, and tell her in the dark.

However oblique or direct Glover's phrasings can be, his poems constantly seek out moments of clear perception; the thing they speak of again and again is vision. Vision is exactly where Glover's Polonius begins:

> Upon the unresponsive eye hammer hard words
> Made crystal in clarity,
> Leaving feathered thoughts to the birds
> And woolliness to handers-out of charity.

If the world's ways of seeing are limited and stale (in *Sings Harry* the eye is 'indifferent', 'accustomed'), the poet's task is to offer another kind of vision. Sight is valuable in itself; but Glover once defined poetry as 'a crystallisation of experience', so insight is important, too. Thus alongside the clear eye of the satirist, there is the weather-wise eye of sailor and climber, the glittering eye of the prospector, the cosmic gaze of the astronomer, the new-kindled eye of the lover, and the mind's-eye of the poet which, fixed in the present, can inspect both past and future by means of memory and imagination. Hence the 'dark-brooding eye' at the end of 'The Chestnut Tree', which sees 'unblinkingly and instantly'. Hence Harry, who sings of what he sees: 'pupil to the horizon's eye', he grows 'wide with vision'; and, in our last glimpse of him, is standing 'hands on hips / [Watching] the departing ships'. In the very last poem in this book, written after he compiled the 1981 *Selected Poems*, Denis Glover mixes his voice with that of a classical shepherd: there he is, above the ocean, his loved one in his arms, contentedly watching his sheep graze.

Polonius also has some words of warning about the poet's material – words:

> Say what you have to say, but beware
> Of nimble-running words that deceive
> Yourself most of all. Words are a snare
> For those who work at a mystery and believe.

Glover speaks as one who has himself occasionally been snared. His love of words is plain throughout his verse – sometimes for better, sometimes for worse. His range of address is rooted in the language he uses: a speaking voice is counterpointed against formal metres, colloquial idioms are mixed with rare and esoteric diction. As Polonius says, it can be a dangerous business: words like 'psephite' may send us in excitement to the dictionary, but too many such will make us close the book. It is hard to know why some phrasings – Gloverisms, they've been called – seem willed and excessive ('Birds nimble the bright air, / Fishes flim in the flood') while others ('The frolic of your dress', 'the inarable, humgruffin sea') seem beyond all argument.

Most of the time Glover had a wonderful ear. Sometimes his liking for risky couplings and hyphenations let him down ('sea-Phoenician-fused'), sometimes alliteration and assonance signal too loudly in the foreground, sometimes his desire to be rid of the superfluous leads to a kind of telegraphese. But his instinct for the half- or slant-rhyme, and for the falling cadence, is always sure. *Sings Harry* has its meanings, but it is the subtle music of the song – the mixed harmonies of certainty and hesitation – that makes us listen:

> To the north are islands like stars
> In the blue water
> And south, in that crystal air,
> The ice-floes grind and mutter
>   *Sings Harry in the wind-break.*
>
> At one flank old Tasman, the boar,
> Slashes and tears,
> And the other Pacific's sheer
> Mountainous anger devours,
>   *Sings Harry in the wind-break.*

The image of the wave-tusked ocean seems beyond dispute – until you try to imagine it being expressed in the less subtle rhythms of prose.

It's sometimes said that Glover never revised his poetry. Certainly he never followed Yeats and set about revising the workings of his younger self. Yet his moments of vision – their articulation in verse – must have depended crucially on the quiet craft of revision. The notes to this selection record some examples: the way in which *Sings Harry* comes into existence over a ten-year period; the artfulness with which the individual parts of *To a Particular Woman* are arranged. They also trace, loosely enough, how various poems passed in and out of his work whenever he set about compiling a new, retrospective collection. Some, like 'Home Thoughts' or 'Electric Love', changed shape as they came and went. And sometimes you can see the crafty poet giving a half-successful poem the breath of life:

>'The rose, the worm, the storm, dark love'
>The Commentator now asks what?
>
>Sickly my rose, wriggles the old worm,
>And dark, dark is love sunrise or storm
>Augmented. (Let the Commentator not
>Fall into suburban spinach leaves to rot.)
>
>His leaves are unimportant, his beliefs
>Are half-explained half-truths.
>
>But here's your three-in-one,
>The god-man-woman toil
>Drilling for oil mirthfully
>And down to earth.
>
>Press then your plastic nose
>To the synthetic rose.
>Stay indoor for the storm.
>In dark, dark love
>A blonde may keep you warm.

'The Sick Rose' appeared in this form in *Landfall* in 1965. It wasn't wanted for the enlarged second edition of *Enter without Knocking* (1971), but some time after that Glover revised it for inclusion in the 1981 *Selected Poems*. One can see why he did eventually retrieve it, and also why he wanted to make changes – in such a small space the tones of voice clash rather than play against one another; and then, alas, the final line sinks the whole enterprise. (The opposite effect is gained by a similar throwaway ending in 'Loki's Daughter's Palace'.) The revised and rescued poem is printed in the present volume. It is a tighter, tougher piece of work, now pruned to the fourteen lines of a sonnet. At the close of the poem the woman's hair no longer comes out of a bottle; rather than a type – a blonde – she is now a plausibly human figure, one whose warmth may even be real:

>Stay indoor for the storm
>In dark, dark love
>Her fair hair may keep you warm.

Anthologists are in the happy position of being able to represent Denis Glover at his best. Reduced to a few perfect things – 'The Magpies', one or two poems like 'Threnody', a few pages from *Sings Harry* – his work can hardly be bettered by anything anywhere. But the happy position is not a true one. Glover sometimes wrote about perfection (in 'Printers', for example), but he knew that the human being was a mistake-making animal, and that his own life as a poet was tied up with imperfections. The best parts of *Sings Harry* depend for their lyric grace on their other, less pure moments. And everywhere in Glover's poetry, the authenticity of statement is guaranteed by a sort of deliberate, muted awkwardness:

> You should have been told
> Only in you was the gold . . .

To see Glover clearly, we need more than the anthologist's half-dozen pages. Glover himself was rather too generous to his offspring each time he compiled a selected poems. If you meet too many of his poems in the one place, the interplay of tones and voices begins to repeat, harmonies grow habitual, the unpredictable gets wearyingly familiar. I have set out here to represent Glover's variety and scope, without – I hope – letting the work wear out its welcome. I have used his own *Selected Poems* of 1981 as a starting point. The major sequences are here, uncut; but otherwise I have whittled down the poet's selection. Where sometimes I have added pieces Glover did not favour, there is some indication in the notes; likewise I have noted my one or two departures from the consistently chronological ordering of the *Selected Poems*.

I like every poem in this book, some more than others. I think that 'The Magpies' deserves its fame, and that *Sings Harry* is one of the few astonishing things in our literature. But I am not at all sure that those poems, or any individual titles one might add to them, constitute the *centre* of Denis Glover's achievement. The Glover I enjoy, and admire even more since making this selection, is somehow dispersed through all the parts of his work. On the page he adds up to more than the sum of his parts. His poetry – in all its distinctive moods and formulations – is greater than his poems.

Introduction to *Denis Glover: Selected Poems* (Victoria University Press, 1995)

AS IF

I start with an advantage. When Andrew Johnston writes of houses, I know, most of the time, exactly what kind of structure to picture – a low, weatherboard bungalow, with a pitched, corrugated-iron roof. New Zealand's suburbs are full of them. I think that I have even visited the house which his opening poem refers to. (The house-to-be exists . . .) Equally, I know that the place evoked and affectionately teased in 'Haiku Beach' is the small coastal settlement of Waikanae, an hour's drive north of Wellington. I know that some of the later poems in this book are set in or around Iowa City and that some of their dedicatees (I'm guessing here) will be poets, possibly novelists, members of the same international writers' programme which took the author of *The Open Window* to North America.

But this is a small advantage, one which – if I clung to it excessively – might become a disadvantage. For beyond all the houses and locations and specific travels in these poems, there is another world which depends for its existence on two words which sound throughout Andrew Johnston's writing: *as if*. Hypothesis, supposition, the playing of a part – these and other imaginative stretchings keep the poet agile, and they have a fuller life in his work than the very particular places he starts from. I find myself wanting to refer his poems back to a whole range of writers, some writing in English, some met by most of us in English translation. I am aware, too, of persuasive contemporaries like Charles Simic and Louise Glück, and through them the informing presence of Wallace Stevens. But most of all I am reminded of Italo Calvino's Mr Palomar, who is named after an observatory. There is the same scrutinising of the world, and with the same result: the reflecting lens of language brings back not only news of what is 'out there' but also an account of the consciousness of the scrupulous, attentive gazer.

In that sense Johnston is a Romantic poet, a watcher of the skies and of the self. Wordsworth's lines in 'Tintern Abbey' about all

> the mighty world
> Of eye and ear, both what they half-create,
> And what perceive . . .

must make perfect sense to him. Perhaps the standard Romantic idea of inspiration might impress him less. His imaginative energies – *as if, as if* – seem to be more usefully triggered by the accidents of language ('There's an echo, / it's you, it's euphony, it's funny') or by the constraints of form. I once read somewhere an interview with John Ashbery which touched on his interest in writing sestinas. Well, he said, you know how it is when you're riding a bicycle downhill and at some point you get up to the sort of speed where you don't know whether your feet are pushing the pedals, or the pedals are pushing your feet . . .

I doubt if there is another contemporary poet who turns as often as Andrew Johnston to the sestina, or who manages the pedals quite so well. It can be a treacherous form – easy to stretch the words too thin at one moment, or to find the poem choked and cluttered at another; easier still to be boring. The poet is under the circumstances, and there he must remain while taking charge of them. The six repeated end-words may mean that nothing is settled until the final stanza, but the mixture of recurrence and variation produces a poem composed of accidents which – of course! – simply had to happen. Security and surprise: the sestina, as Andrew Johnston writes it, works wonderfully well as exploration, as contemplation. A mind is thinking something over.

Then there is the ghazal – or what happens when the Urdu ghazal is carried over into English. 'Four or five couplets trying to dance / into Persia,' is how the Canadian poet, Phyllis Webb, puts it. In Urdu the ghazal (pronounced 'guzzle', not 'gazelle', someone once devastatingly told me) lives in its self-contained couplets, but Andrew Johnston uses the form much more flexibly. The syntax presses forward, the lines reach on, and again there is a sort of two-way tug within a single thing, the tidiness of each couplet playing against the slight untidiness of their number: five.

All this is to say that these poems look settled and predictable on the page, yet go to interesting places, and often in inventive, unexpected ways. They are not so open-minded that their brains have fallen out, but they are always happy – to adapt one of the poet's phrases – to find their moments in momentum. If they yearn to step out of time, they remain aware of change and process. I like the way they are interested in well-being, in families and friends, in pleasure. Over and over they offer a sense of the richness of

As If

human engagements, and of possibility. Things come and go, they say. We can be tongue-tied and articulate, or change tack yet remain on course. Most of all they tell us that the house-to-be exists – its windows reflect, and they are also open.

Introduction to *The Open Window*, by Andrew Johnston (Arc, 1999)

THE POETRY FILE

Rhyme

> The god of love,
> That sits above
> And knows me, and knows me,
> How pitiful I deserve –

> Marry, I cannot show it in rhyme. I have tried. I can find no rhyme to 'lady' but 'baby,' an innocent rhyme; for 'scorn', 'horn', a hard rhyme; for 'school', 'fool', a babbling rhyme. Very ominous endings. No, I was not born under a rhyming planet, nor I cannot woo in festival terms.

Anyone who has seen Kenneth Branagh's screen version of *Much Ado About Nothing* will remember the moment when the love-struck Benedick tries to write a love poem. He needs rhyme to show the song-like harmonies of his heart, but all he can find, despite his cynical glosses, are the most obvious words. In the twentieth century, he might have had to contend with the language of the Hollywood musical: *moon* and *June* and *spoon* (pretty desperate, that last one).

Rhyme wasn't around much at first. Early English verse used a system based on stress patterns and alliteration; it took the remarkable work of Geoffrey Chaucer to establish rhyme as a standard characteristic of English poetry. Plenty of writers have grizzled about it since, including Milton, who talked in his introduction to *Paradise Lost* of the 'troublesome and modern bondage of rhyming . . . the invention of a barbarous age, to set off wretched matter and lame metre'.

But it's only in the twentieth century that rhyming has gone generally out of fashion. Some literary historians suggest big cultural reasons for this. Just as institutional Christianity introduced rhyming as a fairly normal aspect of verse-making in the tenth century, so ten centuries later the breakdown of belief means that – for most of us – rhymes don't ring true. Their harmonies don't reflect the true nature of the world we live in. That sounds impressive, but it's also worth making the more mundane observation that English is simply a hard language to rhyme in. And words that rhyme easily eventually grow predictable: they can make an experience that feels entirely new (like falling in love) seem tired and stale. The American poet Wallace Stevens more or less abandoned rhyme after he caught himself making *breeze* chime with *trees*.

Some languages, like Italian and Russian, are especially generous with rhyming words, but this in turn can produce serious problems for translators. Should you translate a rhyming poem by Mandelstam into rhyming English verse? If the rhymes were effortless in Russian, is the original well served if the rhymes sound forced in English? In many cases, free verse will be the most accurate way of translating rhyming poetry into English.

The problems of rhyme are implicitly acknowledged in the large number of rhyming dictionaries that exist in English. These days computers help the dictionary-makers, as in the recent *Penguin Rhyming Dictionary*. The first extensive English rhyming dictionary appeared in 1775, just a few years after Johnson's *Dictionary of the English Language*. Its compiler, John Walker, followed a sort of alphabetical principle, beginning with words that ended in 'a' and finishing with words that ended in 'z'. He even added definitions:

Waltz	A German dance and its music
Fizz	The face, contracted from physiognomy
To fizz	To make a fizzing sound as a squib
Buzz	A hum; a whisper; a talk
To Buzz	To spread secretly
To Buzz	To hum like bees; to whisper
Fuzz	Dusty volatile matter
To fuzz	To explode and scatter dust

Rhyme in English is often associated with easily memorised texts – nursery rhymes or advertising jingles – and even more with comedy and satire. A piece of 'light verse' – a clerihew or limerick – which failed to rhyme would be a contradiction in terms. Indeed, rhyme often signals a joke, especially when it extends beyond one syllable. When Ezra Pound wanted to be rude about Tennyson, he referred to him as Alfred Venison – not much of a joke really, but the rhyme prompts you to find it funny. The most audacious comic rhyme in English is Byron's couplet from *Don Juan* (textbooks would call it a 'mosaic rhyme' because it needs more than a single word for one of its units):

> But – Oh! ye lords of ladies intellectual,
> Inform us truly, have they not hen-pecked you all?

The quietest, least visible rhyme in English is the one which – especially on Valentine's Day – makes *hearts* and *flowers* and *love* keep such constant company. As the critic Hugh Kenner has pointed out, they translate the Provençal words *cor* and *flor* and *amor*, which were always sounding and chiming together in troubador poetry. The floral industry keeps telling us that flowers are the language of love. But it was rhyming poetry which invented the connection, and still sends moony lovers to the florist.

Words

A New Word

I have a new presence inside me.
You. It is a pale still day.

The tuis are really here,
I have seen them, three of them.

Thrush, tui – which is the most mellifluous?
A word I learned from Phyllis Webb.

'Drunken and amatory, illogical, stoned, mellifluous
journey of the ten lines.' If I could sing

like you, like her, tui, like spring water and
far off a rock falling.

Dinah Hawken's poem appears in a recent issue of *Sport*. I suppose it's the title which makes me want to equate the second line's unspecified 'you' with the word 'mellifluous'. 'Sweetly flowing', says the dictionary, 'sweet as honey', though all sorts of other words – like mellow and melody (and even Phyllis!) – are in there, too. Certainly the poem seems to be interested in song and in what makes singing possible; and the thing that most makes the poet want to sing is the music of 'mellifluous' itself.

Why do some words seem more poetic than others? The satirist Peter

Words

Cook used to have a character called The Misty Mr Wisty who rambled on about whatever was on his mind: his friend, Spotty Muldoon, for example (who became rather a problem for New Zealand broadcasters) or the World Domination League. One routine involved Mr Wisty pattering away about a man who wandered 'o'er the hill and o'er the dale':

> That's where poets wander. He's o'er the hill and dale. Other people wander *over* hill and dale, but not the poets. They go 'o'er'. 'O'er, o'er,' they go. They think it sounds better.

Poetic fashions come and go. There was a stage when poets who would sneer at a word like 'o'er' doggedly used ampersands in place of 'and'. In the 1970s, plenty of poets (mostly Americans) loaded their lines with words like 'stones', 'bones', 'wind' and (gulp) 'wrists'. Were these deliberate monosyllables felt to be somehow more poetic than the ornamental phrasings of late Victorian verse? Back in the eighteenth century, poetry was marked off very deliberately from ordinary speech by the elegant circumlocutions of 'poetic diction': fish were 'the finny prey', birds 'the feathered flock', sheep 'the fleecy care'. No wonder Wordsworth, the original wanderer over hill and dale, rejected 'the gaudiness and inane phraseology' of late eighteenth-century verse in favour of 'a selection of language really used by men'.

Nor was Wordsworth's the first attempt to bring the language of poetry nearer everyday speech. Before him, Dryden had attempted much the same thing, aiming for a poetry that had 'the negligence of prose'. And both the Greek dramatist Euripides and the Roman poet Horace had pursued similar campaigns. By the start of the twentieth century T.S. Eliot and others were repeating Wordsworth's revolution. 'Verse should have the virtues of prose,' said Eliot, 'before aspiring to the elevation of poetry.' It should, said Ford Madox Ford, be 'free of the polysyllabic, honey-dripping and derivative adjectives that make nineteenth-century poetry as a whole seem greasy and "close", like the air of a room.'

Honey-dripping? My hunch is that the Modernist poets would have looked aghast at a word like 'mellifluous'. But then there's nothing fixed about either contemporary speech or the language of poems, and certainly nothing stable about the relations between them. In 1914 Lascelles Abercrombie considered the word 'bicycle', and pronounced it a learned word with no poetic potential: 'I am sure most poets would confess to an instinctive repugnance for using it in poetry.' Well, bad luck Fleur Adcock, Denis Glover, Philip Larkin and any number of other poets.

In fact poets raid both the past and the present for the words which give their poems life. They innovate and renovate in equal measure. They can find (as someone must have once) a new home in poetry for a recent coinage like 'bicycle'. Or they can ransack dictionaries for words which have been lost from both page and tongue – like Seamus Heaney rediscovering 'bone-house', the Anglo-Saxon word for body. As Horace put it a little over 2000 years ago: 'Terms lost in darkness the good poet will unearth for the people's use and bring into the light . . . New ones he will adopt which Usage has fathered and brought forth.'

Incidentally, it's not just Dinah Hawken and the Canadian poet Phyllis Webb who get pleasure from the word 'mellifluous'. Poets may not have used it for a long time; but it's a different matter among consumers. In 1981 the London *Sunday Times* asked its readers to vote for the ten most beautiful words in English, and 'mellifluous' came tenth equal. The others – a rather crepuscular lot – were: melody, velvet, gossamer, crystal, autumn, peace, tranquil, twilight, murmur, caress and whisper.

Light Verse

What is light verse? Usually we think of it as the opposite of serious – light as in lightweight: graceful, probably rhyming, usually amusing, perhaps a bit frivolous, certainly inconsequential. But light verse is a category which is extremely broad and inclusive: it can cover the nonsense rhymes of Lewis Carroll, folk songs, comic parodies and social and political satire, as well as the lyrics of Cole Porter or W.S. Gilbert. Byron's mock epic *Don Juan* is light verse; so are the poems by T.S. Eliot which lie behind the musical *Cats*.

The two forms which have never been used other than comically are the clerihew and the limerick. The clerihew (two uneven rhyming couplets which 'size up' a famous person) has the distinction of being named after its inventor, E. Clerihew Bentley, who died in 1956. Many people have taken up the form; here is one of Bentley's:

> George the Third
> Ought never to have occurred.
> One can only wonder
> At such a grotesque blunder.

The origins of the limerick are more obscure, though there seems to be general agreement that the Irish town of the same name must have something to do with it. All limericks exploit their rhyme schemes, and many are mildly obscene. The first I ever learned was about a young man from Kinleith, about whom the less said the better. The cheekiest development of the form is the prose limerick, invented by Gavin Ewart, who hit on the device of taking well-known limericks and 'translating' them with the help of equally well-known dictionaries. Here is his *Shorter Oxford* version of the limerick about the young man from St John's (a college of Cambridge University):

> There existed an adult male person who had lived a relatively short time, belonging or pertaining to St. John's, who desired to commit sodomy with the large web-footed swimming birds of the genus *Cygnus* or subfamily *Cygninae* of the family *Anatidae*, characterized by a long and gracefully curved neck and a majestic motion when swimming.
>
> So he moved into the presence of the person employed to carry burdens, who declared: 'Hold or possess as something at your disposal my female child! The large web-footed swimming-birds of the genus *Cygnus* or subfamily *Cygninae* of the family *Anatidae*, characterized by a long and gracefully curved neck and a majestic motion when swimming, are set apart, specially retained for the Head, Fellows and Tutors of the College!'

Thoughtful readers will have no trouble translating their way back to the original limerick. A helpful tip: in Ewart's version of the same limerick which follows Dr Johnson's dictionary, the large web-footed birds are 'kept in store, laid up for a future time, for the sake of the gentlemen with Spanish titles'.

The Loch Ness Monster's Song

> Sssnnnwhufffll?
> Hnwhuffl hhnnwfl hnfl hfl?
> Gdroblboblhobngbl gbl gl g g g g glbgl.
> Drublhaflablhaflubhafgabhaflhafl fl fl –
> gm grawwwww grf grawf awfgm graw gm.
> Hovoplodok-doplodovok-plovodokot-doplodokosh?
> Splgraw fok fok splgrafhatchgabrlgabrl fok splfok!
> Zgra kra gka fok!
> Grof grawff gahf?
> Gombl mbl bl –

> blm plm,
> blm plm,
> blm plm,
> blp.

How would we set about translating the song of Edwin Morgan's Loch Ness monster? Presumably we can't: and this is partly why the poem is so entertaining. Here is a nonsense poem which really is non-sense. Yet if this is light verse, it's hardly lightweight. It teases our assumptions about the lyric grace of songs and poems, and it plays with the whole idea of onomatopoeia – is this what monsters sound like? But then it occurs to you that something else is going on: this is a Scottish monster, incomprehensible unless the English language, there in the title, points at – even as it fails to fully explain – what's happening. Among all the possible meanings of its nonsense, the poem is making a wee political gesture. The fact that the monster sinks ('blp'), after what amounts to its own inspection of the reader, also has a certain resonance.

Like T.S. Eliot, New Zealand poets such as Denis Glover and A.R.D. Fairburn used to make a clear distinction between their serious work and their light verse. Allen Curnow even invented a different name, Whim-Wham (the passing fancy that packs a punch), for the part of him which wrote occasional poems. If 'light verse' as a distinctive literary commodity is vanishing from our writing, my feeling is that this is not because we can no longer manage it, but because poets cross borders far more willingly than they used to. Lightness and play are no longer at odds with 'poetry': these days they inhabit the same territory. Witness Jenny Bornholdt's 'Urging Her into the Boat', a poem which, at the very least, leaves the reader with a cheesy grin:

> I'll take some of that expensive brie
> for Beverly, he said.
>
> Beverly? Beverly!
> I cried, quick, get into the
> boat. O shy and beautiful
> Beverly, bring your brie
> and come with me.

Great Scott!

Antarctic

What tale is this which stirs a world of knaves
Out of its grubbing to throw greasy pence
Forth to the hat, and choke with eloquence
In boastful prose and verse of doubtful staves?
Four men have died, gentlemen, heroes, braves;
Snows wrap them round eternally. From thence
They may no more return to life or sense
And a steel moon aches down on their chill graves.

'They died for England.' It is excellent
To die for England. Death is oft the prize
Of him who bears the burden and the load.
So with a glory let our lives be spent –
We may be noble in the Minories
And die for England in the Camden Road.

The poem is by T.W.H. Crosland. It was published in 1917, and commemorates the death – some five years earlier – of Scott on his return journey from the South Pole. Crosland takes the example of doomed heroism, the courage and decency of admirable men making the sacrifice, and applies it to daily life. Glory can be achieved in the mundane world of city streets as well as on the pure white stage of Antarctica. Of course the advice about dying for England has a grimmer resonance if we recall that the poem was published at a time when many young men had already died for England in the war to end all wars.

Crosland has his facts a little wrong, too. Five men died, not four. Here's a case where accuracy would have served assonance rather well, and given truth a fine and icy sound.

There have been plenty of attempts to versify the tale of Scott and his party. Janet Frame recalls keeping an index of her poetry compositions in her second year at Waitaki Junior High School, and there on the list is Robert Falcon Scott, at home among the other sounds of melancholy transience:

DOUBTFUL SOUNDS

> Captain Scott.
> Sand
> A Longing.
> My Rainbow. . .

In fact, the best pieces of writing were produced by the explorers themselves, in their various journals and memoirs: Cherry-Garrard, for example, whose *The Worst Journey in the World* has just been reissued by Picador in its series of travel classics; or Scott himself, who wrote his last words in the certain knowledge of his own impending death, composing the texts of farewell which still govern the way in which we view his expedition.

Most of the early poems about Scott were written by well-intentioned, fairly dreadful writers. Here, for example, is the opening of Ian D. Colvin's 'Dirge of the Antarctic', which appeared in 1913:

> I dreamed I saw the Snow Queen stand,
> The Southern Cross was in her hair,
> And five men's hearts lay in her hand
> Like shining jewels bright and fair . . .

Well, perhaps that's not so bad. But try Chas Moss's 1913 *Commander Scott, RN, at the South Pole*, which labours through the whole exhausting story. In particular, consider Moss on the death of Oates:

> But further trouble lay in wait
> Impossible to over-rate,
> And which exceeded human skill,
> When Captain Oates was taken ill;
> Who grew still worse in fighting on
> Through snow and ice till strength was gone . . .
> 'I'm going out,' said he,
> 'And for some time maybe.'
> Some time?
> Sublime!

Sublime? A range of better poets have tackled the Scott story. One is Douglas Stewart, a New Zealander who shifted to Australia at the age of twenty and wrote *Fire on the Snow*, a verse drama which was broadcast by the ABC in 1941 (war once again complementing the tale of English sacrifice). And one of our best contemporary poets, Chris Orsman, has recently published impressive excerpts from an almost completed sequence,

Great Scott!

South, which looks as if it may prove to be one of the most convincing long New Zealand poems in years.

My favourite account of the Scott expedition – as it gives both silliness and heroism their full due – is a villanelle by the Irish poet Derek Mahon. Villanelles depend on two lines repeating and rhyming across several stanzas, before they come together – often with a wonderful sense of inevitability – at the end. Mahon focuses on the death of Oates, but unlike Moss he quotes the famous exit line correctly. Mahon, too, likes the word 'sublime', but he at least is able to make it count.

> *Antarctica*
> (for Richard Ryan)
>
> 'I am just going outside and may be some time.'
> The others nod, pretending not to know.
> At the heart of the ridiculous, the sublime.
>
> He leaves them reading and begins to climb,
> Goading his ghost into the howling snow;
> He is just going outside and may be some time.
>
> The tent recedes beneath its crust of rime
> And frostbite is replaced by vertigo:
> At the heart of the ridiculous, the sublime.
>
> Need we consider it some sort of crime,
> This numb self-sacrifice of the weakest? No,
> He is just going outside and may be some time –
>
> In fact, for ever. Solitary enzyme,
> Though the night yield no glimmer there will glow,
> At the heart of the ridiculous, the sublime.
>
> He takes leave of the earthly pantomime
> Quietly, knowing it is time to go.
> 'I am just going outside and may be some time.'
> At the heart of the ridiculous, the sublime.

SNOW JOB

The Roman Catholic chaplain at McMurdo, America's main Antarctic base, apparently refers to his flock as the Frozen Chosen. It's not a bad way of describing those who, like Sara Wheeler, develop an obsessive relationship with Antarctica and its history. Wheeler travelled there on a programme run by the American National Science Foundation, which each year takes writers and artists – novelists, poets, painters, photographers – down to the ice. The programme bears fruit in books like her *Terra Incognita: Travels in Antarctica* (Jonathan Cape, 1996), which has already reprinted several times in the United Kingdom.

The human population of Antarctica, as Sir Edmund Hillary has pointed out, consists almost entirely of scientists. But even scientists come from national cultures, and Wheeler has an agreeable habit of bringing out the distinctive qualities of the different groups she visits. The Americans are, as you might expect, expansive and generous, the British – the author's compatriots – misogynist and mind-cramped. The Italians are stylish and have an industrial-sized espresso machine. They scheme to bring the Pope to Antarctica. But, says one of them, 'I cannot really see His Holiness on a snowmobile.'

Then there are the New Zealanders. In her room at Scott Base, Wheeler finds a mug on the bedside table bearing the slogan 'Party Till You Puke' – 'a caption which went some way towards summing up the off-duty philosophy of the base. The Kiwis on the ice had a culture all their own. They held three-legged ski races and painted their toe-nails blue.' On the snowfield used for survival training, besides building the usual things like igloos and snow walls, 'they had carved a life-size bar, complete with barstools, draught pumps and glasses.' (Maybe this should be acquired by Te Papa?)

So Wheeler can be a sort of anthropologist-as-entertainer. But *Terra Incognita* is a far more interesting and intelligent account of the Antarctic than such shrewd comic details. The book's title ('unknown land') recalls one of the designations of the great southern continent which the Greeks first hypothesised and Europeans began to imagine many centuries ago. In some ways the history of the area around the southern pole has involved the discovery that there is nothing there at all – and then that there is plenty once you begin to look for it. The trick is both to examine the human continent, and to look inside yourself.

Indeed, Wheeler's book is most alive when it is informed by her impressive knowledge of human encounters with the Antarctic – which include, as well as the historical dimension of heroic Antarctic exploration, the imaginative worlds of writers as distinct and distinguished as T.S. Eliot, Saul Bellow and Beryl Bainbridge. There's a wonderful skill in her apparently effortless weaving of the details of the past into the tale of her physical journeys in the present.

It has been an extremely good time lately for books about ice. Francis Spufford's *I May Be Some Time: Ice and the English Imagination* (Faber, 1996) is exactly what its title says. It deals with the connections between a particular kind of English behaviour, summed up in the last words of Captain Oates before he stumbled to his death in the snow, and the sublime icy territories at the Arctic and Antarctic poles.

Spufford's book is an examination of the Victorian and Edwardian imaginations, of the cultural assumptions which gave rise to (and which in turn were destroyed by) World War I. It is brilliantly written, deft all the way, a lovely mixture of tactfulness and dazzle. It feels like – and is – a set of separate essays, beginning with a sort of zig-zagging academic account of Ice and the Sublime and ending with the death of Scott, done as an empathising third-person, present-tense set of diary entries. Thus the book concludes, not entirely successfully, by attempting an imaginative inwardness with its own material – as if Spufford, having begun with the desire to write a piece of cultural history, had ended with a half-stifled need to write a novel.

I May Be Some Time is ingenious and interesting, and wonderfully well informed. A more surprising book, however, is the just published *Lonely Planet* guide to Antarctica, all 362 pages of it. Among other things, it includes a large factual section – History, Climate, Ecology, Flora, Fauna, Society and Conduct (if you are a tourist, 'never ask to use the station toilet') – as well as advice about getting there and about South Pole shopping; with chapters, too, on a range of Antarctic gateways, from Christchurch to Punta Arenas.

The *Lonely Planet* book is striking evidence of the burgeoning interest in Antarctica. It's evident in our part of the world in tourist attractions like the Antarctic Centre in Christchurch and Kelly Tarlton's in Auckland; in the fact that one of Australia's bestselling 1996 books was a reissue of the journals of the explorer Sir Douglas Mawson; and in the 300-plus students who enrolled last year for a generalist first-year paper about Antarctica at the University of Canterbury.

Lonely Planet even includes a glossary of Antarctic words, based on the first *Dictionary of Antarctic English* (Dante, for short), which is being compiled by the lexicographer Bernadette Hince. The notion that Antarctica has its own language is matched only by the fact that it has its own, very substantial literature. There is no human population there to produce it, but the continent has already generated somewhere between four and five hundred novels, short stories, plays and poems. In *Terra Incognita* Wheeler describes a poetry group at the US base at the South Pole. Each of the fifteen members puts a word in a box, and then they all write a poem about the first word to be pulled out: 'All the words were white, like marshmallow, or cloud, or chalk.'

It's a pity they didn't have Chris Orsman there to show them how to do it. His long poem, *South,* handsomely produced by Victoria University Press (1996), is a genuinely convincing account of Scott's doomed polar expedition, partly because the words themselves are being used with an intent combination of purpose and delight, and partly because he takes such a patient, courteous, thoughtful approach to a set of human facts which can easily be admired in shallow, dated, Imperial ways or mocked for equally shallow reasons. His book is a major contribution, not only to New Zealand – or even Antarctic – poetry, but also to literature written anywhere which treats the human spirit seriously.

Quote Unquote, 1997

A POET AT THE POLE

The temperature was fifty degrees below, and I was well wrapped up – like the other 195 people at the South Pole. So I had something in common with a famous earlier traveller, Robert Falcon Scott: I did not enjoy, in the heroic explorer's own spin-doctoring words, 'the reward of priority'.

Still, there I was. At the Pole. (Or just 'at Pole', say the Americans, for to them the place isn't so much a mythic destination as just another point on the global network.) I was there as a member of Antarctica New Zealand's inaugural 'Artists to Antarctica' scheme. And I was alone, sort of. My heroic companions, poet Chris Orsman and painter Nigel Brown, had already been sent back to New Zealand. As a contemporary Canadian poet puts it, many are cold but few are frozen. But more likely someone had decided that Brown and Orsman would not be able to cope with a brown paper bag stuffed with jam-and-peanut-butter sandwiches, our rations on the three-hour Hercules flight from Scott Base.

We flew up the two-hundred-kilometre Beardmore Glacier, where Scott and his party had sledged, and looked down on astonishing peaks surfacing like misty, pastel islands through the ice and snow. Then there was the empty white and apparent endlessness of the polar plateau, where, in some places, the ice is so deep you would have to dig a couple of miles to find the land beneath.

Amundsen-Scott South Pole Station, to give it its full name, is a large, unheated geodesic dome. It has been there about twenty-five years and is already half buried in snow. Its predecessor, the Mark I station which dates from the '50s, was abandoned years ago and is now entirely below the surface. Mark II, the dome, was originally designed to accommodate about sixty people. The extra 135 were there because most of them were helping construct the Mark III station, which will be a giant set of pods on legs, looking for all the world like something off the set of *Star Trek*. The Hercules taxis to the dome entrance, and you walk down into a vast space which seems to be full of giant refrigerated chambers. You open the door of one of them, and there you are in the galley, where people are eating. (Traveller's tip: if you would like a latte, just ask for the Polar Ice Cup.) But then you walk out beneath the dome again, protected from the weather but not the temperature, and enter a communications shack, or a berthing (i.e., sleeping) area, or – incongruously – a place where a dentist is about to give someone a filling.

It sounds cosy, and people try to make it cosy, but it is also seriously weird and marginal, real edge-of-the-galaxy stuff. The place feels like a station on the moon or Mars, with only the breathing apparatus missing. Anyway, we had all of forty-five minutes on the ground. The Herc's propellors kept turning while it made a hot load: we ourselves had to get back on board and strap ourselves into the webbing. We lumbered across to the geographical pole itself and took our photographs. I presented a copy of my poem *Hoosh* to the nice man with the frosted moustache, who had just given us the speed-read tour of the facility. He was genuine and effusive in his thanks, and declared that it would be framed and hung above the Base pool table. Well, you can't say fairer than that.

Scientists can seem like embarrassing, marginal figures (almost like poets) in the new corporate New Zealand. But down in Antarctica, they thoroughly matter. Victoria University's Peter Barrett, who leads the Cape Roberts project, is one of the gods of the ice, spoken of in tones of deepest awe. The fact that I had personally spoken to him once or twice in the university Staff Club impressed everyone immensely. I began to swagger along the Scott Base corridor. More generally, talking to scientists down on the ice – from penguin guano analysts to chainsaw-wielding glaciologists – I was struck by the affection with which they describe their research projects and field locations, and just how often their work seems to have an aesthetic dimension. They also work extremely hard. I myself wrote more poems in twelve days in Antarctica than in the whole of the last two years, and in this one I've invented a scientist's love song for a particular place, Lake Bonney, which is a frozen lake at the foot of the Taylor Glacier, on whose banks we camped for four nights. ('Patching' simply refers to field-radio links.)

Deep Field Song

Patch me out to Lake Bonney,
Patch me out to the ice,
Where the glaciers pour,
And suspend at your door,
And the world doesn't look at you twice.

A Poet at the Pole

And patch me through to McMurdo,
To Evans and Royds and Bird,
Where Shackleton and Scott,
By Jove!, did a lot,
While admiring the tabular bergs.

But then patch me right back to Lake Bonney,
Patch me whatever the price;
The ice on the lake
Doesn't hurry, or wait,
And it might be Paradise.

I read that piece along with others during a poetry reading and book-launch at Scott Base. (Chris Orsman had somehow managed to print and publish a book of verse there – *Homelight*, twenty-three signed and numbered copies, hand-sewn, with drawings and a woodcut cover by Nigel Brown.) There was a big audience, including a contingent who had come over from the American base at McMurdo. Someone said that we were just as good as Borge Ousland, who spoke at Scott Base last year after finishing his solo trek across the continent. At the bar after the reading, one of the helicopter crew said to me that he thought this poetry stuff was really interesting. 'It's like you're somehow putting words inside the words.' It was worth going to Antarctica just for that.

Across the Pacific, Vol 8, No 1, Spring 1999

Pengucapan Puisi
KUALA LUMPUR
Poetry Reading

Mr. Bill Manhire,
Department of English,
Victoria University of Wellington,
P.O. Box 600,
Wellington,
New Zealand.

Our ref.: DBP-4/36 K.5 (173)

Date: September 24th. 1990.

Dear Manhire,

THE THIRD KUALA LUMPUR WORLD POETRY READING 1990:
PARTICIPANT'S TICKET

Your ticket is ready! Thank you very much to Malaysia Airlines our main sponsor, with its charm and hospitable has come forward to fly you to Kuala Lumpur, The City of Light to participate in this festival.

2.   Your ticket is already cleared and please re-confirm it and do follow your right date to depart for Kuala Lumpur. At the Subang Airport International (Malaysia) you will be welcomed by a team from the secretariat. Transport to hotel is waiting for you. Although some of you would arrive before 25th. October, please do not worry, we are looking and pay for your accommodation and food.

3.   "SELAMAT DATANG" is Malaysian way to greet you poets of the World. Please come and enjoy every moment of this Kuala Lumpur World Poetry Festival. This is our own festival and we are together responsible to enlighten it.

Until then, warm regards and love.

Sincerely yours,

(AHMAD KAMAL ABDULLAH, Kemala)
Secretary-general,
Third Kuala Lumpur World Poetry Reading 1990,
for Director General.

c.c.:   i. The Chairman.
       ii. The Deputy Chairman.

WINGS OF GOLD

A Week among Poets

> A few years ago one of the present authors, then in Malaysia, was approached by a visiting New Zealand Member of Parliament. 'I have just two important questions for you,' he said. 'What is really going on in this country, and what are the names of the two main types of dress worn by Chinese women here?'
> R.S. Milne and Diane K. Mauzy, *Malaysia: Tradition, Modernity, and Islam*

High above the Australian interior, I sit in a Malaysian Airlines DC10 – knees under my chin, *Wings of Gold* on my knees. I am on my way to the third Kuala Lumpur World Poetry Reading. I open and re-read the letter that came with my flight ticket.

I am faintly confused about my name. In this letter I am addressed as Manhire, but an earlier fax from the organisers came to Billo Manhire. They are probably confused because they had been banking on getting Cilla McQueen. Cilla has had to pull out in favour of her theatre piece, *Red Rose Café*, which is about to premiere in Dunedin. But the Billo is rather good. Friends have debated its appropriateness: does it suggest a failed hobbit or a mild abrasive? Or is Billo built on the model of the missing Cilla? 'From Cilla to Billo' – it has a certain ring. There might be an essay on New Zealand poetry here.

The in-flight magazine, *Wings of Gold*, is written mostly in English. Alas, the only item written entirely in Bahasa Malaysia is the three-page spread devoted to the Kuala Lumpur World Poetry Reading, and I understand none of it, although the word *puisi* has begun to acquire some meaning. Further on, a section called 'Dateline Malaysia' explains that there are two particularly exciting events taking place in Kuala Lumpur in the last week of October. One is the World Poetry Reading. 'More than forty international poets are expected to take part in the Third Kuala Lumpur World Poetry Reading. Twenty-two of the countries confirmed are Jordan, West Germany, Turkey, Soviet Union, Belgium and France.'

The other event is the World Body Building Championships.

The guidebooks give you facts: 330,000 square kilometres, only 40 per cent of it in Peninsular Malaysia, where about 85 per cent of the population live. The population is about 14 million; 54 per cent are Malays and other indigenous people; Chinese are 35 per cent, Indians 10 per cent. Freedom of worship is guaranteed in Malaysia, but it is essentially an Islamic nation. The constitution even defines a Malay as a person who habitually speaks Malay (Bahasa Malaysia), conforms to Malay custom, and follows Islam. And although Kuala Lumpur now calls itself the City of Light (1990 is 'Visit Malaysia Year'), the name in fact means Muddy Estuary. The city is built where a bunch of nineteenth-century tin prospectors set up camp at the confluence of two rivers. (These days the rivers flow through huge concrete drainage channels – gigantic versions of Dunedin's Leith Stream.)

Before I left New Zealand, long before the cabin crew turned on the muzak ('Harbour Lights') and demonstrated safety procedures, I asked people about Malaysia. One friend told me about the *bumiputra* policies. *Bumiputra* means 'sons of the soil' and Malaysia has a range of measures designed to discriminate in favour of the indigenous peoples, mainly the ethnic Malays, so that they can gain a more equitable share of the nation's wealth. There are Malay privileges in business licences, land ownership, government jobs, tertiary opportunities. Someone else explained that Malaysia was one of the powerhouses of the new Asia: its economic success made the New Zealand of Roger Douglas look absurd.

But most people made dark jokes about drugs. One night I turned on a BBC television play, *Among Barbarians*, about young English drug smugglers in Malaysia. I thought there might be some establishing shots, a few images to give the feel of the place: mosques, perhaps, or majestic rainforest. But all I could see was an anxious British family arriving at an airport, then a hotel. I went back to marking end-of-year exams. 'Katherine Mansfield talked of seeing her world in glimpses. How does she make such apparently insignificant moments worth writing about?' After about an hour I flicked on the set again, just in time to see two bodies plummeting through the hangman's trapdoor.

*

Wings of Gold

My arrival card says:

> BE FOREWARNED
> DEATH FOR DRUG TRAFFICKERS UNDER
> MALAYSIAN LAW

And just as we land there is a brief announcement about drug smuggling. 'Such an offence will carry a mandatory sentence. Thank you.'

It is raining as we land, 7.40 p.m. local time, in a steaming, equatorial world. Two men stand around the baggage claim, both wearing face masks, like surgeons in an operating theatre. A young German drifts through the arrival hall asking people to lend him his airfare home. I am luckier than him. Someone holds a sheet of paper saying, 'Manhire'. I have been looked for, I am safe, I do not worry. There are several young men to meet me, and even another poet who has just stepped off a flight from Brunei. One man does all the talking: he is small, all in black, and keeps breaking into nervous, high-pitched laughter. He reminds me of Joel Gray in *Cabaret*.

'Mr Bill,' he says, laughing and thrusting an envelope into my hand. 'Hundred ringgit. Is all for you from us. You sign.'

He has a form which says I have received the money. I sign it. Malaysia will turn out to be a land of forms and form-filling.

'You are at Holiday Inn, okay? Sharing the rooms. This is how it is happening, okay?' There is an edge to his voice. 'Okay?'

I must look faintly puzzled. So he adds: 'Englishman won't. Sebastian! But you are not Englishman, Mr Bill, you New Zealand.' A wild laugh leaves his body in high little ripples. He stops laughing and cries, 'English poet!' Then he says something in Bahasa Malaysia to his colleagues. They all laugh – a sort of anxious hysteria. Then we are in a car, on a motorway, and the neon signs say Guinness, Toyota, Hilton.

At the Holiday Inn, someone darts away with my bag. Someone else tells me that I am sharing a room with a Thai poet. But there is only one key, the Thai poet already has it, and anyway we must go to the dinner! Moments later I am sitting at a table. It is some sort of banquet hall. In fact, many people sit at many tables; there is one of those low ceilings made of smoky steel. The table is set with jugs of water and glasses of orange cordial – which for some reason remind me of a childhood holiday at Pounawea.

I am with a bunch of young Malay men and the poet from Brunei. Food is brought and we smile at one another between mouthfuls. Someone manages to explain that the dinner is sponsored by the Ministry of Tourism and Culture. The Minister of Tourism himself is here. He is pleased: his government has just been re-elected. The idea of poetry as news is news to me – whatever Ezra Pound said about it. But photographers race about the banquet hall, darting out of the way of the arc lights and cables trailed by television news teams. The room is full of poets and photo opportunities. The Minister makes a long speech in Bahasa Malaysia. People chat and sip their orange cordial. The Minister appends a brief English summary. He uses phrases like 'the betterment of mankind'. He suggests that poets should 'highlight positive values'. In a world which is too individualistic, he says, poets 'can act as the stabilising factor that contributes to human development'.

Then the Minister sets off around the room. He shakes hands with the international guest poets, who seem mostly to be clustered at tables masked by a couple of pillars on the far side of the hall. The Minister is trailed by light: subordinates, press photographers and the television crews. Many of the poets are armed with their own cameras and they too join the media throng. By the time the Minister reaches my table, his hand extended, half the banquet hall is travelling with him.

There is entertainment. A Malay band plays music; elegantly costumed men and women dance. Like all the Malay bands I meet during the week, this one has fiddle, flute, piano accordion and an astonishing variety of drums. It is like an Irish pub band with a huge percussion section. The players are all young, except for an elderly bald man on fiddle. His fiddle is painted blue and white, like waves and ocean, like (I think later) doves and clouds crossing a perfect sky. The music itself is both background and foreground: familiar and strange, insistent, swooping through the room and about the heads of the international poets who crowd around the band with cameras.

I meet Kemala, the author of my letter of invitation. He leads me about the room, introducing me to the poets of the world. I hear names but remember countries. Sri Lanka is here, and Turkey. So are Korea, Canada, Nepal, Switzerland, Japan, England, China. Australia is an amiable, slow-motion Tom Shapcott, who is also just off the plane. Then there are Jordan, Romania, the Philippines, Germany – and Pakistan, who will pursue and persecute me during the week with reports on the progress of the New Zealand cricket tour. Also there are Egypt, a couple of Norways, and a small delegation of very big poets from Yugoslavia. No sign of America. I meet my room-mate, the Thai poet, Prayom Songthong. The prayer and song in his name help me remember it. Prayom is in his late fifties or early sixties – courtly, gentle, softly spoken.

I have entered a situation familiar to all New Zealanders who go away from home. I have none of Prayom's language; he has a little of mine. But it is surprising how much we can talk about. Back in New Zealand it is 4.30 a.m., but in Room 1613 in the Holiday Inn, Kuala Lumpur City Centre, it is 11.30 at night, and Prayom explains that he likes to have television on late while he writes. 'Mostly letters,' he says. 'TV and write.' I climb into bed anyway, half aware of an American car chase. I close my eyes and Prayom writes in his notebook. Then there is news. I sleep, or imagine I sleep, very briefly. When I wake, half an hour later, I can hear the over-excited music that signals television news. What is happening in Malaysia round about midnight? Ah, there are the bodybuilders, lines and lines of them, meeting the Prime Minister, bursting out of their jackets. Then there is something about the new Malaysian Cabinet, then something about (I think) Tasmania, then something else altogether: a room full of people sitting at tables, and the Minister of Tourism, Dattuk Sabbaruddin Chik, reaching across to shake my hand.

A Mysterious Poem

From afar we saw the sea flickered
in a festival of lights. Fishermen
told us fluorescent lamps attracted sotongs
to the hook or 'candat' at the end of the line.
The hook reflected in the water.

Sotongs were curious with the way
lights played on the hook. A sotong
wobbled up from the deep
and lingered by it. I waited
till it was close enough

when I jerked the line up
along with the sotong
whose limbs were tangled up
by the hook. The sotong discharged
black liquid all over my face.

26 October
The morning paper, the *New Straits Times*, slides under the door. There is a lot of stuff about the recent Malaysian election and the divvying up of perks and power – who will be in the new Cabinet, and so on. And one fascinating sentence: 'Penang is set to enjoy greater development as the new State Government is composed of intellectuals!' There is a list of Ministers: they all have PhDs.

New Zealand is there on the international page, too. Even in Kuala Lumpur, things look disastrous for Labour.

I bump into a blackboard in the lobby which says there is a registration room for poets. I find it and register. This involves paying a sum of US $100.00 – a good deal more than the 100 ringgits I was given at the airport. I am given an extraordinary folder. It is imitation leather; it has a clipboard and many pockets, and there are many things in the pockets: a fifty-two-page full-colour programme, car stickers promoting the World Poetry Reading, various small booklets and invitations.

I discover that the detail of the formal readings is already settled. I am to read 'Zoetropes' and 'Megasin' (sic) – the last poems I would think to read to a non-English audience normally. The organisers had asked for sample poems, and I faxed them through from Wellington at the last minute simply because they were short. Fortunately I can worry about this later. My first reading duty will be in Shah Alam late tomorrow afternoon. I'm not down to read in tonight's big opening ceremony in the Kuala Lumpur City Hall. Phew!

> WE WILL PROCEED TO CITY HALL AUDITORIUM AT 7.30 P.M.
> PLEASE GET INTO THE BUS FIVE MINUTES EARLIER.
> YOU WILL READ IN YOUR OWN LANGUAGE AND IT WILL BE FOLLOWED BY MALAY TRANSLATION. NO XX INTRODUCTORY SPEECHES ALLOWED.
> PLEASE GO STRAIGHT WITH YOUR READING. ONE POEM ONLY JUST AS STATED IN THE PROGRAMME BOOKLET. THANK YOU FOR YOUR KIND COOPERATION.
>   KEMALA
>   Secretary-general

Introductions
At 3.30, there is an introductions session. 'At the Introductory Meeting, we will introduce you one by one to the other participants. The Director General of Dewan Bahasa dan Pustaka, the principal sponsor of this Festival, will give greetings. Foreign as well as local journalists will freely interview you at this meeting. We appreciate your cooperation. High Tea (consisting

of various tasty local dishes) will be served at 5.00 p.m.' The New Zealand High Commissioner is coming to this session to present books of New Zealand poetry to the Festival organisers. About twenty minutes it should take, one of his staff thinks. It's not clear if I will have to speak.

In the event, everyone will have to speak.

The introductory session begins with a very long speech in Bahasa Malaysia from the Director of the Dewan Bahasa to a room containing almost no Malays but many uncomprehending foreign poets.

Then a Yugoslav woman makes a very long speech in Serbo-Croatian. She is the editor of an anthology of Malaysian poetry translated into Serbo-Croatian. This strikes me as a wonderful cross-city bus – though, as the speech goes on, I realise that the speaker, like many Yugoslavs, is Islamic, and that the poetry bus she travels on is powered by an engine called Islamic Revival. All the same, it makes you realise how few and how predictable are New Zealand's international connections. The editor's speech is then translated into English. Then three poems are read in Serbo-Croatian; then there are English translations. Then there is a long speech of thanks in several languages. There is a formal presentation of the anthology. The editor shakes the hand of the Director of the Dewan Bahasa. The room is suddenly full of photographers; and there are the television crews again.

Now one by one the poets mount the rostrum and introduce themselves. There's competition between the guest poets at flattering the hosts. Something both ingratiating and patronising is going on, but in a long-winded way both sides end up satisfied. 'It is good to make love in Malay,' says a Malay poet, proud of his language. 'I have tried it and it works.' I say something fatuous about being born in Invercargill. Each of us shakes the Director's hand.

We are each given a present, a large bundle wrapped in pink ribbon. There are posters advertising the World Poetry Reading. There is a gold and green cushion, which turns out to contain – or be – a writing pad; there is a Parker pen. There are also several books, mostly about Malay literature, but one turns out to be an anthology of work from the last World Poetry Reading. *Merpati Putih Dan Pelangi/The White Dove and the Rainbow* is 300 pages long, published by the Dewan Bahasa, and has a colour frontispiece showing Kuala Lumpur: 'the city of light and the city of poet'. The poems are all in English and Bahasa Malaysia. The Soviet poet, Bella Akhmadulina, was here last time! Her poems have been translated from Russian into Bahasa Malaysia and thence into English, and have filled with mysterious swerves and wobbles.

> October sums up withering.
> Nature around is heavy and serious.
> In Autumn's late hour – it's so tedious
> Again to hurt my elbows against orphanhood's corner.
> The neighbour couple's overlong visit
> is dragging on and on, and I getting tired with all my soul,
> cannot utter a word – in my throat hangs
> some sort of deaf-and-dumb vagueness.
> In Autumn's late hour – when light is put out
> and all of a sudden, when falling asleep, I hearten up with
>   the guess
> that I was invited to guest
> at an artist's place . . .

From now on, wherever the poets go, presentations will take place. If I remember anything from this week, it will be presentations, flashes of photographic light, little ripples of applause.

Throughout all this, Mike Chilton, the New Zealand High Commissioner, has been sitting on the dais, maintaining an attentive look. Beside him are the Director of the Dewan Bahasa and a couple of the organisers of the World Poetry Reading. Now he is allowed to make a speech. It is nicely judged – elegant and brief, and it generates much goodwill, not to mention genial sounds of envy from Thomas Shapcott (who in an earlier incarnation ran the Australian Literature Board and presumably knows a good move when he sees it). There is a handing over of New Zealand poetry and a shaking of hands. But, alas, the photo opportunities all went to Yugoslavia. The photographers have departed.

Then it is high tea. The High Commissioner detaches himself as fast as decency permits and makes a dash for a waiting limousine. He has to get back to the High Commission, where he is the Chief Returning Officer. They should even have the election results late tomorrow afternoon. Would I like to call round? But tomorrow, along with other poets of the world, I will be in Shah Alam.

Dewan Bahasa Dan Pustaka
The Dewan Bahasa is Malaysia's language and literature agency. It was originally set up as a small government bureau within the old Department of Education. After independence, Malay became an official language of the new nation, and in 1967 the National Language Act made it the sole

official language. Back in 1956 the Dewan Bahasa had a staff of sixty. Now a vast office block houses about 1200 people; the Dewan has grown with the language it fosters.

The history of modern Malaysia could be written as a history of the Malay language. In 1969 hundreds were killed in language riots. The Dewan Bahasa is funded by the government to promote a single tongue, Bahasa Malaysia. It plans language campaigns, and it examines and coins the terms that Bahasa Malaysia needs to cope with the specialist terminologies of science, government, technology. In the last thirty years it has compiled and standardised about 600,000 *istilah* or specialised terms. This has made it possible for Malay to become the language of instruction not only in schools but also at university level.

Dewan Bahasa is also a major publisher. As the whole of the Malaysian education system has moved into Bahasa Malaysia, Dewan Bahasa has supplied the textbooks: over 1000 published for schools (many of them translations of English texts); and, over the next five years, 800 to be published for university courses. Part of the publishing programme is designed 'to encourage literary and creative growth'. The Dewan runs awards and competitions, workshops and literature forums, and has published about 250 literary titles in the last decade. Some of these are Malay texts translated into other languages (French, English).

Translation can be a problem, however, as Bella Akhmadulina might tell you. Because English is the language of the Raj, it is vigorously discouraged. But it is also the language of trade and international chit-chat – not easily avoided. Because Malaysia has not yet stepped fully clear of the shadow of the Raj, it has hardly become clear to most Malaysians that English is a very, very difficult foreign language. Thus Empire has its mischievous aftermath. Even very weak Malay speakers of English believe their command of the language is wonderfully good. Robert Frost said that poetry is what gets lost in translation; but when Malays translate Malay poetry into English, linguistic competence gets lost: the poets sound inept and silly.

A Poetry Spectacular
Standing room only in the huge auditorium of Kuala Lumpur's City Hall. There are speeches of welcome, and a formal launching of *The White Dove and the Rainbow* by the poet Usman Awang (there is a booklet about him tucked into our conference folder). The international poets loll in the front rows while presentations to dignitaries take place.

Suddenly a man rushes up to me and whispers loudly that I am number four.

'You are France! You read, Mr Bill! You read!'

'No,' I say serenely, 'I am New Zealand!'

'No,' he says. 'You read! Tonight you read! I am warning you!'

I open the programme and point. 'Look, France is there. Number four: France.'

'But France is not here!' he cries. 'France never came to Malaysia. It is you, Mr Bill; when you are called, go quickly!'

I look at the stage with renewed attention. A huge perspex screen hangs at the back. The words *Kuala Lumpur World Poetry Reading* are there, along with the logo of the Dewan Bahasa, while a stylised dove tows the Malaysian flag through a clear sky. Further back, a diorama of clouds streams constantly from left to right. At various points on the stage rainbow banners are strung on wild verticals; white doves hang among them. Suddenly a symphony orchestra pours rich muzak through the hall's sound system. Beautiful girls clad all in white leap nimbly about the stage, vaguely courted by men with streamers. For ten minutes they dance – a vision of doves and rainbows. Then the stage is empty.

One by one, we are called – the poet's name and land, and then the poem. One by one we stumble onto the stage. I follow England, Sebastian Barker, whose poem is called 'Thank God Poets Can't Spell'. Because the voice through the loudspeaker says so, I read 'Magasin', a poem about a boy visiting his very sick father, which ends with what must be an impenetrable reference to the second leg at Trentham. Translated into Bahasa Malaysia and declaimed by a very theatrical young woman, it is twice as long as the original and filled with a passion I never knew I was possessed of. The word *Trentham* lingers in the hushed auditorium.

My friend Prayom has a new video camera; he spends the week taking aim around the fringes of events. When I eventually settle exhausted in my seat, he shows me what I look like – swaying among the streamers, muttering nervously as the clouds pour across the sky behind me.

There is theatre in the slow ascent of the elderly Sri Lankan poet, Wimal Abhayasundere, and in his puzzled blinking once he stands in the lights of centre stage. He begins to sing in a quavering voice. The audience break into spontaneous applause as the first notes sound, then begin to talk loudly through the rest of the poem, 'Conquering Hearts', which is indeed rather long. Wimal reads the English version in a thoroughly prose voice:

Wings of Gold

> The King of Ethina in the gambling arena
> Forced in a moment a princess to strip-tease
> Out flowed the wailing of the awakening of
> the offspring of the earth – the female
> Immoralities that prompt the living patterns to go astray
> Makes one to abandon good morals
> And lays the foundations for commitments of misdeeds . . .

The talking goes on. Cameras flash. Eventually Wimal finishes. He makes his way down from the stage. His fellow poets rise to take his hand. 'Very interesting,' says Jordan. 'Very interesting, yes,' replies the poet. He is back in his seat by the time the Bahasa Malaysian translation gets under way; he talks animatedly throughout his own translation.

The Chinese poet, Wang Fei-Bai, reads a rhyming poem filled with quotations from Mayakovsky, Lorca, Mallarmé and Matthew Arnold. He wrote his poem in English, so he does it in English first, then in Chinese. 'The world is a watery star / When we behold it from afar.' Turkey reads. Japan reads. Adam Puslojic – a huge bearded Yugoslavian who is already one of the characters of the week – reads a poem called 'Breath and Ice'. Afterwards he pauses and cries: 'Little poem for Kuala Lumpur!'

> Lord, what age is this one,
> when my love is gone?

Adam dashes from the stage, and a moment later tiptoes back to photograph the young woman who is reading the Bahasa Malaysia version of his poem. The auditorium fills with flashlights and applause. The air is dense with the sound of a hundred films automatically rewinding.

Subdued excitement greets the poet from Indonesia. He is famous – a performance reader – and in Malaysia Indonesians are a kind of family. His poem is comic ('naughty', someone tells me later), which may explain why he delivers it like a general declaring war in some terrible movie. But this is poetry as theatre. He strikes poses – left profile, right profile, head tossed back, eyes widening and narrowing with the meaning of his lines, looking for all the world like the front half of a bulldog.

The Romanian poet, Radu Carneci, gives his name, then says the single English sentence he has learned by heart, 'I am happy to be away from home.'

Thomas Shapcott is the last reader. As he advances towards the stage, the voice cries through the public-address system: 'Thomas Shapcott: the Crippled Poet!' But the reference is not to Thomas Shapcott. 'The Crippled

Poet' is the name of his poem, which is about a visit to the Malay poet, J.M. Aziz.

At refreshments afterwards, I talk to a distinguished-looking man – ex-MP, banker, lawyer and writer of poetry. He has been to Invercargill. We talk about the popularity of poetry in Malaysia. I ask him how well a book of his poems would sell. 'Oh, not well at all. Say ten to fifteen thousand copies.' He asks me why New Zealand never plays any part in the Asia Pacific Film Festival, of which he is one of the organisers. 'We write to them year after year, but no one ever comes.'

27 October
Shah Alam is the new capital city of Selangor – some thirty kilometres west of Kuala Lumpur, the federal capital. It is grand and wealthy, still being carved out of the landscape – a confident invention. The state mosque is huge – blues and whites, spires like rocket ships, and its aluminium dome is said to be the largest of its kind in the world.

New Zealand voters are going to the polls as our international poetry coach glides past the mosque. We draw up outside a modern museum. There is a dance of welcome in the foyer; then we file up a staircase to find ourselves in a lecture hall. This is the morning called 'Poets' Dialogue'. Poets had been invited to prepare papers on 'The Role of Poetry in a World of Cultural Change' or 'My Creative Experience'. It is not wholly clear who will participate in the dialogue. The programme lists several poets' names, then adds an ominous 'etc'. First there are two keynote lectures. Hafiz Arif (aka Harry Aveling, an Australian who is writer in residence at the Dewan Bahasa) gives a brief historical outline of Malay poetry. The Malaysian writer, Baha Zain, delivers a paper called 'Poetry, Poet and Humanity'.

Both men are interested in the question of what is common among cultures and what is culturally distinctive – and what sort of balance needs to be struck between these things. Both clearly believe in belief, and are disturbed, as Harry Aveling puts it, by the common assumption that modern culture is or ought to be secular. Baha Zain refers to Octavio Paz, the latest Nobel prize-winner, as evidence of poetry's importance in public affairs, but the main drive of his speech is against godless ideologies – he attacks several influential but slightly dated Western thinkers: Marx, Freud, Sartre. His paper is a plea for poetry sustained by religious – and especially Islamic – values. 'Poetry was given to us,' he concludes, 'so that we might translate our humanity and the love of God for all.'

Baha Zain's paper is given in Bahasa Malaysia; but we have a typewritten English translation we can follow. During both papers there has been a sort of continuous muttering from the Soviet quarter. Has Baha Zain offended with his comments on Marx? But no, the Soviet poet has a personal translator, Dr Boris Panikov. Dr Panikov has been giving a running translation into Russian; the whole morning's proceedings are accompanied by a low Cyrillic grumble.

In fact, David Kugultinov – though he looks like a man who has just come from reviewing the troops on Red Square – can hardly be upset by attacks on godless ideologies. He is a Buddhist. And he is a Kalmyk, from Mongolia. He published his first book at eighteen, fought in the Second World War, spent ten years in a detention camp under Stalin. Now he is a people's representative and a member of the Presidium of the Soviet Supreme Council. Occasionally he refers to his friendship with Gorbachev.

He reads his paper in Russian. Boris Panikov translates it into Bahasa Malaysia. Words like *perestroika* occasionally float clear. But we can read the printed English translation. Some of what the poet says sounds interesting. He thinks that language has something to do with poetry. Words vary according to region. Thus the Russian word for sun is hotter than the word used by the Arctic coastal tribe, the Yakut. 'Whereas the word "narn" in my mother tongue of the Kalmyk tribe is hotter than the word "matahari" in the Malay language, possibly hotter.' Hotter and possibly hotter? It is hard to follow this sort of English. But it is hardly David Kugultinov's fault. His paper is in Russian; it has been put into English by someone whose English wasn't good enough:

> Word is dynamic in its true sense. Allow me to enlighten participants present regarding an invention advocated by a group of scholars of the Institute of Advanced Neural Activities and Neurophysiology in Moscow, headed by an imminent scholar, Paul Simonov. A group of biologists undertook a research on revival of life of a few humans who were clinically dead in a ward. The revival was indicated by light impulses emitted from the speech section of the brain projected on the TV. I was astounded by this news. A member of the Ovcinnikov Soviet Academy who passed away recently once told the Soviet people regarding a fact of equal importance. He and his colleagues discovered the human speech gene. Whereas the said gene is not found in the organism of the primetes, such as the gorilla and the chimpanzee or in the organism of the dolphins. As such, it is pointless to attempt to teach animals to talk because only human beings have such ability. This is one of the reasons he rejected the Charles Darwin theory of evolution that human beings are the descendents of the apes. We are

the descendents of our parents and our forefathers, and not from the apes. This fact means that the apes that do not possess the speech gene cannot possibly attain the intellectual status of the human being. Although a human possesses the said gene, it can easily deteriorate and be like that of the ape.

This is hard work. Still, as the poet says at the end: 'I feel elated to know that everyone on this earth, be he the follower of Christianity, Islam or Buddhism, whether a capitalist or a communist, can understand our prime need, namely, the preservation of life on our world that is full of beauty and conflict. Long live POETRY!'

Turkey's paper is called 'The Mysterious Sounds Under the Blue Vault (of Heaven)'. He has hardly any English but he is determined to read an English translation he has brought with him. The physical agony he goes through is extraordinary – he makes sounds rather than meanings, his voice tightens and knots; each word, each noise, brings a fresh measure of pain:

> The harmonious order of words leads us to poem, the mysterious thing. Poet wraps the skeleton of poem with tulle and produces this pure and great poem. This poem is the harmonious language of poet's inner world henceforth. Perhaps it is the common voice of humanity rising to the blue vault (of heaven). Which language the poet speaks or what nationality he is is not important because all the poets share the same common and universal language. Poet is the person who sees the thing which we cannot see and understands the language of lines, figures and harmony, and then who teaches us this magical language. Poet constructs new musical structures by adding words to his poem. He sends mysterious messages. He travels us on different climates. In fact, poet is the person who searches for the 'absolute' existence and the poems written by him are the mysterious name of this search.
> And there are many secrets and treasure under this blue vault and the keys of these are given to the poet's tongue to open them.

Afterwards he collapses into his seat – exhausted by language.

During the week my need for 'correct' English vanishes. Talking will do, saying things which mean things. After a day or two I find I have stopped using the definite article. Deviations from the norm become the norm.

Bahasa Malaysia is interesting. Malaysia is a culture without irony, and I find myself wondering what, as it were, lies behind this absence. It may be a matter of belief. But the language makes many of its plurals by repeating words – *buku buku* is books – and it is hard to be sure that such a language could accommodate irony and survive. Nevertheless, there are some interesting repetitions. Someone tells me that *child child* can sometimes mean adult; and *pig pig*, piggy bank.

The poets come and go. 'Ladies and gentlemen, hello from England,' says Sebastian Barker. The Chinese poet mounts the platform at the start of what is announced as an open question session. He stands at the microphone and tells us about himself. He is not supposed to do this; he is supposed to ask questions, but he has a long paper which he had been expecting to read, 'My Creative Experiences'. He explains that he is a translator and Professor of World Poetry. His pen-name means 'spray of the brine'. He was in a camp during the Cultural Revolution. 'I have good luck to experience life in its vivid variety . . . Poetry is the best language of understanding . . . the shortest route between people's hearts.' This is the first time he has left China, the first time he has been able to talk to English speakers in his almost perfect English.

We break for lunch at the Shah Alam Holiday Inn. The lunch is hosted by the Menteri Besar (Chief Minister) of Selangor. There is another poetry reading and, though I am not in the programme, I am summoned to read 'Megasin'.
    Later we visit the mosque. It is impressive, all right – space, water, tiles and silence. I am most impressed by the shoe racks, and the various prohibitions which deal with dress, with menstruating women.
    We look around the museum. There is a wonderful framed enlargement of a photograph showing the Kuala Lumpur flood of 1926. The pith-helmeted men of the British army stand in water up to their waists in the middle of a city street. They face the camera as if nothing unusual is happening.
    The museum has several glass cases full of tiny cannons. 'Ho, ho, excuse me,' says Dr Boris Panikov. 'Do you know, these cannons, they are small. This is because the Dutch are knowing Malays are very little people.' He chuckles and repeats his joke to all who come along.

The poetry coach takes us into the jungle – a rather Disneylandish jungle called the Malaysian Agriculture Park. This is a 1300-hectare project run by the Agriculture Ministry both as a research and education centre and as a tourist attraction. It is divided into various sections: a padi garden, a spice and beverage garden, a mushroom museum, an animal park, even an 'Idlyllic' Village:

> Come to the Idlyllic Village and the visitor may see for himself the various aspects that make up the ideal homestead Malaysian farmers themselves seek to make their own. Peaceful and laid back, yet vibrant in its make up, this beautiful setting is every farmer's dream of the perfect . . .

Our destination is the Peak of Fine Arts, a mid-jungle open-air stage on the Greek model. It is the home of the wonderfully named Agro-Theatre, brainchild of the Minister of Agriculture himself. The Agro-Theatre troupe are all full-time employees of the Ministry of Agriculture. 'They are talented and familiar with the vision of the Agricultural policy. In today's presentation, songs, dances and poetry will be rendered in a message-oriented package, depicting the effort of the government and the people of this country to eradicate poverty.'

We watch the performance, along with large bands of schoolchildren who stay on for the international poetry reading which follows. Serbo-Croatian in the manicured jungle. 'Lord, what age is this one / when my love is gone?' I am listed to read on the printed programme, but am not called. One addition to the programme is Maralia Gozo, 'renowned singer and poet from Brazil'. She attended the last World Poetry Reading with her Japanese husband, who was one of the guest poets. (They met at Iowa – where several of the international poets seem to have spent time as students. So America is here after all.) Maralia is a real performer, and has a range of bright costumes which emphasise her body. She puts her mouth around the microphone and makes moaning noises to a backdrop of electronic sound. Before each performance she says: 'Hello, my name is Maralia. I am from Brazil, and I am happy to share my songs with you.' Her first song has a title which seems to be 'Janola'. She is amplified voice and amplified body: total presence. The small Malay men whoop and shriek; their trousers fill with tiny cannons.

Prayom reads today – a poem called 'Missing', which he performs in three absolutely different styles. The first is a sort of prose rendition of the words; the other versions are sung and chanted. Each seems sadder than the last:

> I nearly cry at the thought of home.
> I've been away because of dismay:
> My home disappeared in the fire;
> Who will wipe the ashes from my eyes.

Prayom lives in Bangkok, but comes from a provincial village in the north which was burned by Communist insurgents:

> 'Sweet vegetables, sweet tamarind, white rice,
> Beautiful women, virtuous men,'
> O the days that sleep forever in the earth,
> Is your name dead or alive, o Nakae?

Throughout the performance I watch him, a small figure in black and white, through the viewfinder of his video camera. I am filming Prayom for his family and friends at home, and vaguely aware that his poem is about the impossibility of going home

At the hotel, he tells me about Thai poetry: the different ways of rendering each poem, the complex systems of rhyme and assonance, cadence and repetition. I always thought skaldic verse must be impossibly difficult to write; but this sounds like the hardest poetry in the world.

We exchange books – and he also gives me a keyring with a tiny Thai cushion attached to it. His wife gave him a plastic bag filled with souvenir keyrings before he left. In my book he writes: 'For Bill, my dear room-mate.'

An evening reading at Central Market. Central Market is in downtown KL. It is rather like London's Covent Garden – an up-market market, a recycled version of a place which was once scruffy, old, real. It is now part of tourist Malaysia; its beautifully preserved exterior houses souvenir stalls, boutiques and restaurants. The poets dismount from their coach and are greeted by a band of small boys doing stylised martial arts.

As we enter the market, young women drape our upper bodies with coloured sashes. We shine in the night, marked out and important, uncomfortably like Miss Universe contestants. We, too, are part of tourist Malaysia. Puzzled shoppers draw back as we promenade among them in our sashes. There is a sprinkling of applause. We pass through a display of our own books and photographs. There is *Zoetropes*. And there is my face beside it: a Robert Cross shot, xeroxed from his book of writers' portraits, faxed through to Kuala Lumpur, then xeroxed once again. Most of the international poets just look ten years younger, but I have dissolved and drifted and am hardly there at all.

The display includes sample verses. Some of the English versions have interesting moments, like this one from a poem by Germany:

> The method of abroad
> just brought me strepafaction
> – not the inner freedom

We leave the market by another door and find ourselves at a small sound shell on the riverbank. We sit, distinctive in our poetry sashes, while Malay and Chinese children perform traditional dances. Lizards scuttle up and down the stage backdrop. It is cute and multicultural. A small Tamil girl reads a poem she has written for the international poets:

> Malaysia is a lovely land
> Everyone will lend a helping hand
> The food is quite massive
> Everything is here to receive

The poets read. Children crowd around asking for autographs. This must be how the All Blacks feel. My pen knocks against something metallic on my sash. It is a badge with a cheerful monkey on it. 'Central Market,' says the monkey. 'Visit Malaysia Year 1990.'

28 October
Today we are travelling to the state of Negeri Sembilan. Meantime, the morning paper carries the New Zealand election results. 'Annihilated' is the word used to describe what has happened to Labour.

There are two coaches, one loaded with international poets, the other with local poets. For a moment we stop by a cemetery. It is a Christian graveyard full of Second World War dead. The large flat field contains many small unmarked stones, like distance markers on a roadway. A car is parked beside one grave. A middle-aged Chinese couple have placed six candles on the slab. They light them and stand still a moment. Then they get in the car and drive across the grass to another grave where they light more candles. They come back to check the first grave. The flames seem to sputter out in the breeze, then spring back to life like trick candles from a joke shop. Now the couple get in their car and drive away.

Negeri Sembilan is south of Selangor. After we cross the state boundary, we stop at a cultural complex, whose main building – though it now houses an exhibition of traditional costumes – was originally constructed as the pavilion for the 1984 International Koran Reading Competition. There is dance and music, some menhirs which I photograph, buildings whose rooflines follow the Minangkabau style, said to be based on buffalo horns. Each of the poets is presented with a hard-boiled egg attached to a paper flower.

The coaches move on. Something must be wrong: the sound of wailing sirens can be heard. But we have been picked up by a police escort – sirens proclaim us as we go, red lights flash. Throughout the day all other traffic pulls over to the side of the road as our poetry motorcade zooms by. We visit a Sultan's palace. Lunch is a banquet with the Chief Minister of Selangor – a diminutive version of David Lange who makes a long, witty, wholly impromptu speech in Bahasa Malaysia which none of the poets understand. The Malaysians roar with laughter. The Chief Minister presents each of us with a specially inscribed lacquered coconut shell. We present him with framed posters promoting the World Poetry Reading. Back on the bus, someone explains that the video team which dogs us everywhere we go is making a permanent record of the week for the Dewan Bahasa. We can order copies: US$10.00.

Much later in the day – after the motorcade has passed through rustic scenery and undulating hills, rubber plantations and palm oil groves – we arrive in the grounds of a pseudo-Tudor guest-house, a seaside retreat which dates from the days of the Raj. We can eat here, swim if we like. There is an abandoned summer house on an island at the end of the pier. It is hot and steamy – vaguely vandalised. Some of the Muslim poets go out to the island and pray.

It is not quite clear who is who; but we are meeting with some of the writers of Negeri Sembilan, the local PEN branch. There is a banquet under marquees; and an impromptu poetry reading through a portable sound system. Norway reads. Switzerland reads. Then there is an interruption. A furious man yells at the compere. The poetry reading has gone on too long; it is preventing people from observing evening prayers. 'So we will be stopped,' says the compere, 'for our ten minutes or so for those of the prayerful to have a wash and say their prayers and then our readings will continue.' The readings never resume, and eventually we are taken by coach, a ten-minute ride through the dark, to Port Dickson's Festival arena. We descend into a giant amusement park. There are lights and crowds of people – sideshows, merry-go-rounds, ferris wheels. The poets are the evening concert's highlight. Seasoned troupers by now, we cheer each other and strut our stuff. I read 'Zoetropes' through a sound system which easily drowns out the chattering teenagers drifting by, the girls screaming from the nearby Horror House, the motorbikes which roar around the Wall of Death.

29 October: Discussion on World Contemporary Issues
In the hotel lobby, poets sign each other's programmes. 'Thank you,' says Sri Lanka, 'it is for my history.' Jordan writes a message in every programme: 'Hello! Be happy, unhappy, be whatever you want. You are a poet.' Someone says that yesterday's lunchtime readings were on television.

Today we visit the Dewan Bahasa. We are greeted by the Director, who makes a speech. We watch a split-screen audiovisual display about the Dewan and applaud when it ends. 'Multivision show,' says the programme. We ascend by lift to the top of the building where we find ourselves in a great council room with a horseshoe-shaped seating plan. The room is full of flags and portable shrubs; there is an expensive parquet floor. It looks like one of those chambers where international conferences take place. But then, we are an international conference: we even sit behind individual microphones. This must be the 'Discussion on World Contemporary Issues'.

The moderator tells us that this is meant to be informal. 'Any topic under the sun except poetry.' He beams.

The international poets who happen to be women have been waiting for a forum like this one. Each of them wants to ask the same question. In the event it is Mousse Boulanger from Switzerland who speaks.

'I wonder if the Malaysian poets here, women or men, will say something about the position of women in this country? Some of us are a little puzzled about it, you see!'

The moderator sits a little straighter. 'All is equal in Malaysia,' he says. 'But let me say, Islam, well, we should have a separate section where we will discuss this. But put aside this question for the meantime, I thank you.'

Black clouds have been gathering at the windows; now the moderator's words are accompanied by rolling thunder. Rain rattles on the roof above our heads.

A long silence produces a more specific question. The questioner is an elegant, middle-aged Japanese woman, with short blue hair. Where has she come from? She wishes to know about polygamy. Is it a Malaysian matter or an Islamic matter? A Malaysian woman at one end of the horseshoe raises her hand – she would like to make a reply, or add a comment. The chair ignores her, looking anxiously around the room. Kemala comes to the rescue.

'In Malaysia, unlike Islam, men have to have first wife's permission before taking another wife. So this is very different from Islam. But actually women are very privileged in our society. It is great privilege here for women.

They are not inferior, they are not even equal, no, in Malaysia they are privileged indeed!'

The Western women look astonished. But now a poet from the Middle East is on his feet, quaking with fury. 'These matters,' he says, 'they are entirely accidental. I know people who sometimes have three wives. For example, the first wife is a cousin who gets no husband and because he is good to his family he has her out of pity. Yes, pity. This is goodness, you see, absolute goodness.' His voice gets louder as he goes on. 'So there was a second wife. *Of course there would be.* So now the second wife, she gets handicapped. And there is the third wife therefore. This is how such things happen. And so I say to you: *Don't you compare cultures!* There are things we do not like in your culture. But do I say them? So this is not a great issue, I think. Three wives, and it is all fine. This is cultures and how they work. The world is a place of conscience and judgement and these are all for us to show. Now let us get rid of this issue and go to other things.'

But the astonished room cannot get rid of the issue. The Malaysian woman – a Tamil, I realise – still has her hand up. There is a sort of smile on her face; she knows she will never get the nod from the chair. Some of the Western men have decided to be peacemakers. Dr Boris Panikov rises.

'I am wishing to warn the women gathered here of the dangers of revolution. Progress, yes. But revolution, it is very dangerous. Very dangerous indeed. I am from Soviet Union, as you know. We know revolution. Oh how we know revolution. So abstain from revolution if you can. This is what I have to say to you women of the world. Thank you.'

He sits but the thunder and the rain go on. People glance around the unlucky horseshoe. Mousse Boulanger decides to defuse things herself. She shifts discussion to the political structure of Malaysia. How many states are there in Malaysia? How do central and district governments work together and divide responsibilities?

At this point a chair is pushed back on my left, and Merlinda C. Bobis (Philippines) walks from the room. She has had enough. On my right, Anne Szumigalski (Canada) has made a page-size doodle on her pad – a giant tree-like woman totters on spindly shoes; her body flaps and flows, giving birth to a hundred faces.

Sebastian Barker asks a question. 'I wonder what is the writer's responsibility to the United Nations and to individual politicians? What is the writer's role really?' Silence. 'What do you think?' says the moderator. 'Oh. What do I think? Well, I'm just asking the question to get the discussion going again. But if you really want to know, I think we need to talk to individual politicians when we meet them. This is what poets everywhere must do.' Anne Szumigalski throws down her doodle and begins to speak into her microphone. Around the horseshoe men look anxious. Then there is a deafening crash from the sky – the lights go out, our microphones go dead, the thunder rolls.

30 October
Prayom departs; we photograph each other and shake hands. The Norwegians and Sebastian Barker are off to Bangkok, too. I find Chinatown's Petaling Street and buy fake designer gear – hammering the prices down by about twenty-five per cent, feeling pleased in the way that only someone who knows he has not really bargained at all feels pleased.

The formalities of the week are over. No more readings. But in the afternoon we are on the coach again. Some poets whisper that the furious Middle Eastern poet had been describing himself. He currently has two wives – each in a different country. Who knows? We find ourselves at the National University. Malay nationalism and Islam are serious on this campus, hard to separate one from the other. Most female students are fully covered, and peer through pillar-box eye openings. The University is devoted to Malay culture, we are told, and is mostly a research institute – no undergraduate students.

We meet the Director of the Institute of Malay Culture, who makes a small speech about Bahasa Malaysia and gives us a book of his own, a collection of polemical pieces on nationalist and ethnic matters.

The international poets take turns reading poems to one another around the table. This impromptu session is the most enjoyable and useful reading of all: something to do with poetry and cultural exchange begins to happen. Our host, the director, listens for a few minutes – then makes his way to an adjoining room where, fully visible and audible through a glass wall, he engages in animated conversation with a colleague.

The final event, the final evening. We are to dine at the house of the poet, Usman Awang. We have been told that it will be possible to drink alcohol this evening: the age of orange cordial is over. The coach will make a special stop at a bottle store. The international poets, led by the Eastern Europeans, descend on the bottle store. I buy half-a-dozen cans of Tiger lager. The Pakistani poet buys two large bottles of cod-liver oil – for some reason sales of cod-liver oil are prohibited in Pakistan. He is happy: already he can see his family rejoicing, running to meet him from the plane.

When we get to Usman Awang's, we are told to leave our purchases on the bus; we may be able to fetch them later – but first someone must ascertain that it is really all right. Usman Awang has a large, elegant residence. There are tables on a patio, a small band, many people milling about, stumbling over the roaming video crew. I find myself at a table next to a man who introduces himself as the Prime Minister's Secretary. Ann Szumigalski is at the table; also Merlinda C. Bobis from the Philippines, Tom Shapcott, and a young North American who teaches law at a local university. We eat and discuss Malaysian fruit – its variety, its abundance.

'And yet the oddest thing,' says the young lawyer. 'I bought some bananas the other day which came from the Philippines.'

'Excuse me,' says the Prime Minister's Secretary, addressing the table generally, 'excuse me but I must tell you that this is untrue.'

'Oh, it's true,' says the lawyer, sipping his orange cordial. 'I saw the little stickers on them: "Produce of the Philippines".'

'We do grow a lot of bananas in the Philippines,' says Merlinda.

'No, no, no, this is impossible! Malaysia does not import bananas, it exports them!'

'But I had to peel the little stickers off.'

'You are wrong! You are wrong! I declare that you are wrong!' The Prime Minister's Secretary will brook no further argument. He rises and leaves the table.

Word is passed around that we may fetch our alcohol. But rain is pouring, and the coach is parked a block away. Anyway, now a microphone has appeared and guests and hosts sing songs. The Malays sing pantoums, which turn out to be lively improvisational choral pieces; the international poets sing their national songs. I grind through a rousing version of 'Tutira Mai', and when the party is about to break up and our hosts are half-heartedly humming 'Auld Lang Syne' to an insecure guitar – at a loss both for words and for melody – I find myself seized by a strange desire to assert whatever cultural heritage I have. Swept forward on the tide of my own foolishness, I seize the microphone and lead the assembled poets in several rounds of 'Auld Lang Syne'. Tom Shapcott is pushed forward to join me, and together we drift around the text. I am beginning to enjoy this – perhaps I could go on to 'Now Is the Hour'? Or 'Ten Guitars'? 'You Are My Sunshine'? – no trouble, just let me get organised here, whatever does Usman Awang put in his orange cordial? – but in fact we seem to be on the bus again, groaning through the night towards the Holiday Inn, downtown Kuala Lumpur, where as I climb into my own wee bed it occurs to me that all of this will be on the official video.

31 October
People are leaving today. Many of the poets have cards and exchange them. Sri Lanka's card says:

> *Pandit Wimal Abhayasundere*:
> Poet, Writer, Lyricist.

Turkey has a printed card which says: *Mehmed Atilla Maras Engineer.* Underneath he has written in blue ink: *poet.*

At breakfast Merlinda C. Bobis talks about the Russians. After the scene at the Dewan Bahasa, David Kugultinov, foe of Stalin and comrade of Gorbachev, explained to her, through his interpreter, Dr Boris Panikov, that such a beautiful girl as she should be having babies, not writing poems. In fact, he explained, it is a well-known fact that to men falls the task of making beautiful poems. It is hard work, man's work. Merlinda does not need to write poems; she can simply look beautiful; she is a poem.

McPimp
I go shopping and come across the Kuala Lumpur McDonald's, where I order a shake and a McRendan, a spiced Malaysian burger. I meet my first dubious fellow, who lurks nearby, then slips across and asks about my shake. 'Is ice-cream in there? How you like Kuala Lumpur? How long you here?' When he discovers I've been here a week and am leaving later today, his face drops, he slides away. I tuck into my McRendan.

Then my friend is back, he sits and gives me his name. I give him mine, and he calls me Mr Bill.

'You would like my sister, Mr Bill. She is going to your country. New Zealand, isn't it? She will study, you can come to our house and tell her all these things. She will be grateful.'

The circumstances of his story grow more elaborate as he goes along. He names the city she will go to – 'Where you from? Wellington? Well, amazing! This is where she is going, Mr Bill, she will be please to see you,' – and throws in a sick mother, whom his sister nurses. He himself is in the import/export business. If only I were staying longer, he would take me to see his sister, I could give her advice, and she is very friendly, very *loving.*

'Do you have time for today perhaps, Mr Bill? A quick visit to my sister?'

No, I say, I must catch my aeroplane and before that I must buy gifts for my wife and children. Can my friend suggest any good places to shop?

'Oh, anywhere at all. Well, very nice to see you.' He shakes my hand and is gone.

Wings of Gold

*

I have hardly seen Malaysia. Air-conditioned coaches, international hotels, lecture halls. But the country is an economic prodigy. Last year the state of Johore created 130,000 jobs and is anxious about how it can fill the 250,000 new job vacancies which are projected in the next decade. The country as a whole expects a ten per cent growth rate during 1991. I have met something of the Malaysia that is trying to create the culture to match the economic growth. The government has made huge investments in culture and education; even its combining of the Tourism and Culture portfolios in a single ministry seems obviously sensible.

When I get back home, I will learn that New Zealand's new Minister of Tourism is John Banks, who is also the Minister of Police.

The Kuala Lumpur World Poetry Reading has very little to do with world poetry. But it is not just an item on the Malaysian tourist calendar. It is mostly about Malay nationalism and self-esteem; a small part of the process by which Malay culture is being transformed into Malaysian culture. Bahasa Malaya is now called Bahasa Malaysia: it is to be the language of all the people of the nation. As for the world, its languages and poets are here as part of that nation-building exercise: our job is to dignify the single language, the single culture, of our hosts. Of course one or two of us, as usual, are learning the extent of our own ignorance.

The Malays are quiet, watchful, generous people. Anxiety and hospitality are equally matched in many of those I meet. In that sense it is just like being at home. The Prime Minister's Secretary's preoccupation with bananas is simply one way in which anxiety surfaces. Throughout the week people ask me if the Fan Club – a New Zealand pop group which has (I think) a Malay singer – is as much admired in New Zealand as in Malaysia. Since I have never heard of the Fan Club, my answers are rather evasive, and the watchful faces grow even more watchful.

On the day I leave Malaysia, it is announced that the price of soft drinks is going up. The Australian and New Zealand Graduates' Association of Malaysia is gathering for a talk on air-conditioning systems by engineer Paul Lau. At the Sapphire Discotheque there will be an attractive gift for the Most Outrageous Halloween guest. My horoscope says: 'You have nowhere to go today but back to the beginning – and where is that? You'll know before the day is out.'

DOUBTFUL SOUNDS

Koala Lumpur

Yesterday Malaysia Airlines – which has just taken on twenty ex-Air New Zealand pilots – made its inaugural flight to Vienna. They imported the Vienna Ladies Orchestra to mark the occasion. The Vienna Ladies Orchestra is a remarkable combo – it can split into three groups to perform in three different countries simultaneously.

And today it is Malaysia Airlines' inaugural flight to Brisbane. My journey home will be via Australia. Glamorous hostesses prowl about the departure lounge, distributing tiny koalas and promotional brochures for the Gold Coast. High above us a large television screen is filled with skyscrapers and ocean, the joys of Surfers.

A giant koala bear is waddling about the lounge. It poses with Japanese tourists for photographs. It snuggles up to a pair of puzzled bodybuilders. Small Malay children scream and burst into tears. The koala bear advances mercilessly through the room, flanked by airline staff, holding out its hand to everyone it passes.

'Giddy might!' says a high-pitched Asian voice.

I look up. The koala bear is standing beside me. 'Giddy might!' says the tiny voice from deep inside the costume. It holds out its paw.

At this very moment – it is exactly 7.00 p.m. – the voice of the muezzin summoning the faithful to prayer calls from the airport public address system. Above us the television screen fills with all the domes and spires of Islam.

I look back at the koala. 'Giddy might,' it says.

'Gidday,' I say, and reach to take its hand.

Sport 6, 1991

THE POETRY FILE

Christmas

Christmas Day

Our Christmas Day is blue and gold,
And warm our Christmas Night.
Blue for the colour of Mary's cloak
Soft in the candle-light.
Gold for the glow of the Christmas Star
That shone serene and bright.

Warm for the love of the little babe
Safe in the oxen stall.
We know our Christmas by these signs
And yet around my wall
On Christmas cards the holly gleams
And snow flakes coldly fall,
And robins I have never seen
Pipe out a Christmas call.

Margaret Mahy

Whatever happened to Christmas? Or, more specifically, whatever happened to Christmas in New Zealand poetry? The season has had plenty of jolly and unjolly moments in drama and fiction – as event and setting it brings people together and drives them apart, just the way good narrative should. Bruce Mason made excellent use of the seasonal ritual in *The End of the Golden Weather*, as did Robert Lord, who even announced the fact in the title of his play: *Joyful and Triumphant*. Perhaps our most memorable and unforgiving Christmas setting is in Maurice Gee's *Games of Choice*, where insults and home truths thrive in an atmosphere of sweltering heat and frayed tempers. My hunch is that most New Zealand writers would willingly assent to Alice Thomas Ellis's droll, desperate prayer: 'Forgive us our Christmases as we forgive those that Christmas against us.'

So the novelists and playwrights have had a great time. But our poets seem to have done less well. At any rate, they have certainly done less – and perhaps this is because the Christmas tradition insists on certain conventional properties. There are the robins and snow which Margaret Mahy mentions, along with all the items associated with the birth of Christ: shepherds, wise men, a star, a mother and baby, oxen. How can a poet be true to a list like that and yet accommodate the world of summer heat, beaches and barbecues?

Margaret Mahy's 'Christmas Day' was written for children – it was first published in the *School Journal* in 1965 – and it focuses this problem. It does so very deftly, too, for it's a kind of reverse sonnet (six lines, then eight), whose back-to-front behaviour nicely mirrors what it has to say. How can we bridge the gap between the world we see and the one we carry in our heads? How can the Christmas proclaimed for us in the songs and poems of the Northern Hemisphere be made to belong in New Zealand?

It's a fairly familiar question in our literature. Some poets, like the Anglican vicar J.R. Hervey, have simply added to the old seasonal production line, offering a kind of placeless Christian celebration. And this may be as good a solution as any, for there has often been something slightly embarrassing about the way others have tried to acclimatise the familiar Christmas tale. For example, Eileen Duggan's 'A New Zealand Christmas':

> Had my Lord been born here in the time of rata
> Three dark-eyed chieftains would have knelt to Him
> With greenstone and mats and the proud huia feather,
> And the eyes of Mary watching would grow dim.

Or there's Peter Cape, setting his poem, 'Nativity', in a roadman's shack, and turning his wise men into gold miners and musterers:

> She sat at the edge of the fernstalk bed,
> And she watched, but she didn't understand,
> While they put those bundles by the baby's head;
> That river nugget into his hand.

Of course, several of our poets have had a go at Christmas. Ursula Bethell did a Christmas poem; there are two by Janet Frame (one of them called

'Christmas and Death') in *The Pocket Mirror*; Hone Tuwhare has produced at least one (his child has a halo but is also a 'shitty-arsed baby'); and Bub Bridger has done a nice piece of seasonal reproof, telling someone off for sending her a photograph as a gift: 'When I want a picture of you / I'll ask you / To buy me a camera'.

But trying to adapt Christmas to 'local conditions' is probably a pointless task. Our *experience* of Christmas – and much else for that matter – is composed of a mixture of inner and outer worlds, and plenty of contradictions come with the mixture. That sense of seasonal contradiction is nicely articulated in John Newton's 'White Manuka', where after 'one of those slow / shitty springs' the manuka is still flowering in late December. 'We cut a branch / and festooned it with the customary / Christmas kitsch,' producing a final image of

> the glass balls
> buried, red and copper,
> among the white manuka flowers.

Newton's lines welcome the incongruous as part of their harmony, and maybe our Christmas poems, those still to be written, need to make a place for the everyday pleasures of incongruity. As Margaret Mahy herself put it in an essay she wrote some twenty-five years after 'Christmas Day':

> The imaginative truth and the factual truth may be at odds with each other but personally I still need those opposites to make Christmas come alive for me . . . the sunny sea in front of me and the simultaneous awareness of short days, long cold nights and snow on dark bare branches.

Mistakes

Strange Type

> I wrote: in the dark cavern of our birth.
> The printer had it tavern, which seems better:
> But herein lies the subject of our mirth,
> Since on the next page death appears as dearth.
> So it may be that God's word was distraction,
> Which to our strange type appears destruction,
> Which is bitter.

Malcolm Lowry, of course, has two strange types in mind: the type of man he was himself (alcoholic, doom-laden, hell-bound – after all, he wrote *Under the Volcano*), and the type that printers use. Thus the printer's error the poem starts with, where 'cavern' becomes 'tavern', is wryly appropriate.

Words have been going wrong ever since people started putting them on vellum and paper. Was it his too, too solid or his too, too sullied flesh that Shakespeare's Hamlet wished would melt? Cack-handed medieval scribes and drunken compositors have kept generations of textual scholars happy trying to decide such things.

Poetry thrives on incorrectness. There's a story about one poet – W.H. Auden, I think – writing the line: 'And the poets have names for the seas.' Grand stuff, full of boom and bombast. But when the proofs came back from the printer, the line went: 'And the ports have names for the seas.' A far more interesting line, and Auden had the good sense to keep it.

I'm not sure what Auden would have made of the printer's error in this translation of the Old Norse poem 'Voluspa' ('The Sybil's Prophecy') which, after a terrifying apocalyptic vision, offers the closing image of a flying monster: 'The dark dragon from Darkfell / Bears on his opinions the bodies of men.' Auden meant 'pinions', and if he had lived would probably have reinstated them. But what a wonderful mistake!

In fact some of the most memorable moments in English poetry are mistakes. Tennyson's famous commitment to change in 'Locksley Hall' – 'Not in vain the distance beacons. Forward, forward let us range, / Let the great world spin for ever down the ringing grooves of change' – came from a failed attempt to be techonologically up to date.

> When I went by the first train from Liverpool to Manchester (1830) I thought that the wheels ran in a groove. It was a black night, and there was such a vast crowd round the train at the station that we could not see the wheels.

Many of the effects we associate with poems are really mistakes. For example, metaphor is a kind of deliberate error. My love is like a red, red rose? Pretty weird, if you think about it – though not as extreme as Martian verse.

Martian verse was fashionable in the United Kingdom a few years ago; the label comes from Craig Raine's poem, 'A Martian Sends a Postcard Home', where the imaginary speaker gets everything wrong in precisely the way poets do. He makes metaphors, and thus makes the familar exotic. Here is how he sees books:

Mistakes

> Caxtons are mechanical birds with many wings
> and some are treasured for their markings –
>
> they cause the eyes to melt
> or the body to shriek without pain.
>
> I have never seen one fly, but
> sometimes they perch on the hand . . .

Another kind of mistake springs from wordplay: some words sound like other words. Gerard Manley Hopkins liked to let words like 'heaven' and 'haven' infiltrate one another, and in the line from Tennyson quoted above, the word 'beckons' is a ghostly presence behind what looks like a mistake, 'beacons'.

Readers can make mistakes, too. Early in T.S. Eliot's *The Waste Land*, there's a passage evoking London, the 'unreal City', just after World War I. City commuters are described, and then a voice says:

> There I saw one I knew, and stopped him crying: 'Stetson!
> You who were with me in the ships at Mylae!'

Learned commentaries on Eliot's poem tell us that Mylae was a Roman trade war back in 260 BC – and that Eliot's point is that all wars are one war. But when I first read *The Waste Land*, the Vietnam War was at its height: I thought automatically of Mi Lai, the village infamously exterminated by American troops; while Eliot's ships reminded me of helicopters.

I suppose my mistake was an anachronism. If so, it was in tune with the rest of *The Waste Land*, which builds a collage of meaning out of jumbled, anachronistic details. Our century's most famous poem is really a network of deliberate mistakes.

English poetry's least deliberate mistake belongs to Robert Browning. A wonderfully innocent man, Browning had the notion that the word 'twat' was part of a nun's attire, somehow equivalent to a monk's cowl. Hence his curious description, in *Pippa Passes*, of late-night woodland revels:

> Then, owls and bats,
> Cowls and twats,
> Monks and nuns, in a cloister's moods,
> Adjourn to the oak-stump pantry!

Long Poems

A long poem is a contradiction in terms. Or so Edgar Allen Poe once observed, probably while taking a short break from horror stories. Poetry's task, he wrote, was to excite, 'by elevating the soul.' But excitements are transient things, almost by definition, and 'cannot be sustained throughout a composition of any length.'

Maybe. But none of this has prevented modern writers running to length any more than it daunted the authors of *Beowulf* or *Paradise Lost*. One can see why poets keep on keeping on: they want to seem at least as important as novelists. Quantity somehow implies substance, and a long poem promises both narrative stretch and the grandeur of public reference. Ezra Pound called the epic 'the speech of the nation through the mouth of one man'. Well, you can't do the speech of the nation in a haiku.

Our century's answer to all this has been the messy, fragmented, modernist splendours of Pound's *Cantos*, or the occasional verse novel, or (most of all) the loose, loosely personal sequence developed out of older sonnet sequences (Baxter's *Jerusalem Sonnets* would be a local example). The Australians have probably been producing more long poems per capita than anyone else in the world lately, but the English poet Craig Raine's *History: The Home Movie* is the most impressive recent venture. Penguin have been promoting it as a novel (it was entered for the Booker Prize), an epic poem, a movie, a masterpiece – and you can't say fairer than that – but really it sits somewhere between the verse novel and the sequence, discontinuous yet focussed, rather like a collection of linked short stories (James Joyce's *Dubliners*, say, or Katherine Mansfield's New Zealand tales).

Raine's book does build up a sense of history. In the course of eighty-seven poems arranged in chronological order, each a few pages long, each with a date as part of its title, we meet two families: the Russian Pasternaks (who include the author of *Doctor Zhivago*) and the Raines, a lower-middle class English family. The public events of history occur, including two world wars, and the poem ends with the pairing of Lisa and Craig, a Pasternak and a Raine – as if to suggest that the designs of history only make sense when they come to rest in the small linkages of the personal.

In fact Raine's *History* is a wonderful interweaving of the public and the personal. The great figures of twentieth-century history – Churchill, Lenin, Haile Selassie – make their appearances, but they are simply actors on the day-to-day stage of ordinary life. Presumably Raine's history constitutes a home movie not only because of its bumpy discontinuities, but also because it is so dense with the trivial domestic detail. He has Janet Frame's gift for preserving the everyday world: he knows the names of implements and household things and vanished brand names; his movie is packed with close-ups of objects which are nearly lost from memory.

Craig Raine is best known, of course, not for epic similes, but for the dazzling tiny comparisons his poems are built on. In his world we are always brought freshly to attention: trout breathe like tweezers; a muscular lizard in the reptile house does its press-ups; a squirrel shudders up a pine. But even Raine's darker moments of comparison make us alert: a bulb 'dangles like a suicide / at the end of its flex'; refugees surrender 'like children / who want to be carried, / lifting their arms'; a rapist shows a woman a razor, and 'a nervous moth of light / flits over the ceiling.'

Raine's history works entirely in the present tense, and can seem less like a succession of events than a network of repetitions: words and phrases repeat, events and people repeat, motifs come and go. There's a great deal of masturbation, and almost every poem seems to have a fly in it (the poem's own voice sometimes seems to belong to a fly on the wall). I guess this is another way of making things particular. In Raine's home movie, flies and masturbation are busy doing duty for the ancient, big-screen visions of mortality and desire.

It's possible to get lost in Raine's book, but that's part of the pleasure. It's especially hard at first to keep track of the characters, and the two family trees which hang like mobiles at the beginning of the poem are a crucial reader-aid. Probably the poem's particularity works against its desire to be a narrative document. Often you feel you're not reading a story but a compendium of lists – successions of scrupulous, astonishing details. Still, history – like God – is in the details, and it is ordinary detail which gives this book its power, its readability and re-readability, and its sense of broader purpose. Craig Raine's poem is witty, violent, tender, wondering, and ruthlessly observant – an instructive lesson in how to write a long poem without being longwinded.

Concentration

There are plenty of definitions of poetry loose in the universe, but the one I like always gets attributed to an anonymous schoolgirl. 'Poetry,' she says, 'is that stuff in books which doesn't quite reach to the margins.'

Part of the joke is the impossibility of defining poetry. The grand definitions are pompous and tell you nothing – so maybe the way poems *look* will do? But there's also a truth in the schoolgirl's definition – to the eye a poem seems crammed onto the page, with plenty of white space round about. All of a sudden I can hear a voice from Treasury, complaining about the waste of paper. But that image of a text unnaturally compressed and concentrated tells us something about the way in which a poem uses words.

The most obvious forms of concentration happen when a poem is short. Brevity can produce astonishing resonance – as in Ezra Pound's famous 'In a Station of the Metro', which is a sort of soundbite that echoes on forever:

> The apparition of these faces in the crowd;
> Petals on a wet, black bough.

But what of this poem by Gerard Manley Hopkins

> *Spring and Fall*
> to a young child
>
> Margaret, are you grieving
> Over Goldengrove unleaving?
> Leaves, like the things of man, you
> With your fresh thoughts care for, can you?
> Ah! as the heart grows older
> It will come to such sights colder
> By and by, nor spare a sigh
> Though worlds of wanwood leafmeal lie;
> And yet you *will* weep and know why.
> Now no matter, child, the name:
> Sorrow's springs are the same.
> Nor mouth had, no nor mind, expressed
> What heart heard of, ghost guessed:
> It is the blight man was born for,
> It is Margaret you mourn for.

At first sight, 'Spring and Fall' is like a syrupy autumnal painting designed for a jigsaw or box of chocolates. But it is almost a textbook example of how a poem can condense vast meanings into a small space.

One way in which this happens has to do with ambiguity. Hopkins isn't in the business of offering ambiguity for its own sake. Rather, when he can find a word or phrase which offers two appropriate meanings, he grabs it. There's the way he manages word order, for example. Which words go with which? In the poem's opening sentence it's impossible to tell whether 'unleaving' refers to Goldengrove, the piece of woodland whose leaves are turning gold and falling, or to Margaret, who seems fixed in the place of her distress, unable to shift her gaze from what upsets her.

Likewise, where does the word 'colder', at the end of line 6, belong? With 'sights' or with 'heart'? Answer: with both. The world will be far, far colder in the future. But Margaret's own heart will be colder, too, for she'll be accustomed to the terrible effects of time. As the rhyme says, older means colder.

There are other kinds of concentration in the poem. The eighth line pushes in (without it the poem would be a sonnet in rhyming couplets), bringing with it a couple of remarkable coinages: 'wanwood' and 'leafmeal'.

Those words don't exist in dictionaries, but we see instantly what Hopkins has in mind: winters where bare and devastated branches hover above a powdery forest floor. Yet if we were to try to write out what Hopkins means in a few, well-intentioned sentences, we would contradict the poem's true power: its ability to give us a complex idea in a moment of instant revelation. (And we would keep finding meanings to add. What else does 'wan' mean? Is the word 'piecemeal' somehow implied? What about 'lie'?)

Sometimes Hopkins overdoes it. His twelfth and thirteenth lines are very difficult. I think that they mean: 'Even if we were unable to articulate all that we sense emotionally and spiritually, it would still be the case that "It is the blight man was born for, / It is Margaret you mourn for".' But it's hard going; you lurch and stumble.

Having started with questions, Hopkins seems to end his poem with answers. But what answers exactly? The last line's lovely turn to the personal, with its thought that Margaret is in fact weeping for her own mortality, is clear enough. But what is 'the blight man was born for'? It helps to know that Hopkins (1844–89) was a Jesuit priest. Most of all it helps to read the poem again.

In fact the poem's 'answer' is waiting quietly in the title, which isn't as innocent as it first seemed. 'Spring and Fall' means more than the seasons, and more than their metaphorical extensions, youth and age. 'Fall' is the 'name' that the poem said didn't matter, the same Fall that James K. Baxter wrote so many poems about. Hopkins has produced a poem about the fallen condition of humankind, everything that follows from Adam and Eve's expulsion from Eden.

So here is a Christian poem about the loss of innocence, which focuses intently on a single child in a single situation. Chekhov once said that rather than try to describe a whole forest at night, you should focus on a piece of broken glass reflecting in the moonlight. Hopkins does just that, concentrating a vast generalisation about human experience into fifteen lines.

AFTERWORD

An E-mail Interview with Andrew Johnston

ANDREW JOHNSTON: Doubtful Sounds *is a big book. Was it a surprise, having gathered the material together, to find you'd written so many essays and reviews and talks over the years?*

BILL MANHIRE: Yes, one of the big surprises. When the project was suggested, I thought that there wouldn't be much there – maybe a few lectures and book reviews – and I began to imagine, with in fact some pleasure, a sort of chapbook version of a book of essays. You know, safely modest, and all that. But then, once I started looking, there was all this *stuff* – which is odd, because I suspect that most of these pieces began as commissions, or were somehow prompted into life by other people. I was asked to write them, not driven to, if that makes sense.

And yet, reading through, there seem to me to be some pretty strong themes, most of all a kind of two-way thing about getting the world into poetry – as in 'Dirty Silence' – and getting poetry into the world, through the Poetry File columns, for example. Do you think those ideas – and accepting commissions to write these essays and reviews and introductions – are part of a general impulse to demystify what writers do?

Well, I think one of the main reasons I've accepted various writing commissions is that it makes me actually do the work. I'm a fatalist, and am sometimes happy to be under the circumstances, especially if I've had some hand in creating them. My innate laziness has to drop away. So that I think over the years I've deliberately put myself, as a writer, into situations where I have felt a sense of obligation to the world around me. Otherwise you find other things to do – family, work, mowing the lawn – and writing of any kind starts to come a long way down the priorities list. It can seem such a

Afterword

selfish thing to want to do. I think that's one reason many people sign up for creative writing workshops: at last someone or something outside themselves is expecting them to deliver the goods – week after week after week. Plus, of course, we've all been trained by the education system to work in terms of deadlines.

'Getting the world into poetry' – I suspect that's my one big obsession. I can't bear the high romantic affectations that are attached to the idea of 'the Poet', and I don't care for poetry that tries to hover above the planet like some abstract mystic flame. In fact, looking over the work in *Doubtful Sounds*, I see that I go on and on about it all the time – dirt, impurity, the muddled dailiness of things. As for the 'getting poetry into the world' thing, that must have something to do with the fact that I've spent much of my life – much to my surprise, really – as a teacher.

The only thing that isn't commissioned – or at least not often – is poetry. It seems to me that the way you use trigger ideas for poems, and encourage others to do so (in the writing course), is a kind of commissioning poems from oneself. Is that to counter that powerful romantic idea that poetry somehow issues forth 'naturally' from the writer's soul or subconscious or heightened sensitivity? Why is that romantic thing – that notion of the 'poetic' – still so powerful anyway?

I guess it's powerful because it's partly true – at least in the sense that anyone who writes poetry discovers that you can never simply produce to order. Good intentions and hard work aren't enough, and there really are moments when you feel inspired. Something beyond the control of your conscious mind prompts you to produce work. Whether it's deep memory, or a damsel with a dulcimer, I don't know. But it certainly happens. It would be stupid, though, just to hang around waiting for the lightning bolt to strike from heaven. It makes sense to somehow tempt and encourage a sort of slow, electrical storm. The ways in which I do this include reading other poets – you get 'inspired' by example, by the atmosphere you're suddenly breathing. Or just by writing a lot. Two pages of inert phrase-making will often produce a wonderful verbal opportunity near the top of the third page. Actually, I think I preach these things more than I practise them. Nor do I use exercise work much myself; but when I use exercises as a teacher it's to oblige new writers to surprise themselves, to stumble on to possibilities they hadn't really anticipated. Constraint prompts accident, which leads to mystery and surprise and imaginative discovery. Maybe mystery is the big thing. People talk a lot about clarity as one of the goals of poetry – but if writers aren't finding their way into mystery, even as they try to clarify something for themselves, then they might as well forget the whole deal. I think I may be starting to contradict myself . . .

But trying to demystify what poets do, while preserving the right of poems to be mysterious – making the world safe for mystery, so to speak – that doesn't sound like a contradiction, or at least, if it is, it's a useful one. What do you make of reviewers who respond to mysterious or difficult poetry by complaining that the poet has nothing to say?

I suppose they mistake mystery for decoration: as if you ought to be able to lift the language surface off and see the sensible statements underneath. But you can't get beneath mystery, all you can do is acknowledge its presence. I assume such reviewers – and it's often the case – don't actually like poetry, either. That's nothing to be surprised at. There are plenty of teachers – in schools and universities – who never read poems, except insofar as they have to sometimes present them in the classroom. The sort of complaint you refer to is a bit more worrying when it comes from writers. That disgruntled, apparently pragmatic grizzle – why isn't X's poem *saying something, and saying it clearly?* – is sometimes just a way of dealing with personal disappointment; you maintain self-esteem by blaming everything on academics or fashion or literary cabals. But it's as if some writers who talk this way don't really love poems; they're much more interested in saying, or being seen to say, important things.

Of course there is the opposite complaint too, about poetry that is not difficult enough – from the world of Language poetry, mainly – according to which the slightest whiff of 'content' is enough to discredit the poem as conservative. There's a huge spectrum from poets who use more or less 'transparent' language to those who try to escape words' referentiality. One thing I find striking in the material collected in Doubtful Sounds *is the sheer range of poets, and poetries, that you're interested in. Of the poets whose work you like, across that spectrum, what are some of the things they might have in common?*

Well, I know what I don't like: aggressive opacity leaves me cold, as does aggressive transparency. More positively, I think a poem simply has to be alive in its language. For me that means that a poem, first of all, has to have some instinct for music. There's an interesting tape recording which Allen Curnow made at the Library of Congress back in the '60s, where he makes it clear that the moa's egg in his famous sonnet, while he describes it as being 'found in a thousand pieces', actually existed in just over 700 pieces. Facts are sacred for Curnow – as you might expect in someone who became

Afterword

a journalist after growing up in a vicarage – so, of course, he makes a mild apology. But essentially he made a decision there on behalf of the poem's music, and at the same time evoked a real sense of discovery in the elaborating chime of 'found' and 'thousand'. In pursuing the music, he made his meaning a little more resonant.

So music matters a lot, and this is probably why my favourite among the Language poets is Michael Palmer. But as well as that musical thing, a poem's words need to be on the hunt somehow, bringing meaning into being even as they find their way to the page. If the words are only there to point directly at what they mean, then – oddly enough – they've become pointless. I like lyric more than narrative; and where narrative is at work I enjoy a quality of obliquity: a few gaps where my own imagination can get to work. (I came across a comment by Louise Glück recently about some lines she'd left out of a poem, to the effect that she had done so because they were busy summarising what the poem needed to suggest. That makes sense to me.) I like melancholy; I like a sense of humour. Maybe it's the mix of these last two things that turns such different poets as Philip Larkin and John Ashbery into curious soulmates.

In 'Breaking the Line' (1986), and in your 1991 interview with Iain Sharp, you mentioned that American poetry no longer held for you the excitement that it had generated, in all its variety, in the '60s and '70s. What has come along in the '90s – in the US and elsewhere – that you find exciting? Has the US creative writing industry succeeded in homogenising American poetry into blandness? Do you think the much-publicised 'poetry boom' in Britain – the New Generation Poets promotion, for example, and the plethora of poets-in-residence – corresponds with a surge in interesting poetry?

Well, I think that all of that immense variety is still there in the States. The creative writing industry hasn't blanded everything out: America is finally just too athletic and continental, to borrow a couple of Whitman's adjectives. Probably any loss of excitement I feel has to do with my own middle age. The fact that poets as different as Mary Karr and C.D. Wright are both at work in the same literary culture is pretty encouraging. And there's a younger writer, Larissa Szporluk, whose work I find really exciting. She's in the line of Emily Dickinson, but in the deep, dark parts of her, rather than the rote feminist drawings-out we've had to witness lately.

I'm not hugely convinced by the idea that poetry is booming or making a comeback – least of all in the UK, where most of the booming comes from. The regeneration of poetry is a piece of news that gets announced every ten years or so, and I'm guilty of having once or twice made the announcement myself. But the fact that – courtesy of lottery profits – British poets can have residencies in law firms or Marks & Spencer or London Zoo doesn't necessarily mean a great deal in terms of the poems that get produced. Of course, it might be nice for the law clerks and the check-out workers and the flamingoes. In New Zealand, the one new thing that seems to be happening – a small shift in the temper of our writing, perhaps also in the make-up of readerships and audiences – is that a number of people who have been involved in performance, in plays and revues and stand-up comedy, are also starting to work on the page. I'm thinking of writers like Duncan Sarkies and Jo Randerson. There's a whole quality of *performance* in their work, which produces results much more oblique and delinquent than a standard short story, but not much resembling conventional poetry or postmodernism-by-numbers either. It's throwaway stuff which is highly moral – anecdote posing as parable; or the other way around.

Across the range of the material in Doubtful Sounds, *it seems to me there's a real commitment to the health of New Zealand writing and culture, a concern with the ability of New Zealand writers to re-imagine and re-invent. And the concern is translated also into the various roles you have within the culture, as writer and teacher but also editor, critic, columnist, anthologist. Is that commitment something you feel strongly about? I'm asking because there are plenty of writers whose participation doesn't go much beyond writing itself.*

That comment/question gives me vast benefit of the doubt. I'd turn it round and say that in many ways I haven't been strong enough, selfish enough, confident enough, about making time for my own writing. I've found it very easy to put time into marking student work, or reading manuscripts for Victoria University Press, or giving a talk here and a reading there . . . I suspect it's evasion activity, displacement activity. I think I actually admire those writers who stick to the main event and don't let themselves get too distracted. Of course, as I think Owen Marshall has said, you also want to give something back to the community, especially if it has encouraged and supported you; you want to live as a civic being, I guess.

When I think of the ways your own writing has re-imagined New Zealand – however ironically – it's the fiction I think of first, the work from the late '80s that is collected in Songs of My Life. *Do you see yourself writing more fiction? When I read* Songs of My Life *I want there to be a Manhire novel to go on to . . .*

Yes, I think New Zealand, various possible versions of it, is the big subject

Afterword

in the stories. It's probably why they seem, at least to me, to add up to more than the sum of their parts. They somehow go on growing. There are things in them, jumps and connections, which I keep finding out about. I have one or two small prose pieces under way, but whether I could manage a novel . . . That involves real stamina. I started one a few years ago, a real entertainment, in which the young Queen Elizabeth II became involved in a series of parallel universes. It began to stutter and slow because there was too much dialogue in it. I'm still keen to go back to that, but I'll have to wait for a proper expanse of time to work on in to.

In the meantime The Brain of Katherine Mansfield *has appeared in 'hypertext' on the Internet (http://www.het.brown.edu/people/easther/brain/), complete with Greg O'Brien's drawings. Its choose-your-path form seems custom-made for the Web. Are you interested in using hypertext as a medium for fiction or poetry?*

Actually, *The Brain of Katherine Mansfield* is much better as hypertext than as a book: you can't cheat and look ahead; you do have to make the choices each time they're presented, and make them in the dark. But I'm not sure that hypertext is something I'll particularly pursue. One part of me thinks that it ought to be a great gift, somehow at one with all my habits and intuitions. But in fact there's something about the computer screen and the Internet which doesn't accommodate time and pace and texture, and doesn't treat the imagination all that well. The page is a much happier place. But then I'm one of those conservative souls who thinks that at the end of the next millennium, when the various artistic forms and mediums will be beyond anything we can currently imagine, we'll all still be debating whether or not the book has a future.

Doubtful Sounds gathers some of the evidence of your interest in how Antarctica figures in people's imaginations. What first triggered that interest? You've also done some work on a bibliography of imaginative writing on the Antarctic – and at one stage was there a plan to put together an anthology?

Well, the anthology's still on the way – there are even publishers competing for it. I suspect I'll never produce the bibliography in any formal way, but that it will have served its purpose by underlying, underpinning, informing, the anthology. Antarctica – the place itself – started life as an aesthetic hypothesis. The ancient Greeks thought that a vast continent ought to be at the bottom of the planet, purely as a matter of balance and symmetry; and long after the great southern continent was tentatively, speculatively, entered on the maps the slow process of exploration brought it actually into being. So the idea with the anthology, which is called *The Wide White Page*, is to represent Antarctica as it has appeared across the centuries to the human imagination. Scientific Antarctica will be there, along with the age of heroic exploration, but so also will be science-fiction, good and bad, and a range of other things. Ursula Le Guin will sit next to Vladimir Nabokov and Robert Falcon Scott; Chris Orsman will keep company with Edgar Allan Poe, Beryl Bainbridge with H.P. Lovecraft.

My own interest in the place must have something to do with having been born in Invercargill. Next stop across the water – a long, long way across – is the ice. And then I was a teenager in Dunedin when the Operation Deepfreeze ships used it as their base – sailors from the ships drank after-hours in our pub; they had exotic things like Polaroid cameras. More generally, I think New Zealanders, certainly southern New Zealanders, have always felt quite closely linked to Antarctica: Scott left from Lyttelton and Port Chalmers, and we have also the distressing connection of the Erebus disaster. More New Zealanders have died down there than citizens of other nations. So the place is a sort of psychic territory for us, much as the desert interior is for Australians: you may not ever go there, but it's there in your mind. It was in my mind long before I got there physically. And Antarctica is the world's last absolutely pure place, and hence quite a challenge to the impurer impulses of the imagination.

Some of the things in Doubtful Sounds *were written for the page, some were written – at least in the first instance – to be delivered as lectures or talks. Yet it seems to me that there's a general movement in the prose towards a more spoken, conversational style. And the book has a strong sense of multiple conversations going on: between you and your readers, among the books and authors and other characters you talk about, and between the pieces themselves. Behind it all – if we can loop back to where we started – were some very real, and perhaps more mundane conversations, with the people who commissioned or prompted these pieces into being. Who can we thank for giving you these topics and suggestions and deadlines?*

I suppose that, with some of the interviews, the promptings came from the interviewers themselves (Greg O'Brien and Rod McGregor, for example). The interview with Iain Sharp was set up by Mark Williams and Elizabeth Alley; and Mark, this time with Graham McGregor, commissioned the 'Dirty Silence' lecture. (There's a bit of sesqui-centennial piety about it, but I still mostly agree with myself.) Lawrence Jones and Jocelyn Harris commissioned 'Stranger at the Ranchslider' as a keynote address for a conference on James

Afterword

K. Baxter at the University of Otago. 'Breaking the Line' was asked for (by Jock Phillips and John Thomson, as I recall) for a Stout Centre conference on NZ-US relations.

Then there's a whole group of magazine editors and review editors and publishers – and of those there are two in particular, 'without whom this book' etc. The first is Robin Dudding, and I think I should probably dedicate *Doubtful Sounds* to him. It mattered to me most that he liked my poems, but during his time at *Islands*, he also commissioned from me a number of review-essays, not all of which I've included. (I've cut 80% from the longest of them, 'Events and Editorials', which was a review of the posthumous Baxter *Collected Poems*, mainly because of an anxiety about overlaps and repetitions.) Robin asked for the *Plumb* review, too.

The second editor – though you might also want to call him a bookworld entrepreneur – is Stephen Stratford. He asked me to do a monthly column on poetry for *Quote Unquote*. 'The Poetry File' was simply a working title I suggested, and neither Stephen nor I got around to thinking of something better, though I think we both wish we had. The idea was to make poetry a bit less intimidating, and I think we managed that. I suspect the *Quote Unquote* column led to the fortnightly spot on the Kim Hill show.

But there are always more people to thank, and more than you can name or even think of when you need to. At Victoria University Press I need to thank Fergus Barrowman and Rachel Lawson, first of all for suggesting the book and then for keeping on at me to get on with it. Iain Sharp did a highly encouraging reader's report, and indeed suggested this long-distance conversation, while Jane Hurley did a very thorough copy-edit at a point where the manuscript was what my mother would call a great big guddle. And I want to thank Sue Brown, the typesetter, and Kirsty Lillico for the cover, and David Cauchi for the index, and Archetype Book Agents.

Of course, you have valuable conversations with people before you write things, and as you're writing them, too – while you're working out what you actually think. And I suppose I hope that that conversational quality has survived into the book itself; and that readers – like the books and authors I've happened to write about – will dip in and out, and wander to and fro, and be pleased to go on talking.

Paris – Wellington: August 1999

INDEX

Abercrombie, Lascelles, 233
Abhayasundere, Wimal, 256
Adcock, Fleur, 150, 178, 191, 233
Akhmatova, Anna, 170
Allen, Donald M., 77
Alley, Elizabeth, 42n, 288
Alvarez, A., 172, 173, 175
Amis, Kingsley, 139–140, 151, 152, 156, 157
Amis, Martin, 144–5
Anderson, Barbara, 112
Angioleri, Cecco, 91–2
Antin, David, 186
Arawata Bill, 221, 224
Archetype Book Agents, 289
Arif, Hafiz, 258
Aristotle, 29
Armstrong, Dave, 218
Armstrong, Louis, 152
Ashbery, John, 38, 77, 181, 228, 285
Auden, W.H., 145, 163, 174, 218, 276
Aveling, Harry *see* Arif, Hafiz
Awang, Usman, 255, 268–9
Aziz, J.M., 258

Bainbridge, Beryl, 241, 288
Ball, Hugo, 44
Banks, John, 271
Barker, Sebastian, 256, 261, 267, 268
Barrett, Elizabeth, 94
Barrowman, Fergus, 289
Barthelme, Donald, 114
Baudelaire, Charles, 180
Baxter, James K., 18, 25, 27, 38, 47, 52, 73, 76, 84n, 94, 100, 101, 142, 184, 199–208, 209–12, 221, 278, 281, 289
Baysting, Arthur, 54n, 81
Beer, Christina, 191

Belitt, Ben, 84n
Bellow, Saul, 241
Bennett, Alan, 151
Bentley, E. Clerihew, 234
Bernstein, Charles, 30
Berry, Wendell, 81
Berryman, John, 77
Bertram, James, 209
Bethell, Ursula, 191, 274
Betjeman, Sir John, 151
Bishop, Elizabeth, 169
Blake, William, 47, 85, 146, 173, 220, 221
Bland, Peter, 48
Bly, Robert, 25, 77, 147, 181
Blyton, Enid, 55–6, 101
Bobis, Merlinda C., 267, 269, 270
Body, Jack, 63
Bolger, Jim, 144
Borges, Jorge Louis, 181
Bornholdt, Jenny, 18, 40, 97, 100, 113, 236
Boulanger, Mousse, 266, 267
Bracken, Thomas, 44
Branagh, Kenneth, 230
Brasch, Charles, 26, 27, 34, 61, 73–4, 75, 200, 220
Brecht, Bertolt, 47, 169
Brennan, Maeve, 156
Bridger, Bub, 275
Brodsky, Joseph, 170
Brooke, Rupert, 31
Brown, James, 186
Brown, Nigel, 243, 245
Brown, Sue, 289
Browning, Robert, 47, 277
Brunton, Alan, 24, 25, 76, 81
Burns, Robert, 210
Byron, Lord, 231–2, 234

Index

Calvino, Italo, 161, 227
Cape, Peter, 274
Carneci, Radu, 257
Carroll, Lewis, 234
Carver, Raymond, 114
Cary, Joyce, 130
Casserley, John, 63
Catullus, 45
Cauchi, David, 289
Causley, Charles, 152, 202
Chapple, James, 118, 124
Chekhov, Anton, 162
Cherry-Garrard, Apsley, 238
Chik, Dattuk Sabaruddin, 251
Chilton, Mike, 254
Coleman, Brunette, 156
Coleridge, Samuel Taylor, 29, 142, 183–4
Colvin, Ian D., 238
Cook, Peter, 233
Creeley, Robert, 25, 78, 84n, 85–6
Crosland, T.W.H., 237
Culbert, Bill, 64, 66–8
Cullen, Christian, 102
Cunningham, Kevin, 24, 26, 200
Curnow, Allen, 18, 31, 38, 42, 70–1, 101, 144, 212, 217, 220, 236, 284
Curnow, Wystan, 30
Cutler, Ivor, 181–2

Dallas, Ruth, 190
Dante, Alighieri, 146
Darwin, Charles, 259
Davie, Donald, 88
Davis, Leigh, 29
Desmond, Arthur, 44
Dickens, Charles, 123
Dickinson, Emily, 188–9, 197, 285
Dickson, John, 24, 28
Dillard, Annie, 185–6
Domett, Alfred, 44
Donne, John, 100
Doyle, Charles, 75
Drew, Elizabeth, 88
Dryden, John, 169, 233
Dudding, Robin, 27–8, 289
Duffy, Carol Ann, 114
Duggan, Eileen, 191, 274

Duncan, Robert, 86
Dunn, Douglas, 174, 178
Durning, Colin, 205
Durrell, Lawrence, 210
Dylan, Bob, 91

Edmond, Lauris, 32, 95, 191
Edmond, Murray, 24, 38, 75–6, 84n
Eliot, T.S., 9, 29, 45, 100, 152, 181, 186, 233, 234, 236, 241, 277
Ellis, Alice Thomas, 274
Ensing, Riemke, 190, 192, 193, 195n
Euripides, 233
Everly Brothers, 76
Ewart, Gavin, 151, 235

Fairburn, A.R.D., 101, 220, 236
Fei-Bai, Wang, 257
Fenton, James, 38, 88, 169, 173, 174, 177–8
Fisher, Arnie, 119
Flammarion, Camille, 33
Ford, Ford Madox, 233
Frame, Janet, 59, 181, 190, 197, 237, 274, 279
French, Anne, 32
Friel, Brian, 166

Gabites, Helen, 109–110
Geary, David, 113
Gee, Lyndahl Chapple, 118
Gee, Maurice, 32, 41, 116, 118–23, 124–32, 273
Geraud, Saint *see* Knott, Bill
Gibson, C.G., 74, 75, 77
Gibson, Colin, 75
Gilbert, W.S., 234
Ginn, Noel, 207
Ginsberg, Allen, 77
Glover, Denis, 12n, 14, 47, 217–26, 233, 236
Glück, Louise, 227, 285
Gozo, Maralia, 262
Grace, Patricia, 116
Gray, Joel, 249
Grey, Zane, 121, 123
Griffin, John, 26
Grigson, Geoffrey, 163

Haley, Russell, 24, 76
Hall, Bernadette, 13
Hall, Donald, 77
Hammond, David, 162
Hardy, Thomas, 46–7, 210
Harris, Jeffrey, 57
Harris, Jocelyn, 201, 288
Harrison, Tony, 149, 169, 174–6
Hawken, Dinah, 40, 181, 202, 232, 234
Heaney, Seamus, 97, 100, 113, 151, 161–5, 169–71, 174–6, 175, 178, 181, 234
Heberley, James, 133
Hejinian, Lyn, 30
Henri, Robert, 185
Herbert, Zbigniew, 163
Hervey, J.R., 274
Higginson, Thomas Wentworth, 188
Hill, Geoffrey, 181
Hill, Kim, 289
Hillary, Sir Edmund, 240
Hince, Bernadette, 242
Holub, Miroslav, 163
Homer, 114, 116
Hopkins, Gerard Manley, 48, 277, 280–1
Horace, 234
Horrocks, Nigel, 29
Horsman, Alan, 200
Hotere, Ralph, 11, 15–18, 25, 27, 57–65, 66–8
Howard Morrison Quartet, 76
Hughes, Noel, 152
Hughes, Olwyn, 159
Hughes, Ted, 159, 173
Hugo, Richard, 116
Hulme, Keri, 32, 45
Humphries, Barry, 87
Hunt, Sam, 81, 101, 183, 184
Hurley, Jane, 289
Hyde, Robin, 191, 194

Ihimaera, Witi, 32
Incertus, 161; *see also* Heaney, Seamus

James, Clive, 172
Johnson, Samuel, 231
Johnston, Andrew, 227–9, 282–9
Johnston, Stuart, 109

Jones, Lawrence, 47, 288
Jones, Monica, 156
Jong, Erica, 194
Joyce, James, 278
Justice, Donald, 81

Karr, Mary, 285
Kavanagh, Patrick, 163
Keats, John, 29
Kemala, 246, 250, 266
Kemp, Jan, 76, 191, 194
Kenner, Hugh, 232
King, Stephen, 160
Kinnell, Galway, 77, 81, 202
Kipling, Rudyard, 23, 45
Kirby, Joan, 84n
Kirkland, Hilaire, 191–2
Knott, Bill, 145
Knox, Chris, 102
Knox, Elizabeth, 113
Koch, Kenneth, 91, 93, 94
Kraus, Karl, 53
Kraus, Lili, 218
Kugultinov, David, 259, 270
Kundera, Milan, 170

Landfall, 27, 41
Larkin, Eva, 155, 156
Larkin, Philip, 38, 47, 151–4, 155–7, 163, 174, 177, 233, 285
Larkin, Sydney, 155
Lau, Paul, 271
Lawrence, D.H., 155
Lawson, Rachel, 289
Le Comte, Edward, 186
Le Guin, Ursula, 114, 116, 288
Leggott, Michele, 41
Leonardo da Vinci, 186
Levertov, Denise, 77, 86
Levine, Philip, 81
Lewis, Day, 218
Lilburn, Douglas, 208
Lillico, Kirsty, 289
Loney, Alan, 60
Lonie, Iain, 27, 200
Lord, Robert, 273
Lovecraft, H.P., 288

Index

Lowell, Robert, 77, 158, 174
Lowry, Malcolm, 276

McAlpine, Rachel, 191
McCabe, Joseph, 124
McCahon, Colin, 61
McCarten, Anthony, 112
McCartney, Colum, 165
MacDiarmid, Hugh, 12n
Macdonald, John, 113
McGee, Greg, 102, 120
McGough, Roger, 150
McGregor, Graham, 22n, 288
McGregor, Rod, 98, 288
McGuckian, Medbh, 178
McKay, Frank, 209
McKenzie, Don, 33, 103
McMurray, David, 147
MacNeice, Louis, 145, 210, 218
McQueen, Cilla, 206–7, 247
Mahon, Derek, 169, 178, 239
Mahy, Margaret, 274, 275
Malouf, David, 111
Mandelstam, Osip, 163, 169, 231
Manet, Edouard, 196
Manhire, Bill, works by:
   'Allen Curnow Meets Judge Dredd', 41
   'The Anglo-Saxon Onion', 33
   'The Asterisk Machine', 41
   The Book for Bookworms, 24
   The Brain of Katherine Mansfield, 37, 287
   'Breaking the Line', 285, 289
   'The Cinema', 80
   'Contemplation of the Heavens', 33
   'Declining the Naked Horse', 92
   'Deep Field Song', 244–5
   'Dirty Silence', 32, 282, 288
   Doubtful Sounds, 284, 286, 287, 288, 289
   The Elaboration, 11, 23, 26, 60–1, 62
   'Fault', 64, 66–68
   Good Looks, 37, 60
   How to Take Off Your Clothes at the Picnic, 61
   'Life with Madame Rosa', 42
   'Loss of the Forest', 60
   'Magasin', 18–19, 252, 261
   Malady, 25–6, 57–63
   Milky Way Bar, 37, 40
   Mutes & Earthquakes, 106
   'A Mysterious Poem', 251
   'New Jerusalem Sonnets', 213-16
   The New Land, 36–7, 65
   Now See Hear! text machine, 41
   The Old Man's Example, 58, 61
   'On Originality', 82–3
   Otago University capping book, 28, 201
   'Phar Lap', 19–22
   'The Proposition', 78
   'Ralph Hotere at the Intensity Centre', 65
   'Some Questions I Am Frequently Asked', 40, 65
   'Song Cycle', 62
   Songs of My Life, 286
   University Arts Festival yearbook (1969), 28
   'The Venus Bird', 11
   'Wen', 33, 183
   'The Wind II', 59
   'Wingatui', 31
   'Wulf', 33
   'Zoetropes', 252, 265
   Zoetropes, 263
Mannion, Robert, 41
Mansfield, Katherine, 134, 248, 278
Margan, Barry, 63
Marsh, Pete, 37
Marshall, Owen, 25, 286
Mason, R.A.K., 69–71, 81–2, 141–3, 192, 220
Maunder, Paul, 204
Mawson, Sir Douglas, 242
Melville, Herman, 134
Merwin, Dido, 159
Merwin, W.S., 75, 77, 81
Middleton, O.E. (Ted), 26, 27
Miles, Josephine, 197
Milligan, Spike, 150
Milosz, Czeslaw, 170
Milton, John, 148, 150, 169, 189, 230
Mintrom, Michael, 186–7
Monteith, Charles, 152
Moore, Lorrie, 114
Morgan, Edwin, 149, 169, 236
Morgan, Robin, 160
Morrison, Blake, 172, 173, 179

Moss, Chas, 238
Motion, Andrew, 155–7, 172, 173, 179
Muir, Gabrielle, 113
Muldoon, Paul, 31, 174, 178
Mullins, Ross, and the Snaps, 202
Murray, Les, 47
Nabokov, Vladimir, 288
Nannestad, Beth, 114
Neruda, Pablo, 72, 84n, 169, 181
Newton, John, 13–14, 275
Niedecker, Lorine, 143, 145

Oates, Lawrence, 238, 239
O'Brien, Gregory, 57, 65, 181, 202, 287, 288
O'Connor, Flannery, 117
O'Hara, Frank, 51, 52
O'Leary, Michael, 16n
Oliver, Bill, 204
Olson, Charles, 25, 77, 86
Orr, Bob, 26
Orsman, Chris, 113, 238, 242, 243, 245, 288
O'Sullivan, Vincent, 18, 181, 190, 194, 212
Ousland, Bruce, 245
Owen, Wilfred, 162

Paley, Grace, 112, 114, 116
Palmer, Michael, 285
Panikov, Dr Boris, 259, 261, 267, 270
Paul, Janet, 26, 61
Paulin, Tom, 166–171, 174, 178
Phillips, Jock, 289
Picasso, Pablo, 152, 180
Plath, Sylvia, 33, 53, 94, 100, 158–160, 163, 170
Plumb, George, 118
Plumb, Vivienne, 112
Poe, Edgar Allen, 278, 288
Pope, Alexander, 146
Porter, Cole, 234
Porter, Peter, 151, 202
Potter, Dennis, 53
Pound, Ezra, 50, 54, 143, 186, 218, 231, 250, 278, 280
Puslojic, Adam, 257
Pym, Barbara, 152

Raine, Craig, 168, 174, 176–7, 178, 276–7, 278, 279
Randerson, Jo, 286
Ranger, Laura, 95–7
Ransom, John Crowe, 48–51, 77
Rawlinson, Gloria, 191, 194
Reeves, Trevor, 27
Reid, Christopher, 174
Reinhardt, Ad, 64
Reverdy, Pierre, 180
Reynolds, Jeremiah K., 134
Rhodes, H. Winston, 121
Rice, Anne, 160
Rich, Adrienne, 111, 169
Richardson, Elwyn, 93, 94, 115, 195
Ricketts, Harry, 84n
Ricks, Christopher, 151
Rilke, Rainer Maria, 181
Rimbaud, Arthur, 180
Rothko, Mark, 64
Rushdie, Salman, 9, 22n
Ryan, Richard, 239
Ryerson, Margery A., 185

Sandburg, Carl, 48
Sappho, 150
Sargeson, Frank, 113, 118, 135–140, 152
Sarkies, Duncan, 286
Saroyan, Aram, 147
Scott, Bob, 119
Scott, Robert Falcon, 237–8, 241, 242, 243, 288
Scott, Sir Walter, 113, 237
Sellers, Peter, 201
Sexton, Anne, 158
Seymour, Rosemary, 192–3
Shakespeare, William, 102, 220, 222
Shand, Jimmy, 76
Shannon, Del, 76
Shapcott, Tom, 250, 254, 257, 269
Sharp, Iain, 23, 285, 288
Shelley, Percy Bysshe, 12, 144, 183
Silliman, Ron, 30
Simeon Stylites, Saint, 52
Simic, Charles, 181–2, 227
Simonov, Paul, 259
Simpson, Louis, 13, 22n, 25, 72, 79, 84n
Smith, Stevie, 47–8, 197, 220

Index

Smither, Elizabeth, 18, 47, 191, 196–8, 199, 220
Smither, Michael, 57
Smithyman, Kendrick, 38
Snyder, Gary, 77, 184
Songthong, Prayom, 250, 262–3, 268
Southgate, Brent, 95, 105, 216n
Spenser, Edmund, 75
Spielberg, Steven, 160
Spufford, Francis, 241
Stafford, William, 81
Stanley, Mary, 191–2, 193, 194
Stead, C.K., 38
Stein, Gertrude, 181
Stevens, Wallace, 9, 15, 114, 116, 227, 231
Stevenson, Anne, 159, 160
Stevenson, Robert Louis, 134
Stewart, Douglas, 238
Stimpson, Mick, 222
Stratford, Stephen, 43, 289
Stravinsky, Igor, 111
Sullivan, Robert, 202
Sweetman, David, 174
Symes, Peter, 149
Szporluk, Larissa, 285
Szumigalski, Anne, 267, 268, 269

Tennyson, Alfred Lord, 52, 144, 184, 276, 277
Thomas, Dylan, 210
Thomson, G.B., 167
Thomson, John, 289
Thwaite, Anthony, 151, 154n
Tomlinson, Charles, 173
Tranter, John, 176
Turner, Brian, 81, 84n
Turner, Professor Fred, 86

Tuwhare, Hone, 15, 22n, 25, 45, 100, 101, 220, 275
Tuwhare, Jean, 204
Twain, Mark, 44, 45

Van Gogh, Vincent, 186
Von Sturmer, Richard, 181

Wainwright, Jeffrey, 174
Walcott, Derek, 163
Webb, Phyllis, 228, 232, 234
Wedde, Ian, 24, 25, 26, 27, 31, 39, 76, 81, 133-4, 176
Welty, Eudora, 116
Wendt, Albert, 134
Were, Virginia, 40
Wevill, Assia, 160
Wheeler, Sara, 240–2
Whitman, Walt, 47, 69, 71–3, 79–80, 82, 90–1, 128
Wilde, Oscar, 93
Williams, Forbes, 113
Williams, Herbert, 11
Williams, Mark, 22n, 42n, 288
Williams, William Carlos, 87–9, 169
Wittgenstein, Ludwig, 29
Wordsworth, William, 48, 99, 146, 178, 227, 233
Wright, C.D., 285
Wright, Charles, 81
Wright, James, 25, 77, 81

Yeats, William Butler, 145, 170, 184, 210, 224

Zain, Baha, 258
Zukofsky, Louis and Celia, 45